Cost Accounting

Augustina Anerville

Cost Accounting

M. W. E. Glautier, B. Underdown

PITMAN PUBLISHING
128 Long Acre London WC2E 9AN

A Division of Longman Group UK Limited

© Guardjust Ltd, B Underdown 1988

First published in Great Britain 1988
Reprinted 1990, 1992

British Library Cataloguing in Publication Data
Glautier, M.W.E.
Cost accounting
1. Cost accounting
I. Title II. Underdown, B.
657'.42 HF5686.C8

ISBN 0-273-02500-7

All rights reserved; no part of this publication may be reproduced, stored in a retrieval system, or transmitted in any form or by any means, electronic, mechanical, photocopying, recording, or otherwise without either the prior written permission of the publishers or a licence permitting restricted copying issued by the Copyright Licensing Agency Ltd, 90 Tottenham Court Road, London W1P 9HE. This book may not be lent, resold, hired out or otherwise disposed of by way of trade in any form of binding or cover other than that in which it is published, without the prior consent of the publishers.

Printed in England by Clays Ltd, St Ives plc

Contents

Preface

The purpose of this book is to provide a thorough and comprehensive introduction to cost accounting. Its underlying theme is the role of cost accounting information for management planning, control and decision making. Accordingly, the principles of cost accounting are related to management theory, and cost accounting techniques are discussed and explained in the context of the purposes for which cost information is needed.

We hope that this approach will provide realism to the study of cost accounting, and instil in our student readers an awareness of the significance of modern cost accounting techniques for the management of business enterprises.

Our objective is to cover the examination syllabuses of the major professional bodies. For this reason, we have gone beyond the usual coverage of textbooks in this area in that we have extended the discussion of the more practical aspects of cost accounting. The examples used, the illustrations given and the test questions selected are all intended to prepare students to pass their professional examinations.

Our intention is also to provide students of cost accounting at universities, business schools and polytechnics with a basic textbook that not only explains the techniques of cost accounting, but provides a theoretical structure to which explanations are referred.

Acknowledgements

We express appreciation to Graham Axelby for giving us the benefit of his experience and knowledge.

Our sincere thanks also go to the editors and staff of Pitman Publishing Ltd, in particular to Eric Dalton and David Carpenter.

We gratefully acknowledge permission to quote from the past examination papers of the following bodies:

Association of Accounting Technicians (AAT); Chartered Association of Certified Accountants (CACA); Chartered Institute of Management Accountants (CIMA); London Chamber of Commerce and Industry (LCCI).

Part 1 The Framework of Cost Accounting

The purpose of Part I is to explain the nature of cost accounting and its role in the management of business enterprises.

Chapter 1 discusses the objectives of cost accounting and relates them to the management process. Chapter 2 explains cost accounting concepts and cost classifications in terms of management information needs. This chapter prepares the way for the discussion of the techniques of cost accounting that follows in subsequent parts.

1 The Objectives of Cost Accounting

This chapter deals with the following topics:

1.1 The origins of costing.
1.2 Cost accounting and the management process.
1.3 The nature of cost accounting.
1.4 Cost accounting and financial accounting.

The purpose of this chapter is to discuss the objectives of cost accounting in terms of management needs for cost information. Cost accounting is distinguished from financial accounting in its focus upon providing cost information to management for planning, control and decision-making purposes. Financial accounting is concerned with external reporting to shareholders and the investment public at large, and relates to recording financial transactions and the preparation of financial statements in the form of balance sheets and profit and loss accounts.

1.1 THE ORIGINS OF COSTING

Historically, cost accounting developed as a response to the need for management to determine factory product costs for pricing purposes. Thus, it was the inability to determine product costs that led to firms going bankrupt during the Industrial Revolution. It was this problem that inspired early attempts at costing. With the advent of large-scale factory production at the beginning of this century, rapid progress was made in developing costing methods. Ultimately, the idea appeared of providing information that could be used by managers of business firms for planning, control and decision-making purposes. Business success is interpreted in terms of profits, defined as the excess of revenues derived from sales over the cost of sales. Accordingly, success in business means making management decisions that result in increases in profits.

In competitive markets, prices are largely determined by the level of demand. Business firms are assumed not to be able to control market prices, but they are assumed to be able to exercise control over costs and in this way achieve greater profits. The concern with cost control as a major factor in managing for profitability explains the importance attached to cost information for management decisions.

This century is generally regarded as the age of science. Developments in the physical sciences seized the imagination, and inspired businessmen and academics to consider how management itself could become more efficient in the utilization of resources. Since scientists relied on objective information, particularly expressed in the form of measurements, it was realized that the 'scientific management' of resources required objective information. Cost measurements are needed, therefore, as objective information making possible the scientific management of resources by business organizations. These are expected to be objective and reliable measurements of resources, interpreted as financial inputs, necessary for attaining business objectives in the form of financial products derived from the sale of goods and services.

Consequently, although product costing remains an important purpose of cost accounting, the subject matter of cost accounting has extended much beyond its initial concern with product costing to the provision of cost information relevant to a broad range of management decisions addressed to notions of profit planning and control.

Non-profit organizations, such as universities and hospitals and government agencies and departments, such as the Post Office and the Ministry of Defence, are also concerned with cost control given that funds allocated to them are limited in supply.

Although this book examines cost accounting in terms of business organizations, many of the topics discussed are also relevant to non-profit organizations and government bodies. Accordingly, the objectives of modern cost accounting can best be understood by reference to the management process.

1.2 COST ACCOUNTING AND THE MANAGEMENT PROCESS

The management of organizations consists of three types of inter-related activities – planning, organizing and controlling.

1.2.1 Planning

Planning may be defined as the thinking process that precedes action: it is directed to making decisions now with the future in mind. Its purpose is twofold:

(a) To ensure that management decisions reflect the objectives of the enterprise.

(b) To improve the quality of management decisions by ensuring that all relevant factors are considered prior to making decisions.

Planning consists of the following five stages:

(a) Setting objectives, for example, the profit objective and the sales objective.
(b) Assessing the business environment in which these objectives have to be realized. This implies making forecasts of external factors that may affect the firm, as well as weighing the likely impact of changes in its policy.
(c) Evaluating the resources available and needed for achieving business objectives.
(d) Establishing an overall plan (strategy) for achieving these objectives. Strategic decisions are concerned with relating the firm's objectives to the business environment.
(e) Developing long-range and short-term action programmes to realize the strategic plan. Long-range planning covers a period of years, whereas short-term (operational planning) deals with the 1-year period defined by the annual budget.

Cost accounting information produced by the firm's costing system is combined with other available information, and is used in making planning decisions that affect the firm's financial position. Typically, cost information will be needed for profit planning purposes, when management is preparing the budget for the forthcoming year.

1.2.2 Organizing

Organizing means setting up an administrative structure for implementing the firm's strategy. It involves defining the chain of command in terms of lines of authority and managerial responsibility. It results in designing an organizational chart in which the authority and responsibility of respective management levels and respective managers are determined.

Exhibit 1.1 illustrates a typical organizational chart. The managerial structure is divided first into functional segments, for example, production, sales and finance. Next, each functional segment is divided into departments, for example, production is divided into extrusion, printing, etc.

Management decisions at all levels have to do with the use of organizational resources, defined as costs. The purpose of the organizational chart is not only to define the decision-making responsibility of different managers, but also to provide a framework for a *management information system* which will supply each manager with cost information relevant to his area of responsibility.

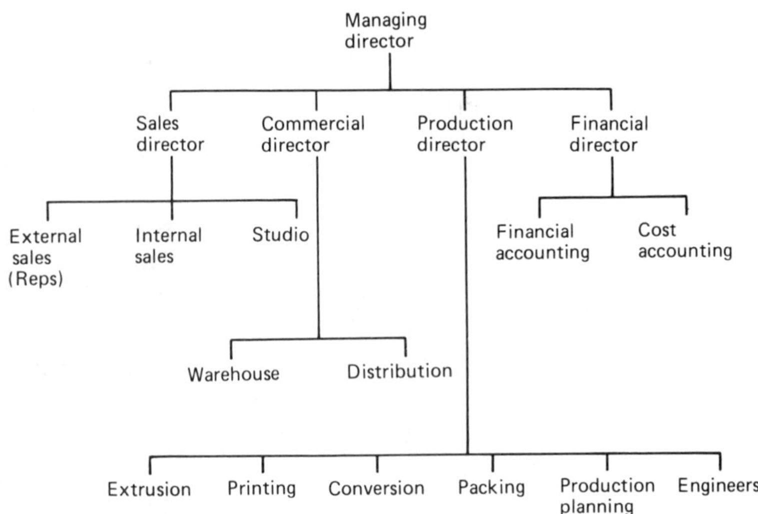

Exhibit 1.1 Organizational chart. KRS Packaging plc.

Superimposed upon the organizational chart, the management information system identifies the information flow through the enterprise. Information for decision making flows from one manager to another manager. Lower-level managers must be given adequate information from their superiors to carry out their duties: they must also provide their superiors with the information they need themselves. For example, managers are 'given' a budget that defines a spending limit (costs) that should not be exceeded in relation to an expected level of activity. Such information will be stated in terms of budgeted costs. All managers are required to make periodic reports to their superiors detailing how they are managing their budget.

The collection (accumulation) of cost information is effected in terms of managerial areas of responsibility, defined as 'centres'. Lower-level managers who are responsible for the management of costs only are known as cost centre managers: those higher in the hierarchy who are responsible for revenue are known as revenue centre managers: those higher still who are responsible for profit areas are known as profit centre managers: those who are at the highest level of responsibility and are responsible for the profitable investment and utilization of the firm's resources are known as investment centre managers.

In terms of Exhibit 1.1, the manager of the extrusion department would be designated as a 'cost centre manager': the sales director would be designated as a 'revenue centre manager': the managing director would be a 'profit and investment centre manager'. The exact definition of the status of the managing director would depend on whether the firm is an independent one, or a subsidiary of another firm.

1.2.3 Controlling

Controlling involves ensuring that management decisions throughout the organization have been directed towards achieving the planned objectives. It consists of comparing results with the targets stated in the plan (budget), noting and investigating deviations prior to deciding what corrective action, if any, should be taken. As illustrated in Exhibit 1.2, planning and controlling are closely linked in a cycle of managerial activities by means of feedback systems.

By comparing the plan (budget) with the results of operations, deviations (variances) are highlighted. Control is effected by investigating variances, determining their cause and taking corrective action. Since only variances require managerial action, management control 'by exception' is made possible. This means that management assumes that all is going according to plan, *except* if a variance indicates otherwise. Corrective action is limited to the elimination of the variance.

Managers throughout the firm are given budgets that reflect their respective share of resources for the planning period. If they are 'cost centre managers', their effectiveness as managers will appear evidently in terms of variances between budgeted costs for their department and actual costs incurred. Hence, cost control through the investigation of budget variances has become a topic in cost accounting.

The interrelationship and interdependence of the three elements of

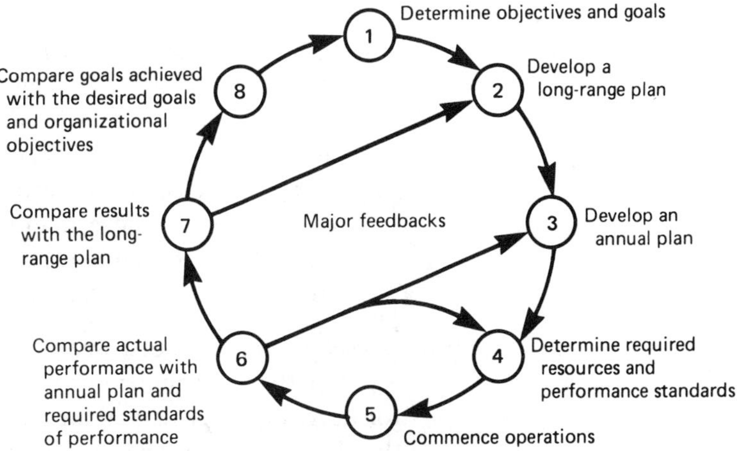

Exhibit 1.2 Planning, control and feedback systems.

the management process – planning, organizing and controlling – is made manifest in the operation of management information systems. Cost accounting information, that measures organizational resources as costs, is clearly an important element in management information systems.

1.3 THE NATURE OF COST ACCOUNTING

Cost accounting is concerned with the provision of cost information, for management purposes. It embraces the following objectives:

(a) *Cost determination.* Cost information is needed for product costing, and for establishing organization costs in the form of departmental costs for the purposes of budget planning and control. A 'budget' is a quantitative expression of managerial plans.

Product costs are required for:

(i) *Stock valuation.* The cost of goods manufactured cannot be determined without a costing system that measures product costs in the form of raw material, labour and other costs. Stock valuation records provide the firm with information relating to the cost of goods manufactured, to determine the cost of goods sold from such records and to ascertain the cost value of the stock remaining on hand at the end of the accounting period.

(ii) *Determining selling prices and preparing estimates and tenders.* Product costs are an important element in pricing. Although other factors are involved, product costs set a floor below which prices should not fall if losses are to be avoided.

(iii) *Assessing product profitability.* By comparing the cost of different products with the prices at which they can be sold, the firm is able to identify unprofitable products, and make appropriate decisions.

(iv) *Diagnosing inefficiencies.* Product costs are used in a variety of ways to diagnose manufacturing inefficiencies in the form of unacceptably high costs, and selling inefficiencies that result in significant over- or under-pricing.

(b) *Budget planning.* As discussed earlier, planning is an important aspect of the management process that relies on cost information for drawing up plans that are stated as budgets. Firms plan for the short, medium and long term. Close attention is given to short-term (annual) budgeting for which detailed cost information is needed. As we shall see in Chapter 14, planning through budgeting involves relating levels of activity to costs for establishing profit targets. In addition to budgeting for on-going operations, cost information is also required to non-routine decisions, such as the acceptance or rejection of a special order. 'Special decisions' are discussed in Chapter 13.

(c) *Budget and cost control*. Budget and cost control is the regulation of the costs of running a business through management action. Effective cost control involves:

   (i) Setting up cost centres throughout the firm and identifying clearly the responsibility for costs with the respective cost centre managers.
   (ii) Establishing efficient cost standards for planning purposes which ensure that all possible cost savings have been considered, and for producing actual costs to be compared with budgeted costs.
   (iii) Devising a reporting system that will allow the communication of feedback cost information to the appropriate management level.

1.4 COST ACCOUNTING AND FINANCIAL ACCOUNTING

Cost accounting has its origins in the need of manufacturing firms to establish product costs. Subsequently, the idea of cost control through budget planning extended the usefulness of costing to non-manufacturing firms, such as trading and service companies by focusing upon the control of costs in the form of expenses. Today, cost accounting is concerned with the costing of services as well as manufactured goods. Its relevance to trading firms, government agencies and non-profit organizations, as well as manufacturing enterprises has been emphasized in the context of budgetary planning and control at the departmental level, in addition to the control of costs at the product level.

Cost accounting relates to the accumulation of cost information inside the firm, and the provision of that information to management. Costs are accumulated in costing systems that are designed to fit the business objectives of particular firms and their organizational structure. By contrast, financial accounting is concerned with recording the transactions of the firm in the form of the acquisition of resources, including the purchase of raw materials and finished goods, labour, and a variety of services, as well as the sales of its own products and services.

The objectives of financial accounting are not only to record financial transactions, but also to provide periodic information in the form of balance sheets and profit and loss accounts that indicate the financial status of the firm and its overall profitability. Such information is not only used by management, but also by shareholders, investors and other interested parties.

Cost accounting information flows into the financial accounting system through stock valuation based on the accumulation of product costs. The best example that may be given in this respect is the manufacturing firm that has to sell its products. Its formal cost accounting system will accumulate the cost of the units produced that will appear in the cost of goods sold and the closing stock. Indeed, the interdependence of cost accounting and financial accounting systems is extensive. Raw material, labour and other costs are recorded in the financial accounting system through transactions under which they are acquired as resources by the firm. The process by which they are transformed into products is the concern of cost accounting, but their eventual sale will appear in the financial accounting system.

The formal cost accounting system just described generally provides cost data for stock valuation and control purposes. Such data is essentially historic in nature and is of limited usefulness for management planning and decision-making purposes. In order to meet these objectives such data must be reclassified, reorganized and supplemented by other relevant economic and business data from outside the formal cost accounting system.

Questions

1. Explain the origin of cost accounting.
2. Describe briefly the elements of the management process.
3. Relate the purpose of cost accounting to the management process.
4. Define cost accounting.
5. What do you understand by product costing?
6. Discuss the importance of cost determination for management decisions.
7. Why is cost information so important to planning?
8. Explain briefly what you understand by cost control.
9. Distinguish cost accounting and financial accounting.
10. Explain the interdependence between cost accounting and financial accounting.

2 Cost Accounting Concepts

This chapter deals with the following topics:

2.1 Main cost classifications.
2.2 Functional costs.
2.3 Product costs.
2.4 Activity level costs.
2.5 Controllable costs.
2.6 Relevant costs.
2.7 Cost codes.

Costs are routinely identified by their nature, for example, raw material costs, labour costs, heat and light, depreciation, etc. This classification by nature is derived from financial accounting. Cost accounting classifies them in different ways depending upon the purpose for which such costs are to be used. When cost accounting is directly concerned with providing information for decision making, costs are prepared specifically for particular types of decisions. This chapter examines alternative cost classifications and their use.

2.1 MAIN COST CLASSIFICATIONS

It is important to stress that the objective of all cost classifications is to analyse the *same monetary value* in alternative ways.

Four main cost classifications are:

(a) functional costs;
(b) product costs;
(c) activity costs;
(d) relevant costs.

2.2 FUNCTIONAL COSTS

Costs may be classified according to the functions of the organization with which they are associated. In effect, this means that costs are identified with major segments of a business that have specific activities. Functional costs are as follows:

(a) *Production costs*, which are the costs incurred in the activity of production involved in transforming raw material into the finished product. They are sometimes referred to as 'factory costs'.
(b) *Selling costs*, which relate to the activities of securing orders.
(c) *Distribution costs*, which are the costs incurred in warehousing finished products and delivering them to customers.
(d) *Administrative costs*, which are associated with the overall management of the enterprise, and which cannot be identified with specific functions such as production, selling, distribution and research. For example, the salary of a factory manager would be assimilated into product costs, but the salary of the company accountant would be included in administrative costs.
(e) *Financial costs*, are the cost of financing the business, such as interest on loans.
(f) *Research and development costs*. Research costs relate to discovering new products or processes or ways of improving existing products and processes. Development costs are those incurred after management has decided to adopt the new product or process.

The classification of costs into broad functional categories provides management with an overall view of major segments of the business in order to assess their relevant impact on total enterprise costs. For example, firms commonly look at functional costs as a percentage of total costs in expressing a judgement about the extent of their financial effort in particular directions. Thus, selling costs or research and development costs may be deemed to be too high or too low in a judgemental sense.

2.3 PRODUCT COSTS

The major concern of manufacturing business is to have information about product costs. Firms need product costs for pricing purposes. In addition, they need to track product costs to ensure that they are not excessive. In competitive markets, the control of product costs and the search for cost reductions is a key factor for business survival. The cost of particular products is also important with respect to assessing the relative profitability of different products, and making decisions accordingly.

2.3.1 Direct and indirect costs

The problem of product costing is how to trace or identify costs according to products. For this purpose, costs are classified in terms of their *relationship* with the product. These relationships are shown in

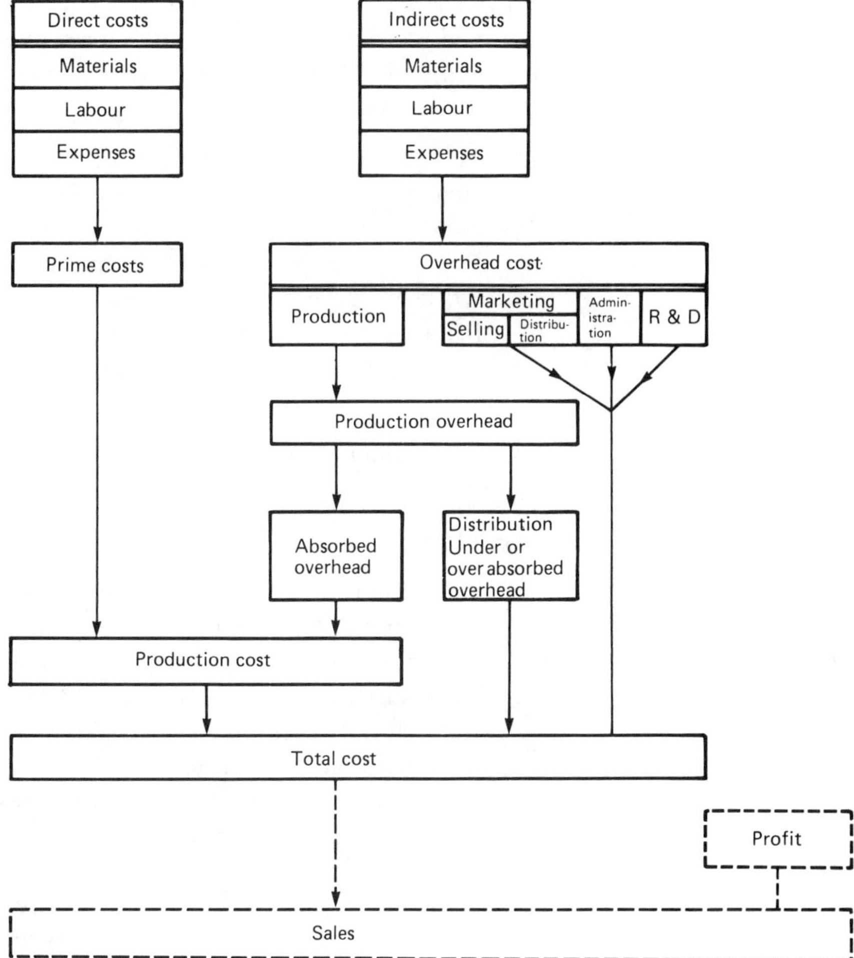

Exhibit 2.1 Elements of cost. OIMA terminology.

Exhibit 2.1. Costs that are traceable only to the product are called *direct costs*. Costs that are not immediately traceable to the product are called *indirect costs*.

Direct costs comprise:

(a) *Direct material costs*, which are the materials that go into the product.
(b) *Direct labour costs*, which are the wage costs of workers engaged in the making of the product.
(c) *Direct expenses*, which are expenses other than direct material and direct labour costs, such as the hire of tools or equipment for a particular job.

Indirect costs comprise all other factory costs that have not been classified as direct costs. The terms *overhead costs* or *production overheads* are commonly used when referring to indirect costs of production.

Indirect costs include:

(a) *Indirect material costs*, such as lubricants and supplies used in the factory, and not used specifically for a particular product.
(b) *Indirect labour costs*, such as the salaries and wages of factory inspectors, foremen, timekeepers and workers who do not work on specific products, such as cleaners.
(c) *Indirect expenses*, such as factory heat, light and power, as well as the depreciation of factory buildings, plant and equipment.

2.3.2 Production costs

The purpose of product costing is to determine production costs. The following points should be noted:

(a) For the purpose of profit determination product costing is concerned with determining the production cost of products. These are defined as factory costs, and do not include non-production costs, such as selling, distribution, administrative, financial, and research and development costs. Accountants have traditionally excluded non-production costs from products for measuring profit mainly because they are not as readily identifiable with products as production costs. Therefore, the inclusion of non-manufacturing costs in products would make the process of matching revenue and costs less precise.
(b) Production costs comprise direct costs and production overhead (factory indirect) costs only.
(c) In the case of a one-product firm, it is evident that *all* production costs are direct costs. The distinction between direct and indirect production costs relates only to multiproduct firms.

2.3.3 Prime costs and production overhead costs

The term 'prime costs' refers to the total of direct costs in the form of direct material, direct labour and direct expenses. Where the firm produces more than one product, production overhead costs have to be allocated to the different products to arrive at their production cost. Production overhead costs which are allocated in this way are known as '*absorbed overheads*'.

2.3.4 Conversion costs

Another cost classification involves the distinction between direct material costs and conversion costs. In this context, conversion costs express the totality of costs that a firm has to incur in converting raw materials into the finished product. Conversion costs include all costs other than direct material costs, namely direct labour cost, direct expenses and overhead production costs.

2.3.5 Cost units

In order that product costing should be useful for such decisions as pricing, it is necessary to relate production costs to units of output. A cost unit is defined as the *quantitative unit of product or service in relation to which costs are ascertained.*

A cost unit may be:

(a) a unit of production expressed as a relevant quantity, volume or weight of the product;
(b) a unit of service, for example, passenger-mile, hospital bed, number of students enrolled;
(c) a job or contract for a specified client.

2.3.6 Product costs and financial accounting

The aggregate product costs of the finished cost units flow into the financial accounts of the enterprise and appear as the cost of production of finished units. They are added to the existing stocks and, in financial accounting terms, represent goods available for sale. Therefore, product costs are recorded in the financial accounting system and provide the following information:

(a) cost value of opening stock;
(b) cost of production of the current period;
(c) cost of goods sold during the current period;
(d) cost value of closing stock.

EXAMPLE 2.1

B Company manufactures two products for which the following cost information is known:

Product description	*Type 1*	*Type 2*
	£	£
Direct material cost per unit	0.20	0.30
Direct labour cost per unit	0.35	0.15
Direct expenses per unit	0.10	0.05
Prime cost per unit	0.65	0.50
Allocated overhead cost per unit	0.35	0.20
Production cost per unit	1.00	0.70

There are no stocks on hand at the beginning of the year. Production during the year consisted of 1000 completed units of type 1 and 2000 completed units of type 2. Seven hundred and fifty units of type 1 and 1800 units of type 2 were sold during the year.

From the foregoing cost, production and sales information, the financial accounting records will show the following:

	Type 1	*Type 2*	*Total*
Cost value of opening stock	—	—	—
Cost of current production	1000	1400	2400
Cost of goods sold	750	1260	2010
Cost value of closing stock	250	140	390

2.3.7 Period costs and financial accounting

Period costs are costs other than the production costs that have been identified as product costs. They usually include:

(a) non-production overhead costs, such as selling, distribution, administrative, financial, and research and development costs;
(b) under- or over-absorbed production overhead costs.

Period costs are not included in production costs. Consequently, they are not included in the cost of stock and of the cost of goods sold. Instead, they are charged as expenses in the profit and loss account.

EXAMPLE 2.2:

During the period ended 31 March 19X0, C Company sold 100 units of their product at a price of £1 per unit. Production cost per unit was £0.60. Selling, distribution and administrative costs amounted to £18, and unabsorbed production overhead costs totalled £2. C Company's profit and loss account for the period ended 31 March 19X0 will appear as follows:

	£	£
Sales		100
Cost of sales (product costs)		60
Gross profit		40
Selling, distribution and administrative costs (period costs)	18	
Under-absorbed product overhead costs (period costs)	2	20
Net profit for the period		20

2.3.8 Under- or over-absorbed production overhead costs

The under- or over-absorption of production overheads is a phenomenon arising from the method used in cost accounting for allocating production overhead to product costs.

EXAMPLE 2.3:

Consider the data given in Example 2.1 where B Company has two products type 1 and type 2 for which estimated production costs were:

	Type 1	*Type 2*
	£	£
Prime cost per unit	0.65	0.50
Allocated overhead costs per unit	0.35	0.20
Production cost per unit	1.00	0.70

The calculation of the estimated direct cost elements making up the prime cost is a simple matter, since such costs result from the actual production of each unit of a product. Thus, each unit of the product will require a given quantity of material priced at the cost per weight.

The calculation of the estimated overhead costs per unit requires knowledge of the following two key factors:

(a) the total production overhead costs to be allocated to both products;
(b) the total number of units of type 1 and type 2 which will 'absorb' such production overhead costs.

Since production overhead costs are indirect costs, that is, they are incurred independently of the number of units actually produced, calculating the total production overhead costs to be allocated involves making an estimate of the total production overhead costs for the period. In the example given, the total production overhead costs were estimated at £750, and allocated to each unit of type 1 and type 2 with the following result:

	Type 1	*Type 2*
Allocated overhead cost per unit	£0.35	£0.20
Number of units actually produced	1000	2000
Production overhead costs *absorbed*	£350	£400

Under- or over-absorption of production overheads results from the following differences:

(a) a difference between the estimate made of total overhead costs to be allocated to the products prior to actual production and the actual total overhead costs incurred;
(b) a difference between the estimated (budgeted) number of units of each product to be produced and the actual number of units produced.

Under-absorption will result from:

(a) an under-estimation of the production overhead costs that were ultimately incurred;
(b) an under-estimation of the number of units that were ultimately produced.

Over-absorption will result from:

(a) an over-estimation of the production overhead costs that were ultimately incurred;
(b) an over-estimation of the number of units that were ultimately produced.

EXAMPLE 2.4:

Prior to the commencement of the period of production, it was estimated that production overhead costs would total £750. This estimate resulted in the allocation of £0.35 and £0.20 to each unit of these products as and when they were produced.

At the end of the period, the actual production overheads incurred were found to amount to £800. The production overhead costs *under-absorbed* were £50. Since these costs had not been absorbed into product costs, they may be charged as an expense in the profit and loss account.

2.3.9 Accumulating production costs

Products are normally processed through several departments before they emerge as a completed product and are transferred into stock. As we noted in Chapter 1, such departments are described as *cost centres* for the purpose of accumulating (recording) production costs. For product costing purposes, a cost centre is defined as *a location, function or items of equipment in respect of which costs may be ascertained and related to cost units.*

Two types of cost centres are involved in the accumulation of costs for product costing:

(a) *Production cost centres*, which are departments directly concerned with the manufacturing process, for example, the cutting department, the machining department, the assembly department and the finishing department.
(b) *Service cost centres*, which are departments that provide services to the production departments, for example, the maintenance department, the factory administration department, the canteen and the transport department.

Direct costs are accumulated with the products themselves as they move successively through the production cost centres. Indirect costs, in the form of the overhead costs of production cost centres and the totality of the costs of service cost centres have to be allocated to the products.

The allocation of indirect costs to products is effected in three stages:

(a) First, total production costs are allocated between production and service cost centres. Some of these costs are directly identifiable with particular cost centres, for example, wages costs of personnel working in a cost centre are allocated directly to that cost centre. Costs that cannot be traced directly to a cost centre, because they are associated with the provision of benefits to several cost centres, have to be *apportioned* to these cost centres pro rata to the benefit received.
(b) Second, indirect costs accumulated in the service cost centres are assigned to production cost centres by pro rata apportionment based on the benefit received.
(c) Finally, indirect costs accumulated in the production cost centres are allocated to cost units, and absorbed into their total production cost.

As will be seen in Chapter 5, the apportionment of indirect costs to different cost centres requires the use of an appropriate apportionment base, as does the allocation of indirect production cost centre costs to cost units.

Exhibit 2.2 illustrates the accumulation of production costs by cost centres and cost units. There are two production cost centres – drilling and assembly, and one service cost centre – maintenance. Direct costs for all three cost centres represent those costs that were traceable directly to these cost centres. Indirect costs in the form of rates and administration were apportioned to the three cost centres on the basis of benefit received. Also shown under indirect costs is the apportionment of maintenance totalling £1700 to the two production cost centres.

Exhibit 2.2 also shows the accumulation of production costs by cost units. The assembly department worked on two jobs during the period. Their production costs amounted to £7800, representing the

Exhibit 2.2 Direct and Indirect Production Costs

	Drilling	*Assembly*	*Maintenance*
	£	£	£
Direct costs:			
Raw materials	5 500	1 500	—
Direct labour	2 000	3 000	—
Production overhead:			
Indirect labour	300	400	500
Indirect material	400	400	300
Depreciation	100	200	50
Total direct costs	8 300	5 500	850
Indirect costs:			
Production overhead			
Rates	600	500	150
Administration	1 500	1 300	700
Apportioned service	1 200	500	1 700
Total production cost	11 600	7 800	

	Job 1	Job 2
Direct costs:	£	£
Raw materials	1 000	500
Direct labour	2 000	1 000
Indirect costs:		
Production overhead	2 200	1 100
Total job costs	5 200	2 600

totality of costs accumulated in the assembly department. Direct costs of £4500 in the form of direct material and direct labour that are directly traceable to job 1 and job 2 were £3000 and £1500, respectively. Indirect costs amounting to £3300 are apportioned as to £2200 to job 1 and £1100 to job 2. The basis of apportionment for estimating the benefit received by these jobs from the assembly department is the 'direct labour cost basis'. Thus, since two-thirds of the total labour costs of £3000 incurred by the assembly department were traced to job 1, so two-thirds of total indirect costs of £3300 were apportioned to job 1.

2.3.10 Further applications of direct/indirect cost analysis

Classifying production costs between direct and indirect costs is useful not only for product costing purposes, but also for calculating the cost of running departments, divisions or other business segments. We have seen, so far, that *at the product level*, costs are direct or indirect depending upon their relationship to a particular and identified product. Costs which are indirect to the product *at the product level* may be direct costs *at the department level* at which the product is being processed.

Where a factory comprises several production departments, it is important to know where production costs are being incurred. Consequently departmental costs will consist of direct and indirect costs associated with the products being processed in the department *plus* the factory costs which are identified as being direct to the department. In addition, departmental cost will include factory costs which are indirect to the department. This process of moving upward through the organizational structure requires identifying direct and indirect costs with the organizational level in question.

Exhibit 2.3 illustrates the manner in which the direct/indirect cost classification depends on the reference level involved.

Exhibit 2.3 Cost classification and organizational level

Cost	*Direct to*	*Indirect to*
Top corporate management	Company	Divisions, departments, products
Division management	Company, division	Departments, products
Direct departmental overhead	Company, division, department	Products

2.4 ACTIVITY LEVEL COSTS

The direct/indirect cost classification assumes that costs will remain constant irrespective of the level of activity. It is known, however, that some costs change as activity levels change. For example, some costs remain constant irrespective of the level of activity, whereas other costs increase with the level of activity.

The purpose of classifying costs into fixed costs and variable costs is to provide management with information of the behaviour of costs at different activity levels. In particular, this information is important for setting output level targets that will enable the firm to improve profits. Given that fixed costs are constant, the firm should seek to maximize profitability by reducing costs. One way is to obtain the maximum output from given fixed costs.

Fixed costs are defined as *those costs which in aggregate remain constant through different activity levels.* They include rent, rates, depreciation and the salaries of managers and supervisors. Variable costs are defined as *those costs which in aggregate vary at different activity levels.* They include such important elements of product costs as direct material and direct labour costs.

Exhibit 2.4 illustrates the nature of fixed and variable costs by means of simple graphs for a paint manufacturing business. Salaries are assumed to be fixed at £50 000 irrespective of the activity level, expressed in litres of paint. The slope of the cost curve is perfectly horizontal, indicating that salaries will cost £50 000 *irrespective* of the volume of output. Direct material costs are variable costs. The slope of the cost curve indicates that one cost unit of paint (1 litre) costs £1, and at an activity level of 50 000 litres, direct material costs are £50 000. For simplicity, it is assumed that the variable cost curve is linear, and, for example, that the purchase price of direct materials does not change as larger quantities are purchased.

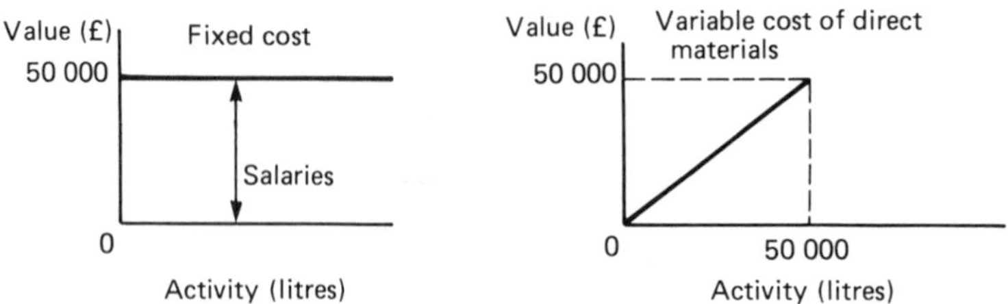

Exhibit 2.4 Fixed and variable costs.

2.4.1 Implication of cost behaviour for product costs

From Exhibit 2.4, it will be noted that if the firm produces only 1 litre of paint, product costs will amount to £50 001 (£50 000 of salaries plus £1 of direct material). If however the firm produces 50 000 litres of paint, product costs will fall to £2 (£50 000 of salaries + £50 000 of direct materials divided by 50 000 litres of output).

2.4.2 Cost behaviour at the unit level

As explained above, costs are classified as to fixed and variable cost at the aggregate level. When applied to the unit level (cost unit), fixed costs behave as variable costs and change as output increases or decreases.

EXAMPLE 2.5:
Consider the data shown in Exhibit 2.4. Since salaries are fixed costs, they remain constant at £50 000 irrespective of the activity level. However, at the cost unit level, salaries allocated to 1 litre fall from £50 000 when only one cost unit is produced to £1 when 50 000 cost units are produced. Therefore, at the unit level, fixed costs are seen as variable costs. Following the same reasoning, variable costs are fixed costs at the unit level since they remain constant at £1 per unit.

2.4.3 Profit planning and cost behaviour

Since product costs per unit will be affected to the extent that some elements of costs are fixed costs and others are variable costs, product costs will be a function of activity levels. Hence, profit planning implies seeking the lowest product costs per unit in order to maximize total profits that result from the formula:

Total profits = market price per unit − (unit production costs × number of units produced)

2.4.4 Semi-variable costs

To make the foregoing analysis possible, all production costs must be classified into fixed and variable costs. Some production costs, however, are neither fixed nor variable. They are described as semi-variable costs. For example, electricity supply costs may consist of a fixed standing charge per period and a variable charge relating to consumption. Exhibit 2.5 illustrates the nature of semi-variable costs, using electricity supply costs as an example.

As will be seen in Chapter 5, it is necessary to split semi-variable costs into their fixed and variable components for the purpose of analysing cost behaviour at different activity levels.

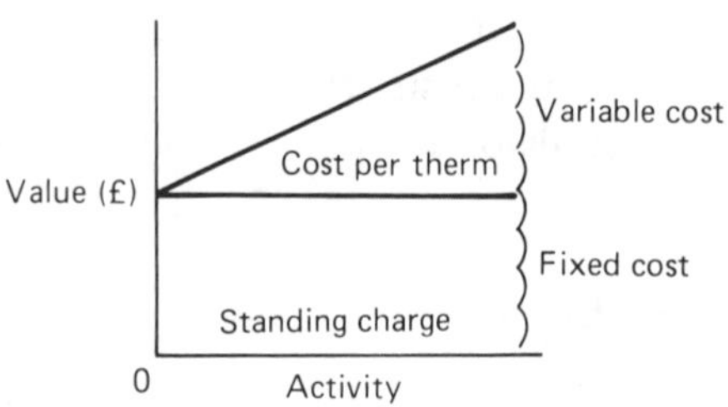

Exhibit 2.5 Semi-variable costs.

2.4.5 Product costs and activity level costs

Product costing requires the distinction between direct and indirect costs. Typically, direct costs consist of material costs, labour costs and direct expenses: indirect costs consist of insurance salaries, rent, depreciation, etc. Activity level costing requires the distinction between fixed and variable costs.

Consequently, there is a tendency to assume that direct and variable costs are the same costs, and that indirect and fixed costs are also the same costs. Nothing could be more erroneous. Direct costs refer to the relationship of costs to a cost unit. Some direct costs may be variable in relation to activity levels, such as material costs, but other direct costs may be fixed, such as the depreciation of equipment used solely for a particular cost unit. Similarly, some indirect costs may be variable costs in relation to activity levels, such as the variable portion of electricity costs, and other indirect costs may be fixed, such as insurance and rent costs.

2.4.6 Further applications of activity level costs

In addition to examining the impact of activity levels on unit product costs, the analysis of cost behaviour in relation to different activity levels may be applied to non-production costs, such as selling, distribution, administrative, and research and development costs. Such analysis helps management to understand how functional costs respond to activity level changes, as part of a global approach to the management of all enterprise resources.

2.5 CONTROLLABLE COSTS

We mentioned in Chapter 1 that one important aspect of the management process is concerned with control which is aimed at ensuring that management objectives are attained. Financial control is directed at achieving planned (budgeted) targets, which themselves reflect the desired level of efficiency in the use of resources.

Cost control within the enterprise is effected in two related ways:

(a) At the departmental level, defining the responsibility for the management of costs in terms of cost centres. Cost centre managers are given a 'total cost allowance' that is related to an accounting period. This cost allowance is stated as the *budgeted costs*.
(b) At the product level, determining limits of resource usage that represent desired standards of efficiency in the use of production resources. A 'unit cost allowance' is calculated in advance of production for each cost unit. This cost allowance is stated as *the standard cost per cost unit*.

2.5.1 Budgeted costs and standard costs

The introduction of cost control requires the firm to undertake cost studies designed to determine efficient cost levels. The budgeted costs of production and non-production cost centres will be related to planned activity levels. Control is exercised through periodic budget reports in which cost centre managers account for the budgeted costs for which they are responsible.

The budgeted costs of production cost centres will be a function of the planned level of output and will correspond to the aggregate of the standard cost of the cost units to be produced during the budget period. Control is exercised through periodic reports that enable variances between standard costs and actual costs to be investigated, and subsequent corrective action to be taken.

2.5.2 Controllable and non-controllable costs

Responsibility for costs extends only to costs over which individual managers are able to exercise control. Hence, it is the managerial level that determines the extent of cost responsibility. For example, the supervisor of a factory production cost centre can only be held accountable for the costs incurred in his department over which he has control. Hence the term *controllable costs* is defined in terms of a manager's position in the hierachy. He is not responsible for costs over which he has no control. *Non-controllable costs* would include costs incurred on processing the product prior to transfer to his department, as well as costing resulting from the action of his superiors. Non-controllable costs also include costs influenced by external factors, such as market prices for raw materials and wage rates.

The organizational structure is often described as reflecting *the pyramid of control*. The level of managerial authority increases as one rises up the pyramid of control. Accordingly, the extent of controllable costs is at maximum at the level of the board of directors, since managerial authority is the most complete at that level.

2.5.3 Controllable costs and performance reports

The effectiveness of cost control systems depends on the quality of information included in feedback reports. One important objective of cost control systems is the evaluation of the performance of managers in respect of the costs (resources) under their individual control. It follows that controllable and non-controllable costs should be distinguished in performance reports. Chapter 16 reviews the principles upon which cost control and management information systems should be established.

2.6 RELEVANT COSTS

In Chapter 1, we noted that the management process could be explained in terms of decision making. In this chapter, we have seen that different cost concepts are needed for the following different types of decisions:

(a) *stock valuation*, for which a distinction is required between direct and indirect costs;
(b) *profit planning*, requiring knowledge of cost behaviour through activity level changes, and hence that fixed costs and variable costs be distinguished;
(c) *cost control*, based on the notion of predetermined levels of cost efficiency reflected in the concepts of budgeted and standard costs and a system of performance evaluation requiring a distinction between controllable and uncontrollable costs.

2.6.1 The nature of relevant costs

Although the foregoing cost concepts are all related to various aspects of the management process involving decision making, the term *relevant costs* has a special meaning in cost accounting. Relevant costs are those costs that will be affected by management decisions.

2.6.2 Relevant costs as future costs

Since decisions are intended to affect the future, rather than the past, relevant costs will be incurred in the future as the result of the decision presently to be made. Costs that have already been incurred, described as *sunk costs* are irrelevant costs.

EXAMPLE 2.6:
D Company has equipment costing £100 000, presently being used to 60 per cent of capacity. The annual rate of depreciation is 20 per cent. Z Inc. an American company places an order for 100 000 units of the product made solely by that equipment. Acceptance of that order would involve increasing capacity usage by 10 per cent and additional costs of 10p per unit for raw materials, labour and other direct expenses. The costs relevant to considering acceptance of that order total £10 000 (100 000 × £0.10). The relevant costs do not include any proportion of the depreciation that is already being charged in full against current production.

2.6.3 Relevant costs as differential costs

Decisions are assumed to reflect choices between at least two alternatives, and are intended to assist making a decision in favour of one alternative as against the other(s). Since, all things being equal, management will select the least costly alternative, the relevant costs are those that will differ as the result of preferring one alternative to another.

EXAMPLE 2.7:
D Company has equipment which could be used for manufacturing product X or product Y. These two products are mutually exclusive, since they require operatives with different skills. At full capacity, the equipment uses £500 of power per annum. Wages costs for product X and product Y would amount to £10 000 for Product X and £15 000 for product Y per annum. The annual depreciation costs of the equipment are £10 000.

The costs relevant to making a choice between product X and product Y are limited to the differential costs. Hence, only the wage costs are the relevant costs for that decision.

2.6.4 Relevant costs and opportunity costs

In economic theory, *opportunity costs* are defined as the benefits forgone as the result of preferring one alternative to another.

EXAMPLE 2.8:
F Company owns premises currently being used as a selling outlet and producing annual profits of £20 000. These premises could be leased to G Company at an annual rent of £30 000.

In deciding whether it is more advantageous to continue using the premises or leasing them, F Company must take account of the opportunity costs of seeking the most profitable alternative. The opportunity costs are the annual profits of £20 000 which will be forgone as a result of opting to letting for £30 000. F Company is better off by £10 000 (£30 000–£20 000) as a result of choosing to lease.

2.6.5 Relevant costs and accumulated costs

Relevant costs appear only when alternative decisions are being considered. They are not accumulated (recorded) as costs, for their usefulness disappears as soon as decisions have been made.

2.7 COST CODES

We noted earlier that the accumulation (recording) of costs is made at two levels:

(a) cost centre level;
(b) product level.

Costs are accumulated at cost centre level for the purposes of establishing managerial responsibility for costs, and at the product level in order to calculate product costs. A basic requirement for accumulating at these two levels is an appropriate coding system that enables costs to be identified with respective cost centres and products.

Establishing cost codes for identifying costs with cost centres involves the following stages:

(a) ensuring that the organizational chart clearly represents the boundaries of responsibility and authority in the firm;
(b) ensuring that the organizational chart clearly models the processes particular to the firm;
(c) superimposing managerial responsibility for costs in the information reporting system that relates the processes of the firm with the manager responsible for their control;
(d) establishing an appropriate reference code that identifies each cost centre within the functional area in which it is located.

It should be noted that coding systems are in general use and are not limited to coding cost centres. The extensive use of computers in businesses today implies data coding systems that make computer applications possible. Coding systems are necessary for computer applications in the general accounting area, for stock control, for sales control as well as personnel records, etc.

Example 2.9 illustrates the cost coding system designed for use in a packaging company. Other types of businesses would need cost codes designed to fit their particular processes.

EXAMPLE 2.9:
From the organizational chart for KRS Packaging plc shown in Exhibit 2.6, it is seen that the firm is structured on the basis of four functional areas – production, sales, commercial and administration. Each is designated as a cost centre and given a code number expressed as a digit, as follows:

Production	1
Sales	2
Commercial	3
Administration	4

Next, subordinate cost centres are coded. For example, within the production function, there are six cost centres. These are coded as follows:

extrusion	1.1
printing	1.2
conversion	1.3
packing	1.4
production planning	1.5
engineers	1.6

The next stage is to devise appropriate codes for costs by nature, i.e. materials, labour and overhead. Most companies have a system of

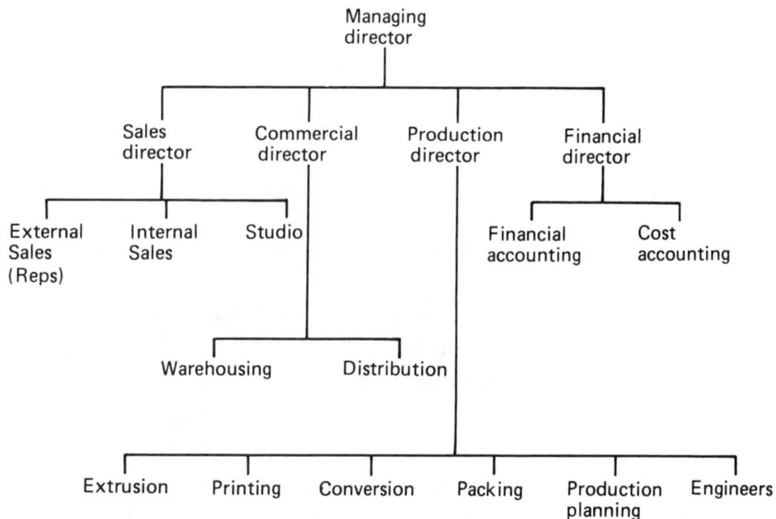

Exhibit 2.6 Cost centre cost coding. KRS Packaging plc.

accounts codes for every item of expense and income. Usually the system will serve both the financial and cost accounts. The code was made up of five digits as follows:

Field A		*Field B*		
0	0	0	0	1
1	1			
2	2			
3	3			
4	4			

Field A =	Balance sheet	0		
	Production cost centres	1	Extrusion Department	1.1
			Print department	1.2
			Conversion department, etc.	1.3
	Sales cost centre	2	Sales department: External	2.1
			Internal	2.2
	Commercial cost centre	3	Warehousing	3.1
			Distribution	3.2
	Administration	4	Financial accounts	4.1
			Cost accounts	4.2
Field B =	Fixed assets	Codes	000	
		to	100	
	Current assets		101	
		to	200	
	Capital		201	
		to	300	
	Current liabilities		301	
		to	400	
	Materials		501	
		to	600	
	Labour		601	
		to	700	
	Overheads		701	
		to	999	

The code for a material cost charged to the extrusion department could be coded 11501; that for a salary cost for administration could be 41601; stock in current assets, 00101; creditors, 00301.

Example 2.9 shows that there are two major classifications, balance sheet items and profit and loss account items. The balance sheet is further divided into assets and liabilities, then fixed assets and current assets and long-term liabilities and current liabilities. The profit and loss account comprises sales codes, cost of sales codes and expense codes. The level of detail required from the coding system is dependent on the various managers' needs of the system. Common sense principles should also be applied. These should be related to the main purpose of the coding system, i.e. to provide a database for management decision making.

Questions

1. Explain briefly the four main cost classifications.
2. Define clearly the elements of product cost.
3. Distinguish direct from indirect costs.
4. What are prime costs?
5. What do you understand by conversion costs?
6. What is a cost unit?
7. Is there a difference between product costs and production costs?
8. What costs are included in production costs?
9. Is the 'direct/indirect cost' classification limited in its usefulness to product costing? Explain.
10. Why do production overhead costs have to be 'absorbed'? What happens if they are not absorbed?
11. What are 'activity costs'?
12. Give examples of variable costs, direct costs, fixed costs and indirect costs.
13. Give one example of a cost which is:

    (a) variable and *not* direct;
    (b) indirect *and* variable;
    (c) fixed *and* direct;
    (d) variable *and* direct;
    (f) fixed *and* indirect.

14. At the product level, is it true that:

    (a) variable costs are fixed;
    (b) fixed costs are variable?

15. What are semi-variable costs? Are these the same costs as semi-fixed costs?
16. What is the relevance of the 'fixed/variable cost' classification?
17. Explain the connection, if any, between product costs and activity costs.
18. Define 'budgeted costs' and 'standard costs'.
19. What are 'controllable' and 'non-controllable' costs?
20. What is a relevant cost?
21. Discuss the importance of the relevant cost concept for management decisions.
22. Explain the role of cost codes for cost accounting purposes.

Problems

1. Classify the following production expenses as either direct or indirect costs:
   (i) rates of the factory;
   (ii) raw materials;
   (iii) production director's salary;
   (iv) production operatives' wages;
   (v) canteen staff wages;
   (vi) consumable stores;
   (vii) lighting of the factory;
   (viii) production administration expenses.
2. Analyse the following costs between:
   (i) direct materials;
   (ii) direct labour;
   (iii) production indirect expenses;
   (iv) selling and distribution expenses;
   (v) general administration expenses.
   (a) Solicitors charged for collecting debts;
   (b) expenses of hiring a tank and military uniforms for advertising promotion;
   (c) motor tax and insurance on fleet delivery vans.
   (d) wages of chargehands;
   (e) hotel bills for salesmen;
   (f) running costs of managing director's Rolls Royce;
   (g) cost of electricians used to install and maintain all electrical systems in the company;
   (h) cost of fork-lift trucks used to transport materials from one department to another;
   (i) commission charges from bank;
   (j) foremen's wages;
   (k) repairs to factory buildings;
   (l) depreciation of a firm's computer;
   (m) overtime premium for direct employees;
   (n) materials traceable to jobs;
   (o) hire of equipment for a specific job;
   (p) sales director's bonus;
   (q) fire insurance on plant and machinery;
   (r) purchase of discs for computer;
   (s) setting up wages in machines;
   (t) heating costs of accounts office;
   (u) salary of managing director's secretary;
   (v) postal charges on sample goods sent to customers;
   (w) maintenance wages in the factory;
   (x) cost of market research survey commissioned by the sales director.

3. From the following prepare a schedule highlighting:
prime cost;
production cost;
total cost.

			£
(i)	Expenses of the administration function		60 000
(ii)	Materials used in producing products		220 000
(iii)	Depreciation in:	£	
	Office equipment	5 000	
	Machinery (production)	29 000	
	Delivery vans	18 000	
	Showrooms	6 000	58 000
(iv)	Direct labour costs incurred		155 000
(v)	Indirect factory expenses		17 000
(vi)	Wages of truck driver		30 000
(vii)	Salaries and expenses of salesmen		100 000
(viii)	Salaries of the production function		30 000
(ix)	Salaries of the administration function		40 000
(x)	Expenses of delivering goods		50 000

4. (a) 'Fixed costs are really variable: the more you produce the less they become.'

Explain the above statement and state whether or not you agree with it.

(b) You are required to sketch a separate graph for each of the items listed below in order to indicate the behaviour of the expense. Graph paper need not be used but your axes must be labelled.

(i) supervisory labour;
(ii) depreciation of plant on a machine-hour basis;
(iii) planned preventive maintenance plus unexpected maintenance;
(iv) monthly pay of a salesman who receives a salary of £15 000 per annum plus a commission of 1 per cent paid on his previous month's sales when they exceed £100 000; assume that his previous month's sales totalled £150 000.

(Chartered Institute of Management Accountants)

5. The graphs in Exhibit 2.7 reflect the pattern of certain overhead cost items in a manufacturing company in 1 year. The vertical axes of the graphs represent the total cost incurred, whilst the horizontal axes represent the volume of production or activity. The zero point is at the intersection of the two axes.

   Required:
   (a) Identify which graph represents the overhead cost items shown below.
   (N.B.: a graph may be used more than once.)

Ref.	*Brief description*	*Details of cost behaviour*
1	Depreciation of equipment	When charged on a straight line basis.
2	Cost of a service	£50 annual charge for subscription, £2 charge for each unit taken, with a maximum total charge of £350 per annum.
3	Royalty	£0.10 per unit produced, with a maximum charge of £5 000 per annum.
4	Supervision cost	When there is one chargehand for every eight men or less, and one foreman for every three chargehands, and when each man represents 40 hours of production, thus: *Hours* Under 320 one chargehand 321–640 two chargehands 641–960 three chargehands, etc. plus one foreman.
5	Depreciation of equipment	When charged on a machine-hour rate.
6	Cost of a service	Flat charge of £400 to cover the first 5000 units: *Per unit* £0.10 for the next 3000 units £0.12 for the next 3000 units £0.14 for all subsequent units
7	Storage/carriage service	*Per ton* £15 for the first 20 tons £30 for the next 20 tons £45 for the next 20 tons No extra charge until the service reaches 100 tons; then £45 per ton for all subsequent tonnage.
8	Outside finishing service	*Per unit* £0.75 for the first 2000 units £0.55 for the next 2000 units £0.35 for all subsequent units

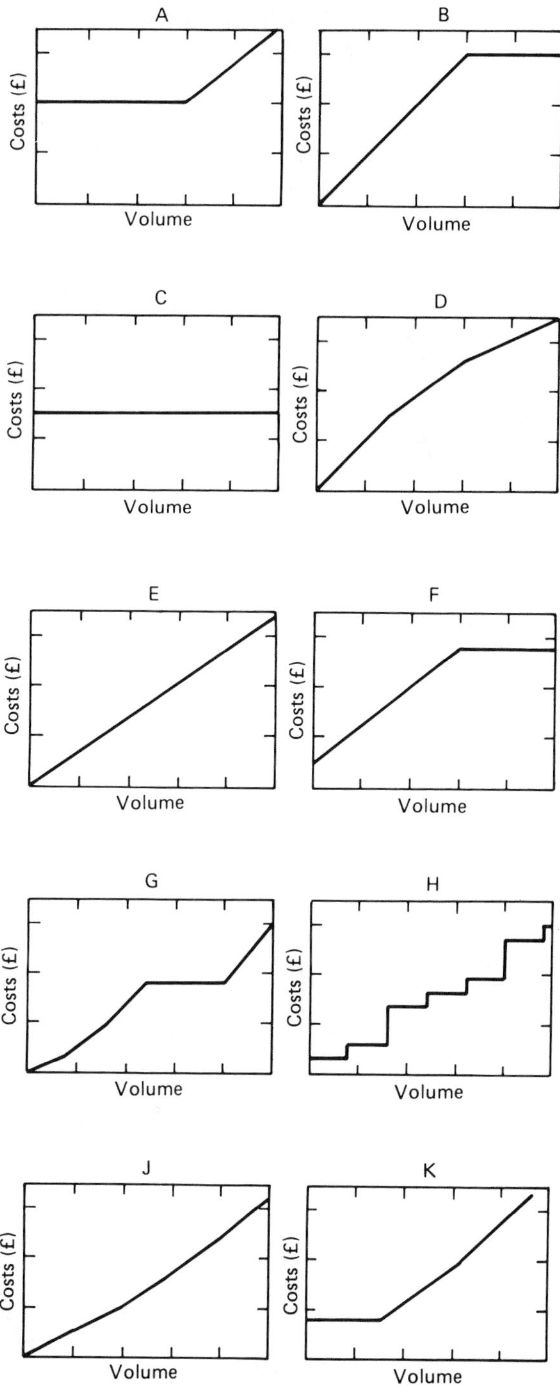

Exhibit 2.7

(b) Give an example of an overhead cost item that could represent those graphs to which you do not refer in your answer at (a) above.
(c) Draw one graph of a pattern of an overhead item not shown and give an example of an overhead cost item that it would represent.

(Chartered Institute of Management Accountants)

Part 2 Accounting for the Elements of Costs

Product costing requires costs to be distinguished on the basis of their relationship to the product. Costs that can be directly identified with the product are direct costs. They consist of direct labour, direct materials and direct expenses. Costs that cannot be directly identified with the product are indirect costs. They consist of production overhead costs that relate to all the products being produced in a particular factory or the services provided by an agency.

Product costing involves analysing and accumulating costs to permit the cost of production of each product to be calculated. Where only one product is being produced, direct materials, direct labour and overhead costs are all direct costs. This is because they all relate to a single product. Where multiple products are being produced within the same factory, direct material and direct labour costs can still be identified with individual products, but overhead costs cannot be so identified. It is for this reason that they are indirect costs.

In order to determine and record the total production cost of each product, a way has to be found of allocating production overhead costs to individual products. Once that has been achieved, the allocated overhead costs are added to the direct material and direct labour costs in the calculation of the total production cost of each product.

The purpose of Part II is to discuss these several elements of product costs, as follows:

Chapter 3 discusses accounting for material cost.
Chapter 4 examines accounting for labour costs.
Chapter 5 reviews the several areas of difficulty relating to accounting for overhead costs.

3 Material Costs

This chapter deals with the following topics:

3.1 The definition of material costs.
3.2 Cost accounting objectives for material costs.
3.3 Materials coding.
3.4 Recording and documenting materials transactions.
3.5 Stock control.
3.6 Costing stores issues.
3.7 SSAP 9 stocks and work-in-progress (1975).
3.8 Stock ratios.

The purpose of this chapter is to explain the cost accounting techniques relating to materials. As we noted in Chapter 2, material costs may be direct to the product if used in its manufacture, and may be indirect if their utilization cannot be related to a particular product.

3.1 THE DEFINITION OF MATERIAL COSTS

The term 'material costs' may be used to refer to the cost of the following:

(a) raw materials used in making products;
(b) components used in assembling products;
(c) consumable materials, such as small tools, cleaning materials, paint and other items too small to assign separately as costs;
(d) stationery and office supplies;
(e) finished products available for immediate resale, such as stocks held by retailers.

3.2 COST ACCOUNTING OBJECTIVES FOR MATERIAL COSTS

Although the relative importance of material costs in production costs varies widely in different industries, statistical data shows that, on average, they amount to 50 per cent of production costs. It follows that an enterprise must instal a system of materials cost control for the purpose of achieving satisfactory profits.

This chapter deals with the following features of an efficient system of materials cost control:

(a) materials coding;
(b) documenting and recording materials transactions;
(c) valuing stores issues and closing stocks;
(d) stock control.

3.3 MATERIALS CODING

A code is defined as a 'system of symbols designed to be applied to a classified set of items, to give a brief, accurate reference facilitating entry, collation and analysis' (Chartered Institute of Management Accountants, 1982).

The use of symbols allows data to be gathered more speedily, and coded data is readily processed in computer-based control systems. A digit code can be developed to replace a label. For example, material that is labelled as '0.5 mm mild steel wire' can be coded as 1105, denoting in this way the description 'mild steel wire' as 11, and the diameter 0.05 mm as the next two digits. Mild steel wire 0·6 mm in diameter would be coded as 1106. If stainless steel is coded as 12, then stainless steel wire 0.5 mm in diameter would be coded 1205.

Codes can be assigned to each identifiable material that is significant in cost terms. Materials of small value and of limited usage can be designated as 'sundries' and coded appropriately. Computerized stock control systems have led to simplifications in coding systems. In the example noted above, the numeric code 1105 that uses only four digits to describe '0.5 mm mild steel wire' replaces a narrative code in a manual coding system of 17 digits. Materials coding systems must be capable of expansion to provide sufficient space for coding new material specifications in the same groups of materials. Numeric coding systems provide that flexibility. Coding systems may be developed to serve different purposes. In addition to coding materials, coding systems may be extended to refer materials usage to cost centres, products and divisions.

Responsibility for developing and controlling coding systems will rest with the accounting department. The extent of the coding systems will depend on the level of detail required. Periodically, data gathered under each code will be used to prepare reports on the total cost of materials used by each cost centre or product, and the stock of each material remaining on hand. This information will also serve to prepare periodic control reports and profit and loss accounts.

3.4 RECORDING AND DOCUMENTING MATERIALS TRANSACTIONS

The responsibility for buying materials at the lowest prices consistent with required specifications rests with the purchasing department. It is also responsible for arranging delivery schedules that avoid interruptions in production due to material shortages.

The following materials transactions require documenting and recording:

(a) material purchases;
(b) receiving and inspecting in-coming materials;
(c) valuing material purchases;
(d) issuing materials to cost centres;
(e) materials returned or transferred;

Exhibit 3.1 illustrates the phases and the documentation involved with the normal cycle of material transactions.

Exhibit 3.1 The material cycle

Phase	*Documentation*
Request for materials	Purchase requisition
Purchase	Purchase order
Reception and inspection	Goods received note
Valuing material purchases	Supplier's invoice
Storage	Bincard/stores ledger
Issue of materials	Materials requisition

3.4.1 Purchase requisition

Exhibit 3.1 shows that the first stage in the material cycle is the request for materials supported by a purchase requisition. On receipt of the purchase requisition, the buyer will place an order with a regular supplier in which the quantities, price and terms are stated. Alternatively, he may seek quotations or ask for bids before placing an order.

The following details appear on a purchase order (see Exhibit 3.2)

(a) reference number and date of the order;
(b) full description and quantity of materials ordered;
(c) price per cost unit, and total value of the order;
(d) terms of payment;
(e) required date of delivery;
(f) location where delivery is to be made;
(g) authorization signature.

PURCHASE ORDER

Lydgate Engineering Ltd
Davy Road
Whitechapel
London WH6 2PY

No.: 4832
Date: 18/6/19X7
Reqn No.: 756
Delivery: At once

To: Hughes and Howe Ltd
Titan Works, Ipswich IP9 2EB

Please supply, in accordance with the conditions stated overleaf:

Quantity	Description	Price	Per	Amount
50	1 foot diameter cyclops	£150	each	£7500·

Please quote order number on invoice and advice note.

To be delivered free at our works.

for Lydgate Engineering Ltd
W. Small
Buyer

Exhibit 3.2 Purchase order.

A copy of the purchase order bearing a cross reference to the materials requisition is sent to the accounting department. This copy will be used for checking and approving the supplier's invoice. Other copies will be sent to the receiving department, the inspection department and to the department which initiated the purchase requisition.

3.4.2 Reception and inspection

Authorized deliveries are inspected on arrival for conformity with the purchase order as to quality and quantity by the receiving and inspection department. The delivery note is signed only when inspection is completed. A *goods received note* is prepared showing:

(a) reference number of the goods received note;
(b) date of receipt;
(c) supplier and carrier;
(d) description, quantity and material code number;
(e) corresponding purchase order reference number;
(f) signature of person authorized to accept delivery.

Copies of the goods received note are sent to the purchasing and the requisitioning departments as well as the accounting department for matching with the purchase order.

3.4.3 Valuing material purchases

The purchase price of materials consists of the price per unit agreed with the supplier less the following discounts normally allowed to the buyer:

(a) the trade discount allowed to the purchaser which recognizes that he will be incurring further costs in trading;
(b) the quantity discount allowed to the purchaser which recognizes the cost savings realized by the supplier as a consequence of being able to supply larger quantities.

The purchase price may include further charges for carriage and insurance, depending upon the contract price quoted.

Commercial contracts take two general forms:

(a) carriage paid, where the supplier is responsible for delivery costs to the buyer. Sometimes, the term FOB (free-on-board) is used;
(b) carriage, insurance and freight (CIF), where all delivery costs are borne by the buyer. Sometimes, the term 'ex factory' is used also.

The supplier's invoice, which is generally received with the delivery of the materials, records the following:

(a) name of the supplier and the buyer;
(b) supplier's VAT (value added tax) registration number;
(c) supplier's reference number for the order;
(d) date of the invoice;
(e) buyer's purchase order reference number;
(f) description of the goods;
(g) quantity, price and total value.

The invoice is sent to the accounting department for matching with the purchase order and the goods received note. Once checking is complete, it is authorized for payment.

3.4.4 The issue of materials

Materials delivered to the firm are placed in stores and held until required for use. Stores are defined as a cost centre and the storekeeper's accounting responsibility as a manager includes safeguarding the materials stored against losses from theft and deterioration. Stores accounting requires that proper records be maintained of receipts and issues of stores, and that these records be supported by proper documentation. Issues of materials from stores for use by a cost centre require an authorization in the form of a material requisition note issued by the requesting cost centre. Exhibit 3.3 illustrates a material requisition note.

MATERIALS REQUISITION

To: West Stores — No: 8146

From: Drilling department — Date: 16/1/X6

Charge code: 2518

Code	Description	Units	Rate	£
1105	0.5 mm mild steel wire	150	£8	1200.00

Requisitioning foreman:	Issued by: B.Bracewell
I.Wright	Date: 16.1.X6

Exhibit 3.3 Material requisition note.

As may be noted, the following details appear on the material requisition note:

(a) requisitioning cost centre's reference number for the note;
(b) date of the note;
(c) description of the materials;
(d) material code number;
(e) quantity required (and issued, if different);
(f) job number or cost centre code;
(g) stores from which issued;
(h) signature of the person requisitioning.

The columns 'rate' and '£' are left blank by the requisitioning cost centre and the stores, since these cost centres are not concerned with recording the cost of materials.

Material requisition notes are in triplicate form – one remaining in the requisitioning cost centre, one kept by the stores as a record of material issued, and one going to the costing department. The costing department completes the material requisition form by inserting in the 'rate' and '£' columns the cost value per unit of the material and the total cost of the materials issued in connection with the requisition note. Costing methods are discussed later in this chapter.

3.4.5 Materials returned and transferred

Materials that are returned to stores must be accompanied by a *materials returned note*. It is usually designed in the same form as the material requisition note, but is coloured red to assist document identification. It is in triplicate, one copy for the cost centre returning the materials, one copy for stores records and one copy for the costing department.

Materials that are transferred from one cost centre to another cost centre must be accompanied by a *materials transferred note*. It gives details similar to those of the materials returned note. It is in triplicate form, one copy for the transferring cost centre, one copy for the cost centre receiving transfer and one for the costing department. In this way, correct costing is maintained of material used in particular cost centres and on particular jobs.

3.5 STOCK CONTROL

Efficient stock control implies:

(a) determining required stock levels;
(b) determining the re-order level and re-order quantity;
(c) maintaining proper stock control records;
(d) ensuring adequate audit procedures for checking physical quantities with stock control records.

3.5.1 Determining stock levels

The following considerations generally apply to the management of stocks:

(a) Steps should be take to ensure that stocks never run out, thereby causing cancellation of orders and loss of goodwill.
(b) Stock levels should be closely integrated with production planning schedules to ensure smooth production flows.
(c) Goods may deteriorate or be affected by obsolescence if held too long in stock.
(d) The cost of holding stocks may be seen as equivalent to an interest charge calculated with respect to the total investment in stocks. Moreover, stocks as investments produce no financial returns to the firm, since they represent idle money.

For the foregoing reasons, the determination of stock levels is a matter of fixing minimum and maximum quantities within which limits actual stock levels should be maintained.

(a) *The minimum stock level* is the lowest point at which stock should ever fall. It represents the quantity of buffer stock for an item calculated by reference to normal periodic usage and the normal delivery time. There is a danger of 'stock out' if the level should fall below this point. It is calculated as follows:

re-order level − (normal usage × normal re-order period)

(b) *The maximum stock level* is the maximum point beyond which stock will never rise. Factors that are taken into account in determining the maximum stock level are:

(i) usage rate;
(ii) risk of deterioration and obsolescence;
(iii) market supply factors;
(iv) storage space available;
(v) cost of financing stockholding.

In practice, the maximum stock level is linked to the re-order level and re-order quantity (see below) and is calculated as follows:

maximum stock level = re-order level − (minimum usage × minimum re-order period) + re-order quantity

(c) *The average stock level* is simply:

$$\frac{\text{Maximum level} - \text{Minimum level}}{2}$$

3.5.2 Determining the re-order level and the re-order quantity

The management of stock levels focuses on the re-order level and the re-order quantity.

(d) *The re-order level* is the point at which a purchase order should be placed. It is calculated to take account of the probability of 'stock out', as follows:

re-order level = maximum usage × maximum re-order period

(e) *The re-order quantity* is the quantity that should be purchased once the re-order level has been reached. It is calculated as follows:

re-order quantity = maximum stock level − re-order level − (minimum periodic usage × minimum delivery period)

The notion of the re-order quantity has been developed further into the concept of the economic order quantity which recognizes the costs of placing orders and holding stocks and relates these costs to usage.

(f) *The economic order quantity* is the optimal quantity that should be purchased at any one time and is calculated as follows:

$$\sqrt{\frac{2 \times \text{cost of placing an order} \times \text{usage per annum}}{\text{cost per unit} \times \text{carrying costs per annum}}}$$

3.5.3 Maintaining proper stock control records

Stock control records are kept in two locations – on bin cards in the stores and in the stores ledger kept in the cost department.

(a) *A bin card* records deliveries and issues of materials and assists the storekeeper to control stocks. There is a bin card for each item on which minimum and maximum stock levels are stated, as well as re-order levels and re-order quantities. Exhibit 3.4 illustrates a bin card.

BIN CARD

Material code No.: 1105 — Re–order level: 400

Material description: 0.5 mm — Re–order quantity: 800

Maximum stock: 1100

Minimum stock: 300

Date	Reference	Receipts	Issued	Balance
1 Jan				350
5 Jan	8014	400		750
16 Jan	8146		150	600
25 Jan	8185		100	500
31 Jan	8192		100	400

Exhibit 3.4 Bin card.

(b) *The stores ledger* reflects the same information as shown on the bin cards, and additionally records the unit price and total value of all stock deliveries and issues. It comprises three sections containing detailed records of raw materials, identifiable work-in-progress and products in finished goods stock. In each of these three subsidiary sections there is recorded the balance of stock in hand and the value of the balance for each item. The summarized subsidiary records are reconciled with the materials accounting in the nominal ledger (see Chapter 6). Exhibit 3.5 illustrates a stores ledger account.

3.5.4 Stock audit procedures

Verifying that actual quantities in stores correspond with the stock

STORES LEDGER ACCOUNT

Material code no.: 1105 Location: West Stores

Material description: 0.5 mm mild steel wire Re–order level: 400

Re–order quantity 800

Maximum stock 1100

Minimum stock: 300

Date	Receipts				Issues				Stock balance		
	Ref.	Qty	Price	Value	Ref.	Qty	Price	Value	Qty	Price	Value
1 Jan									350	£8	2800
5 Jan	5014	400	£8	400					750	8	6000
16 Jan					8146	150	£8	1200	600	8	4800
25 Jan					8185	100	8	800	500	8	4000
31 Jan					8192	100	8	800	400	8	3200

Exhibit 3.5 Stores ledger account.

ledger records is a central feature of stock control and a main objective of stock audit procedures. It will be recalled that financial accounting stock records may be kept on a periodic or perpetual basis. Similarly, stocktaking may be on an annual or on a continuing basis.

(a) *Annual stocktaking* implies that at any time during the year, the quantity recorded on the bin card is an accurate statement of the physical quantity in stores. This assumption is verified at the year-end by a physical stocktake. The following disadvantages are associated with annual stocktaking.

 (i) It may be necessary to stop operations while stocktaking is in progress.
 (ii) The count may be inaccurate since staff required to assist in stocktaking may be unfamiliar with the items in stores.
 (iii) Discrepancies revealed will have occurred during the year, and their subsequent investigation may prove difficult.

(b) *Continuous stocktaking* is the verification of the recorded stock shown on the bin cards and the stores ledger account with the physical quantity in stores, whenever it is felt appropriate. The timing of the physical stocktake depends on the value of the item, the cost of checking, etc. The advantages of continuous stocktaking are as follows:

 (i) Stocktakers are able to work round the production process, thereby avoiding shutdowns and consequent losses in production and profits.

(ii) Discrepancies are quickly discovered and investigated.

(iii) Financial losses resulting from obsolescence and stock deterioration are reduced.

(iv) Regular monitoring of stocks improves the quality of control and limits losses resulting from misappropriation.

(v) Stock information produced for management purposes commands a higher level of confidence by reason of regular verification.

(vi) The competence of personnel employed in the stores and in the stock recording process is evaluated on an on-going basis. However, to avoid collusion between stores management personnel, independent auditors should be involved in the physical verification of stocks, particularly items of high value.

3.6 COSTING STORES ISSUES

Product costing requires that issues of materials be costed at the appropriate value. Under conditions of changing market prices, items in stock may have been purchased and recorded at different prices. The following five alternative methods may be used for costing out materials to products:

(a) FIFO (first-in, first-out);
(b) LIFO (last-in, first-out);
(c) weighted-average cost;
(d) standard cost;
(e) replacement cost.

EXAMPLE 3.1:
The following data is used to illustrate these methods:

Purchases:		
2 April, 19X0	200 units at £4.15	830
7 April, 19X0	200 units at £4.20	840
15 April, 19X0	300 units at £4.30	1290
22 April, 19X0	100 units at £4.40	440
28 April, 19X0	200 units at £4.65	930
		£4330

Issues for April totalled 800 units and goods transferred out of stock were as follows:

3 April, 19X0	250 units
10 April, 19X0	200 units
16 April, 19X0	250 units
23 April, 19X0	100 units

FIFO (first-in, first-out)

The main characteristic of this method is that issues from stock are priced at the purchase price of the earliest batch received. When all the receipts relating to that batch have been issued, then the purchase price of the next batch is used. The method follows the actual physical issue of stock, namely, that the oldest stock is used first. Exhibit 3.6 illustrates this method, which is used by the majority of companies in the United Kingdom. During periods of inflation, however, the value of the closing stock under this method is likely to approximate current replacement cost. Whilst this characteristic is relevant to the current valuation of closing stock on the balance sheet, it leads to an overstatement of reported profits.

Exhibit 3.6 FIFO Method

Date	*Receipts*			*Issues*			*Stock balance*		
19X0	*Quantity*	*Unit cost*	*Total cost*	*Quantity*	*Unit cost*	*Total cost*	*Quantity*	*Unit cost*	*Total cost*
		£	£		£	£		£	£
1 April							100	4.00	400
							200	4.15	830
2 April	200	4·15	830						
3 April				100	4.00	400			
				150	4.15	622			
7 April	200	4.20	840				50	4.15	208
							200	4.20	840
10 April				50	4.15	208			
				150	4.20	630			
15 April	300	4.30	1290				50	4.20	210
							300	4.30	1290
16 April				50	4.20	210			
				200	4.30	860	100	4.30	430
22 April	100	4.40	440				100	4.40	440
23 April				100	4.30	430	100	4.40	440
28 April	200	4.65	930				200	4.65	930
				Total cost of issues		3360	300	Closing stock	1370

LIFO (Last-in, first-out)

Under LIFO valuation procedures, the closing stock will be at the value of the earliest purchases constituting stock. Accordingly, stock values tend to be progressively understated. Advocates of this method claim that the most current costs are being matched against revenue, leading to more accurate representation of profit. Changes in stock levels, however, can lead to fluctuations in the cost of sales. This system is rarely used in the United Kingdom. The Inland Revenue does not regard it as an acceptable basis for tax purposes. Exhibit 3.7 illustrates the method.

Weighted-average method

This method avoids the extreme assumption of the FIFO and LIFO methods and attempts to avoid the excessive distortions in either the cost of issues or the value of closing stock implied by these methods. This method is at best an expedient which does not really solve the

Exhibit 3.7 LIFO Method

Date	*Received*			*Issues*			*Stock balance*		
19X0	*Quantity*	*Unit cost*	*Total cost*	*Quantity*	*Unit cost*	*Total cost*	*Quantity*	*Unit cost*	*Total cost*
		£	£		£	£		£	£
1 April							100	4.00	400
2 April	200	4·15	830				200	4.15	830
							100	4.00	400
3 April				200	4.15	830			
				50	4.00	200			
7 April	200	4.20	840				50	4.00	200
							200	4.20	840
10 April				200	4.20	840	50	4.00	200
							300	4.30	1290
15 April	300	4.30	1290						
16 April				250	4.30	1075	50	4.00	200
							50	4.30	215
							100	4.40	440
22 April	100	4.40	440						
23 April				100	4.40	440	50	4.00	200
							50	4.30	215
28 April	200	4.65	930				200	4.65	930
				Total cost of issues		3385	300	Closing stock	1345

problems of valuing stock. Exhibit 3.8 shows that the average price is calculated after every receipt.

At this point, a comparison of the valuations achieved by the three methods will be useful. If we assume that the firm used in our illustration is a retailer 'issues from stock' will appear as 'cost of goods sold'. Exhibit 3.9 summarizes the different valuations of the cost of goods and the closing stock using the three alternative methods. During a period of rising prices the FIFO method produces the highest profits because the prices used for calculating cost of goods sold are the lowest. On the other hand, the value of closing stock is highest under the FIFO method because the most recent prices are used.

Standard and replacement cost methods

A standard cost is a predetermined cost which is usually only altered if there is a significant change in price. The preparation of a standard price will be discussed in Chapter 15.

Exhibit 3.8 Weighted Average Method

Date	*Received*			*Issues*			*Stock balance*		
19X0	*Quantity*	*Unit cost*	*Total cost*	*Quantity*	*Unit cost*	*Total cost*	*Quantity*	*Unit cost*	*Total cost*
		£	£		£	£		£	£
1 April							100	4.00	400
2 April	200	4.15	830				200	4.15	830
							300	4.10	1230
3 April				250	4.10	1025	50	4.10	205
7 April	200	4.20	840				200	4.20	840
							250	4.18	1045
10 April				200	4.18	836	50	4.18	209
15 April	300	4.30	1200				300	4.30	1290
							350	4.28	1499
16 April				250	4.28	1071	100	4.28	428
22 April	100	4.40	440				100	4.40	440
							200	4.34	868
23 April				100	4.34	434	100	4.34	434
28 April	200	4.65	930				200	4.65	930
				Total cost of sales		3366			
					Closing stock		300	4.55	1364

Exhibit 3.9 Comparison of Stock Pricing Methods

	FIFO	*LIFO*	*Weighted average*
	£	£	£
Cost of goods sold	3360	3385	3366
Closing stock	1370	1345	1364

The replacement cost method prices material issues and stock values at the current replacement cost of material. This method of accounting has attracted many supporters in recent years and has figured prominently in the inflation accounting proposals of the Accounting Standards Committee. The cost of goods sold it is argued, should be calculated on the current cost of replacing stock, otherwise reported profits will be inflated by rising prices rather than by increased efficiency. The balance sheet will show stocks valued at current replacement costs, the true value of the assets to the business.

3.7 SSAP 9 STOCKS AND WORK-IN-PROGRESS (1975)

SSAP 9 requires that stocks and work-in-progress should be valued at the lower of cost and net realizable value, taking each item or group of items separately. Cost is further defined to mean 'expenditure incurred in the normal course of business in bringing the product or service to its present location and condition'. Related production overheads (those costs not associated directly with the product) should be included in cost, as should other overheads attributable to bringing the product to its present location and condition. The allocation of overheads for this purpose should reflect current and expected future levels of activity. Net realizable value is defined as

> 'the actual or estimated selling price of the stock net of any trade discount, from which is deducted any cost incurred to put the stock into a saleable condition, and to which is added all costs to be incurred in the marketing, selling and distribution of such stock.'

SSAP 9 allows the use of several methods of approximating actual costs. They include unit cost, average cost and FIFO. If standard (predetermined) costs are used as production costs and for the valuation of stocks, they should be reviewed frequently to ensure that they bear a reasonable relationship to actual costs. The use of selling price less the profit mark-up is allowed only if it can be shown to give a reasonably close approximation to actual cost. LIFO is not a permissible method of stock valuation because it does not normally provide a sufficiently close approximation to actual costs. In this connection, it will be recalled that LIFO understates the valuation of stock in hand, since the earliest purchases remain in stock and the more recent purchases are treated as issues. Consequently, under conditions of rising prices, stock values fall in relation to current replacement costs.

SSAP 9 also requires the disclosure of the main categories of stock. Accounting policies used for stock valuations must be disclosed. In this connection, it should be noted that the Companies Act 1985 requires the disclosure of separate figures for raw materials, work-in-progress and finished goods stock.

3.8 STOCK RATIOS

Management will seek to evaluate the effectiveness of stock control systems, and a number of techniques are employed in this regard. Stock ratios are important for providing benchmarks with respect to stock figures. The following stock ratios are in common use:

(a) stock turnover for raw materials;
(b) stock turnover for finished goods;
(c) input–output ratio for raw materials;
(d) stock–out ratio.

3.8.1 Stock turnover for raw materials

This ratio provides an indicator of the rate at which materials are being utilized. It is calculated as follows:

$$\text{rate of stock turnover} = \frac{\text{value of materials issued}}{\text{average value of stock}}$$

EXAMPLE 3.2:

The accounts of McClure at the end of the year show: opening stock £4000, purchases £30 000, closing stock £6000.

$$\text{rate of stock turnover} = \frac{£4\,000 + £32\,000 - £6\,000}{(£4\,000 + £6\,000) \div 2}$$

$$= \frac{£30\,000}{£5\,000} = 6$$

Therefore, the stock turns over six times a year, and, on average, stock is being held for 2 months. This calculation may reveal the presence of slow-moving stocks. Materials which are lying in stock for long periods not only are subject to deterioration, but are incurring storage cost in the form of locked-up capital, storage space, etc.

3.8.2 Stock turnover for finished goods

This ratio indicates the rate at which finished goods are sold. It is calculated as follows:

$$\text{rate of stock turnover} = \frac{\text{cost of goods sold}}{\text{average value of stock}}$$

This ratio may reveal slow-moving stocks of finished goods.

3.8.3 Input–output ratio for raw materials

This ratio indicates wastage (or the efficiency of usage) of raw materials.

EXAMPLE 3.3:

Reverting back to Example 3.2, McClure estimates that the raw materials content of the finished product is £25 000.

$$\text{input–output ratio} = \frac{£30\ 000}{£25\ 000} = 1.2$$

This indicates an inefficient use of raw materials because 12 per cent of the input has been wasted.

3.8.4 Stock-out ratio

This ratio could indicate inefficient stock control or the need to review stock holding levels or delays in supplier deliveries. It is calculated as:

$$\frac{\text{orders held up by stock shortage}}{\text{orders received}}$$

EXAMPLE 3.4:

Grime estimates that of 500 orders received in the previous year 50 were held up by stock shortages.

$$\text{stock – out ratio} = \frac{50}{500} = 1.0$$

This indicates that 10 per cent of Grime's orders were held up by stock shortages. This situation could jeopardize the success of his enterprise.

Questions

1. What cost items are included in the term 'material costs'?
2. State what is meant by a 'code' in cost accounting.
3. What is the purpose of using codes for materials?
4. What are the materials transactions that require to be recorded? Describe the documentation that these transactions require.

5. What is the importance of the purchase requisition?
6. Describe the discounts normally allowed with respect to materials purchases.
7. Describe the two general forms of commercial contracts for materials purchases.
8. Distinguish the purchase requisition and the material requisition.
9. What do you understand by 'efficient stock control'?
10. Define the following:

    (a) the minimum stock level;
    (b) the maximum stock level;
    (c) the average stock level.

11. Define the re-order level. Explain what is meant by the re-order quantity in that regard.
12. Explain the economic order quantity.
13. What information is disclosed in:

    (a) the bin card;
    (b) the stores ledger account.

14. Compare and contrast annual and continuing stocktaking.
15. List the valuation bases relevant to material stocks.
16. State the requirements of SSAP 9 with respect to stock valuation.
17. Explain the significance of the following ratios:

    (a) the stock turnover for materials;
    (b) the stock turnover for finished goods;
    (c) the input–output ratio for raw materials;
    (d) the stock–out ratio.

Problems

1. A company manufactures shoes and slippers in half sizes in the following ranges:

	Sizes
Men's	6 to 9½
Ladies'	3 to 9
Boys'	1 to 5½
Girls'	1 to 5

The company uses a seven-digit code to identify its finished products, which, reading from left to right, is built up as follows:

Digit *one* indicates whether the products are men's, ladies', boys' or girls'. The numbers used are:

1 – men's;
2 – ladies';
3 – boys';
4 – girls'.

Digit *two* denotes type of footwear (shoes or slippers).
Digit *three* denotes colour (5 is green; 6 is burgundy).
Digit *four* denotes the material of the upper part of the product.
Digit *five* denotes the material of the sole.
Digits *six* and *seven* denote size.

Examples:

Code 1613275 represents a pair of mens slippers, brown suede, rubber sole, size 7½.

Code 1324195 represents a pair of mens shoes, black leather, leather sole, size 9½.

Required:
Set suitable code numbers to the following, stating any assumptions you make:

(a) boys' shoes, brown leather uppers, rubber soles, size 4;
(b) ladies' slippers, green felt uppers, rubber soles, size 4½;
(c) girls' shoes, burgundy leather uppers, leather soles, size 3½.

(*Chartered Institute of Management Accountants*)

2. (a) From the following information relating to component BCD you are required to calculate:
   (i) the re-order level; (4 marks)
   (ii) the re-order quantity (4 marks)
   (iii) the minimum level; (4 marks)
   (iv) the average stock held: (4 marks)

Maximum stock has been set at:		5500 units
Usage per month:	Maximum	1100 units
	Minimum	900 units
Estimated delivery period:	Maximum	4 months
	Minimum	2 months

(b) What do you consider to be the essential practices of efficient storekeeping? Explain by giving at least four examples.
(6 marks)
(Total 22 marks)

(Association of Accounting Technicians)

3. (a) A company is reviewing its stock policy and has the following alternatives available for the evaluation of stock number 12789:
   (i) purchase stock twice monthly, 100 units;
   (ii) purchase monthly, 200 units;
   (iii) purchase every 3 months, 600 units;
   (iv) purchase every 6 months, 1200 units;
   (v) purchase annually, 2400 units.

   It is ascertained that the purchase price per unit is 80p for deliveries up to 500 units. A 5 per cent discount is offered by the supplier on the whole order where deliveries are 501 and up to 1000, and a 10 per cent reduction on the total order for deliveries in excess of 1000. Each purchase order incurs administration costs of £5. Storage, interest on capital and other costs are 25p per unit of average stock quantity held.

Required:
Advise management on the optimum order size.
(9 marks)

(b) Concerning stock, explain:
   (i) purchase requisition;
   (ii) continuous stocktaking;
   (iii) stock turnover.

(6 marks)

(c) An audit of the stocks in your organization shows many discrepancies between the actual quantities counted and the quantities on record.
   State the possible causes of these differences from receipt of items to depatch of finished products and how you might remedy these weaknesses.
(7 marks)
(Total 22 marks)

(Association of Accounting Technicians)

4. On 1 January Mr G started a small business buying and selling a special yarn. He invested his savings of £40 000 in the business

and, during the next 6 months, the following transactions occurred:

Yarn Purchases			*Yarn Sales*		
Date of receipt	*Quantity*	*Total cost*	*Date of despatch*	*Quantity*	*Total value*
	Boxes	£		*Boxes*	£
13 Jan.	200	7 200	10 Feb.	500	25 000
8 Feb.	400	15 200			
11 March	600	24 000	20 April	600	27 000
12 April	400	14 000			
15 June	500	14 000	25 June	400	15 200

The yarn is stored in premises Mr G has rented and the closing stock of yarn, counted on 30 June, was 500 boxes. Other expenses incurred, and paid in cash, during the 6-month period amounted to £2300.

Required:

(a) Calculate the value of the material issues during the 6-month period, and the value of the closing stock at the end of June, using the following methods of pricing:
   (i) first-in, first-out;
   (ii) last-in, first-out; and
   (iii) weighted-average (calculations to two decimal places only).

(10 marks)

(b) Calculate and discuss the effect each of the three methods of material pricing will have on the reported profit of the business, and examine the performance of the business during the first 6-month period.

(12 marks)
(Total 22 marks)

(Chartered Association of Certified Accountants)

5. The managing director of a company manufacturing one product, a standard-sized office desk, asks you as the recently appointed works accountant to investigate the material control procedures operating in the factory. You have arranged for a physical stock count of raw materials, work-in-progress and

finished goods to take place at the beginning and end of April. The results of this stocktaking and other data relevant to the consumption of material during April are shown below.

Physical stocktaking	*Opening stock at beginning of April*	*Closing stock at end of April*
Finished goods	650 desks	925 desks
Work-in-progress	300 desks	160 desks
degree of completion:		
Timber	66.67% complete*	75.0% complete
Varnish	25.0% complete	37.5% complete

(* That is, the 300 desks had been issued with 66.67 per cent of the timber necessary to complete the desk).

Raw materials:		
Timber	40 000 ft^2	55 000 ft^2
Varnish	1 600 litres	700 litres
Other Data		
Sales	4600 desks	
	Timber	*Varnish*
Works manager's estimate of material consumption per desk, including an allowance for normal waste	30 ft^2.	0.47 litres
Purchase price of opening stock	£1.40 per ft^2	£1.20 per litre
Purchases of materials:		
5 April	125 000 ft^2 at £1.50 per ft^2	400 litres at £1.10 per litre
19 April	70 000 ft^2 at £1.70 per ft^2	1800 litres at £1.30 per litre
Value of material issued to production:		
12 April	£120 000	£1200
26 April	£164 000	£1550

The value of material issued to production has been obtained by using the following methods of pricing material issues:

Timber – last-in- first-out,
Varnish – first-in, first-out.

Required:

(a) Calculate the quantity of timber and varnish issued on *each* of the dates shown in the question and the consequent book-stocks of each material at the end of April. Compare the closing book-stocks of each material with the results of the physical stock counts.

(9 marks)

(b) Calculate the total quantity of each material which, according to the works manager's estimates, should have been consumed and compare with the quantities of materials actually consumed.

(6 marks)

(c) Discuss the possible reasons for any differences revealed by your comparisons in (a) and (b) above.

(7 marks)

(Total 22 marks)

(Chartered Association of Certified Accountants)

6. Nicholl commences the manufacture of model railway engines on 1 January 19X0. His trading account for the first year is as follows:

	Units	£	£	£
Sales	50 000			500 000
Cost of sales				
Raw materials:				
Opening stock		—		
Purchases		500 000		
		500 000		
Less: Closing stock		(50 000)	450 000	
Labour			160 000	
Production overheads			80 000	
Cost of production	80 000		690 000	
Less: Closing stock	(30 000)		(240 000)	
	50 000			(450 000)
Gross profit				50 000

Notes:

(1) Stocks of both raw materials and finished goods have increased uniformly over the year.

(2) The raw materials content of finished goods is £5.00 per unit.

(3) Nicholl was ill during August, when he received orders for 6000 units which were held up by stock shortages and subsequently cancelled. He had a further 4000 orders on his books at the year end.

(a) (i) inventory turnover for raw materials;
(ii) inventory turnover for finished goods;
(iii) input–output ratio for raw materials;
(iv) stock–out ratio.

(8 marks)

(b) Comment briefly on these four ratios.

(4 marks)
(Total 12 marks)

4 Labour Costs

This chapter deals with the following topics:

4.1 Framework for effective labour cost control.
4.2 The personnel department.
4.3 Timekeeping.
4.4 Methods of remuneration.
4.5 Incentive schemes.
4.6 The wages department.
4.7 Accounting for labour costs.
4.8 The cost of labour turnover.

The purpose of this chapter is to discuss the accounting techniques relating to labour costs. Labour costs are similar to material costs in that they may be direct or indirect in relation to the product itself. Unlike material, labour cannot be stored. Therefore, the complex notions of accounting for raw material stocks have no place in the discussion of accounting for labour costs. Instead, the focus is on people and on the manner in which people are employed. In this chapter, we deal with the various techniques employed in this connection.

In most organizations, labour costs are a significant proportion of total costs, and control over the usage of human resources expressed as labour costs is an important objective of cost accounting. The techniques utilized in this context are discussed in Parts III and IV.

4.1 FRAMEWORK FOR EFFECTIVE LABOUR COST CONTROL

Effective labour cost control is achieved through:

(a) satisfactory procedures for selecting, training and assigning workers to jobs;
(b) efficient production planning for scheduling work to production departments;
(c) establishing desired standards of performance based on budgeted labour costs reflecting labour cost standards;
(d) controls that not only ensure the performance of tasks for which

wages are paid, but allow variances between expected and actual performance to be highlighted;

(e) rewards systems that provide appropriate payments for employees and include incentives to improve productivity.

The effective control of labour cost through these various management activities concerns several different functions. The cost department is responsible for recording and controlling labour costs and relies on the personnel department, the production department and the wages department for several of the important tasks stated above. An adequate system of responsibility accounting is required that clearly identifies managerial responsibility with respect to labour costs throughout the firm.

Hereunder, we examine the basic procedures involved in labour cost accounting. Setting performance standards, controlling labour cost and allocating labour costs to products or cost units are topics covered in later chapters.

4.2 THE PERSONNEL DEPARTMENT

The primary responsibility for providing the firm with an efficient labour force rests with the personnel department. Its responsibility covers the following areas:

(a) recruiting personnel – advertising jobs, interviewing applications and making offers;
(b) maintaining personnel records – name, address, grade and rate of pay of each employee;
(c) training personnel – in-house and by external programmes;
(d) determining the wage rate for each task/job;
(e) industrial relations – settling disputes and dealing with wage negotiations;
(f) administering welfare programmes, safety and medical facilities;
(g) discharging and retiring personnel.

4.3 TIMEKEEPING

The most obvious indicator of labour usage is labour time. This indicator may be used to cost out the utilization of different grades of employees by reference to their appropriate wage rates and the time committed to different products.

It follows that systematic timekeeping is necessary to track labour usage and to account for labour costs. Accordingly, the timekeeping function is a separate department that reports to the cost accounting department, as well as to the wages, production and personnel departments. It maintains records relating to:

(a) hours worked by each employee;
(b) work done by each employee, units produced and time spent on tasks.

This information is essential to the cost accounting department for identifying labour costs with products and departments, and to the wages department for preparing the payroll.

Two common documents are used for recording labour time:

(a) Clock cards that record the actual time spent at work. This includes basic hours and overtime hours, and forms the basis for the calculation of gross earnings.
(b) Job cards that record the actual time spent on each job. A job card is prepared for each job, unlike the clock card that is made out for each employee.

Production workers may be remunerated on the basis of time or on the basis of output. Under the time system, time is the only determinant of labour cost and proper timekeeping is essential for the control of labour costs. Under the output system, commonly known as the piecework system, production workers are paid solely on the number of units produced, irrespective of the time spent. Even though timekeeping appears redundant for labour cost accounting under the piecework system, correct timekeeping is still essential for the following reasons:

(a) Pieceworkers are required to work to specific times to maintain an even flow of production in the factory. Requiring pieceworkers to clock in at specific times and in the same way as time workers maintains the discipline needed to maintain the even flow of production.
(b) Many production overhead costs vary with time. Hence, allocating overhead production costs to products requires records of labour time usage with respect to particular products or cost units.
(c) As will be seen in the following section, most wage incentive schemes base the bonus on time worked and quantity produced.

4.4 METHODS OF REMUNERATION

The main methods of remunerating labour are:

(a) Payment on a time basis, irrespective of output achieved.
(b) Payment by results (piecework), irrespective of the time taken.
(c) Payment under incentive schemes that combine time rates and payment by results are designed to improve productivity.

Workers are paid a basic minimum rate based on time worked, and a bonus related to output achieved, once the minimum standard of output has been reached.

4.4.1 Time rate method

The time rate (or day rate) method is simple and easy to apply. It is calculated by multiplying the hours recorded on the clock card with the employee's rate of pay. The disadvantages of this method are:

(a) Since the weekly wage is calculated regardless of output, there is no productivity incentive.
(b) If overtime can be worked, some workers will tend to work slowly during the basic time, and then request overtime. This will increase labour wages without increasing output.

Hence, this method is rarely used when output can be measured, and where high output and high efficiency is needed. Conversely, it will tend to be used where output is difficult to measure or when quality is important.

4.4.2 Piecework method

This method is also relatively easy to apply, since wages are calculated by multiplying the units of output recorded for each worker by a rate per unit. For example, an employee producing 35 knitted garments during a particular week payable at a rate of £3 per garment will earn £105 (£3 × 35) in respect of that week.

The piecework method places the entire responsibility for production on the worker. If – for any reason, even those beyond his control, such as a shortage of materials – he produces nothing, his wage is zero. To alleviate this problem, this method is modified by incorporating a guaranteed time rate to ensure that the worker earns a basic wage for clock hours, irrespective of output.

EXAMPLE 4.1:
An employee works 35 hours a week and produces 40 garments. The guaranteed time rate is £2 per hour and the piecework rate is £1 per garment. His total weekly wage for that week will amount to £110 (35 hours × £2 plus 40 units at £1 each).

A further refinement of the piecework method is the use of differential piecework rates, that may be decreased or increased with different levels of output.

EXAMPLE 4.2:
A firm uses the following differential piecework rates:

1–10 units	£1.50 per unit
11–20 units	£1.25 per unit
21–30 units	£1.00 per unit
31 units and above	£0.75 per unit

Applying these rates to the data shown in Example 4.1, the worker's weekly wage would be:

35 hours × £2	= £ 70.00
plus 10 units × £0.75	= £ 7.50
plus 10 units × £1.00	= £ 10.00
plus 10 units × £1.25	= £ 12.50
plus 10 units × £1.50	= £ 15.00
	£115.00

The differential piecework rates have an in-built incentive to produce more, since the first units are paid at £0.75 per unit, whereas the fortieth unit is paid at £1.50. The advantages of this method are:

(a) individual workers can increase their earnings by increasing their output;
(b) workers are remunerated on their individual merit, and the cost of wasted time is eliminated;
(c) overhead cost savings can be realized by the firm by spreading the fixed and semi-variable production overhead costs over a larger output, thereby reducing unit product costs.

Some disadvantages are:

(a) difficulties may arise in finding equitable piecework rates agreeable to the workers;
(b) slower workers may become discontented;
(c) work quality may be sacrificed for higher output.

4.5 INCENTIVE SCHEMES

As mentioned above, remuneration can be modified to provide incentives for workers to increase output and at the same time increase their own wages. Firms have been concerned to improve productivity by means of such schemes, and several variants are found. These are discussed below.

4.5.1 Premium bonus scheme

A premium bonus scheme is a compromise between the simple time rate and the straight piecework systems. It relates wages to the recorded hours and the output achieved by individual workers.

There are several commonly used alternative premium bonus schemes. The three best-known schemes are named after their original inventors: Halsey, Halsey and Weir, and Rowan. They are similar in the following respects:

(a) a time is set for each task;
(b) the time taken by a worker is compared to the allowed time, and a bonus is paid if the time taken is less than the time allowed;
(c) the bonus is shared between the worker and the firm, the amount of the bonus depending on the scheme used as follows:

Halsey:	one-half of the time saved,
Halsey and Weir:	one-third of the time saved,
Rowan:	$\frac{\text{time taken}}{\text{time allowed}} \times \text{time saved}$

(d) payment is usually based on the time rate, but may be subject to separate negotiation.

EXAMPLE 4.3:
An employee is allowed 30 min. to produce each knitted garment. The time taken to produce a week's output of garments is 25 hours. The day rate is £3 per hour and the basic week is 35 hours.

The bonus under each method would be as follows:

	£
(a) *Halsey* = 25 hours × £3	75
plus ½ time saved × hourly rate	
$= \frac{35 - 25}{2} \times £3$	15
Total wage	£90

	£
(b) *Halsey – Weir* = 25 hours × £3 per hour	75
plus ⅓ time saved × hourly rate	
$= \frac{35 - 25}{3} \times £3$	
$= 3\frac{1}{3} \times 3$	10
Total wage	£85

(c) *Rowan* = 25 hours × £3 per hour £75

plus $\frac{\text{time taken}}{\text{time allowed}}$ × time saved × hourly rate

$= \frac{25}{35} \times 10 \times £3$ £21.43

Total wage £96.43

4.5.2 High day rate scheme

This scheme is distinguished from the time rate method by the payment of a significantly higher rate per hour if a standard level of output is achieved. It developed from experience in the use of the piecework and premium bonus schemes over a number of years. This experience showed that workers' motivation is linked to a high hourly rate and is loosely linked to the level of output.

EXAMPLE 4.4:
In Example 4.1 we noted that the time rate was £2 per hour and that 40 garments were produced. Under the high day rate scheme, if the standard level of output is fixed at 45 garments and the high day rate is fixed at £4, then that rate would only be paid if the output achieved is 45 garments.

4.5.3 Group bonus scheme

The incentive schemes discussed so far focus on the individual worker. In some industries where workers tend to work as teams, for example, motor car manufacture, coal mining, steel, paper and wall-covering, it is difficult to separate the output of one individual from that of another.

A group bonus scheme focuses on the team for the purpose of calculating the incentive bonus. It may be based on the piecework method or the premium bonus method, and the calculation of the bonus is similar to that of the individual bonus, the only difference being that the data is aggregated for the group. It may also be based on the number of direct production workers in the team.

EXAMPLE 4.5:
Standard production is set at 50 units per day and it is agreed that for every 10 per cent increase in production a bonus of £40 will be paid. This will be divided equally among the 30 members of the group. In one day, 60 units were produced. The bonus is calculated as follows:

$$\frac{60}{50} \times £40 = £48$$

Each person in the group receives £1.6 (£48 ÷ 30) as bonus.

The advantages of a group bonus scheme are:

(a) It encourages team spirit, and any deviant behaviour in the form of absenteeism, lateness and slow working will be discouraged by the rest of the group.
(b) There is a saving in the elimination of the need to keep individual records, since it is only the production of the group which has to be recorded for the purpose of calculating the bonus.
(c) The group may be expanded to include ancillary workers who can directly influence the output of the group and consequently increase motivation, for example, electricians, engineers, plumbers and fork-lift drivers.

The acceptance of a group bonus scheme may be more problematical than that of an individual bonus scheme. Some workers are able to work harder and find tasks easier. In effect, they will be subsidizing other members of the group and will be penalized in being prevented from obtaining higher earnings.

4.5.4 Guidelines for implementing bonus schemes

The incidence of disputes is likely to be higher in companies that have bonus schemes rather than companies paying workers on time or piecework rates. Such disputes may be about the allowed time, the rate per unit, etc., and may require lengthy negotiations between workers and management to find acceptable solutions. The following guidelines have evolved to ensure the successful implementation of bonus schemes:

(a) The scheme should be agreed by management, unions and employees. Any grievance about perceived bias in the scheme towards either the employer or employee should be resolved at this stage.
(b) The performance level(s) set for bonus payment should be attainable by the average employee, and there should be no limit to the amount of bonus that can be earned.
(c) The rules laid down in the scheme should be clear enough to allow each employee (or group) to make a calculation of the bonus, and to confirm the accuracy of the bonus payment. The bonus should be closely related to effort.
(d) The work environment should not place obstacles to earning the bonus. Management should ensure the smooth flow of work to employees, machine breakdowns should be speedily repaired, output should be removed from the work area, etc.

(e) The bonus should be paid as soon as possible after the output has been produced.
(f) The scheme should not be made the subject of frequent modifications. Frequent changes of time allowed, bonus rates, etc. will lead to loss of confidence in the scheme and lack of trust in management.
(g) The benefits of the scheme should always outweigh its costs. Consequently, the cost of operating the scheme should be known, for example, wages of bonus clerks, work study costs, etc.
(h) The design and implementation of a bonus scheme should conform to the model illustrated in Exhibit 4.1.

4.5.5 Profit sharing and co-partnership

A profit-sharing scheme enables employees to share in the profit of the firm. Normally, an agreed percentage of company earnings is allocated to employees as a group and apportioned to individuals on some equitable basis that takes account of such factors as status, annual wages or salary, and length of service.

A co-partnership scheme gives employees a stake in the company

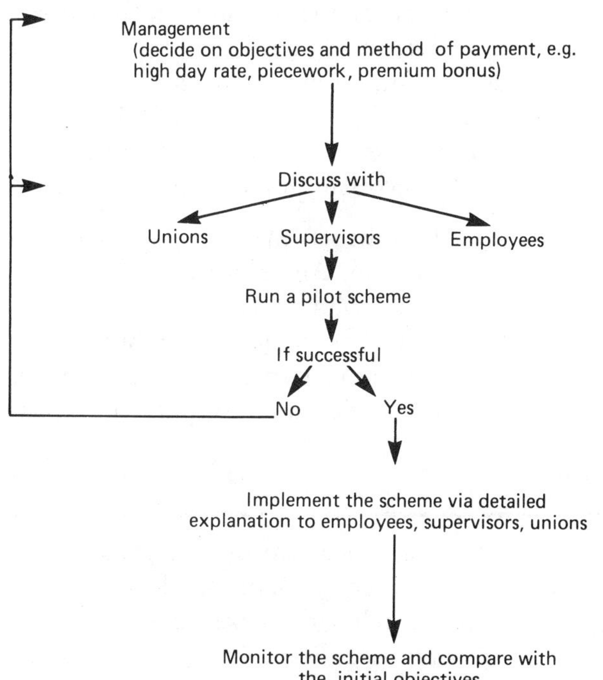

Exhibit 4.1 Model for designing and implementing bonus schemes.

which may be in the form of shares and loans with the company at generous interest rates. Co-partnership schemes may operate in conjunction with other incentive schemes, such as profit sharing and bonus schemes, the amounts earned by employees being invested in shares of, or loans to, the company.

The objectives of such schemes are:

(a) increased productivity;
(b) better industrial relations;
(c) reduced labour turnover;
(d) high employee morale.

4.5.6 Summary of benefits and limitations of incentive schemes

The major benefits of incentive schemes are:

(a) employees are able to increase their earnings as a result of their own efforts;
(b) reductions in production overhead costs per unit occur as production rises, leading to increased profits;
(c) there is pressure on management to improve efficiency in production planning which is encouraged to avoid stock–outs, lost production, fall-back payments and apathy.

The costs of designing and implementing a scheme are usually significant. At the design stage, work study staff are needed and a great deal of time is invested in liaising with management, supervisors and employees. As the scheme is likely to form part of the wage negotiation process, discussions with the trade unions may be protracted.

The successful implementation of the scheme requires:

(a) That the scheme be seen to be of equal benefit to employees and the firm. Any perceived bias will be a backcloth to which disputes will be referred.
(b) That the scheme be unambiguous, there being only one way in which to interpret how the scheme is to be applied. Any ambiguity will lead to disputes and to exploitation of the scheme.

4.6 THE WAGES DEPARTMENT

The wages department is responsible for preparing the payroll and paying wages. Exhibit 4.2 illustrates the data on which payroll accounting relies, the make-up of the individual's paysheet, the financial accounts used for recording payroll transactions, and the cost accounts to which labour costs are charged.

4.6.1 Gross pay

As illustrated in Exhibit 4.2, the inputs into the calculation of gross pay are based on the following:

(a) clock card (time records, flexitime recorders) that show the time spent at work;
(b) piecework tickets (production schedules, etc.) that record the number of units produced;
(c) job cards that record the time spent on each job: these may be substitutes for clock cards or piecework tickets;
(d) employee record cards that gives details of rate of pay (basic and overtime), holiday pay entitlement and sick pay entitlement.

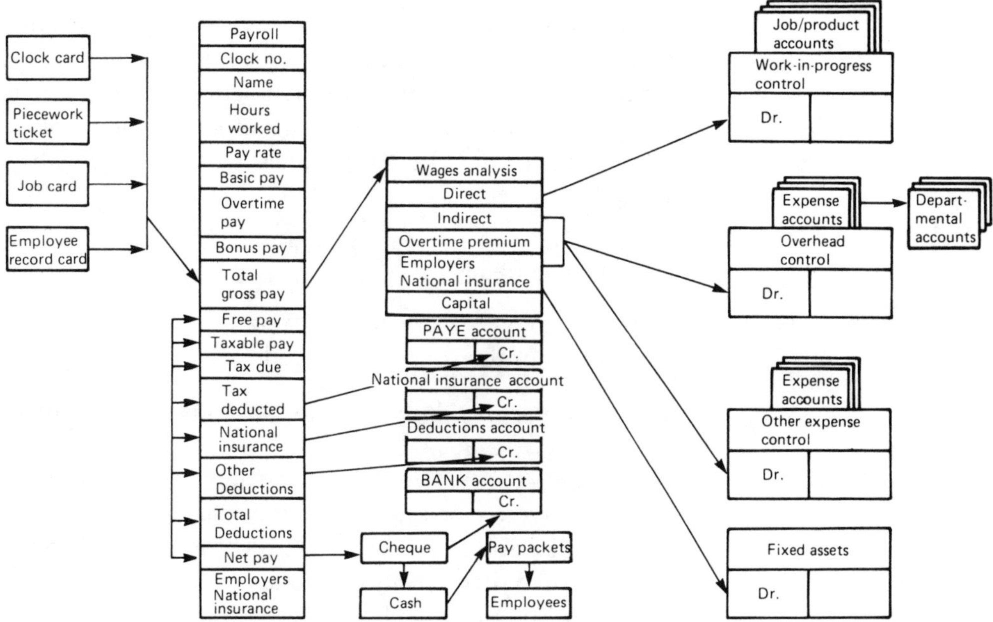

Exhibit 4.2 Labour cost accounting chart.

4.6.2 Net pay

Once the gross pay has been calculated, a number of deductions are made to arrive at the net pay. Some of these deductions are statutory, some are obligatory, and others are voluntary.

Statutory deductions are:

(a) pay as you earn (PAYE) tax;
(b) employee's national insurance contribution.

Obligatory deductions usually are limited to employee's pension fund contributions. Firms having an approved pensions scheme usually make it obligatory for their employees to join the pension fund.

Voluntary deductions are:

(a) trade union subscriptions;
(b) health scheme contributions;
(c) charity deductions;
(d) social club deductions;
(e) savings deductions.

4.6.3 Paying out wages

The cashier's office is usually responsible for the payment of wages and salaries. Wages paid in cash are drawn from the bank by the cashier's office, made up in individual wage packets and distributed to workers. Wages paid by cheque are drawn by the cashier's office and distributed. A more common practice for the payment of salaries is the bank credit transfer by means of which the employee's bank is advised to credit the employee's account with the net salary advised.

4.6.4 Wages fraud

Appropriate controls are needed to prevent wages frauds, which could occur in a number of ways, as follows:

(a) manipulating clock hours by entering more hours than actually worked;
(b) employees clocking in and out for other employees;
(c) employees clocking in and out and not working;
(d) manipulation of production records, for example, more units recorded than produced, bonus paid twice for the same output;
(e) 'dummy' personnel entered on the payroll;
(f) manipulating pay rates and tax codes;
(g) inflating the value of the wages cheque and pocketing the difference;
(h) unclaimed wages being claimed by an unauthorized person.

Most of these frauds can be avoided by close supervision, division of duties, rotating duties, ensuring that wages related personnel take holidays, etc.

4.7 ACCOUNTING FOR LABOUR COSTS

Labour costs borne by the firm comprise the gross wages of employees and additional direct and indirect costs.

Additional direct costs include the employer's share of national insurance contributions, holiday pay entitlement and company pension fund contribution in respect of each employee.

Additional indirect costs include the cost of the various service cost centres that are related to labour, for example, personnel department costs and wages department costs.

The procedure for accounting for labour costs is explained in Exhibit 4.2. The wages analysis gross wages plus other direct and indirect labour costs are allocated to various cost accounts on the basis of data recorded when preparing the payroll, for example, the jobs on which the worker was engaged. The total shown on the wages analysis should agree with the total wages paid as shown on the payroll.

In addition, accounting for labour costs involves dealing with the following:

(a) *Idle time*. Defined as the difference between the time spent on production work and the time for which the worker is paid.

Normal idle time (such as time lost between the completion of one job and the start of another) may be ignored and treated as part of direct labour costs. Alternatively, it may be treated as indirect labour costs and included in production overhead costs.

Abnormal idle time (such as due to work stoppages, production holdups, etc.) should be identified and debited to a separate overhead cost account.

(b) *Overtime*. The correct accounting treatment of overtime depends on circumstances. If overtime working is normal, it should be included with the base pay and debited to direct or indirect labour costs. If overtime was worked on the customer's instructions, the cost should be debited to the job. Where overtime is due to circumstances beyond the control of any department, for example, as a result of a national strike, it should be charged to the profit and loss account.

(c) *Holiday pay*. Two methods of costing holiday pay are available:

 (i) it may be charged to production overhead costs and recovered over total production;
 (ii) wages costs may be inflated to include an appropriate portion of holiday pay.

(d) *Accounting entries*. The payroll and wages analysis form the basis on which accounting entries are made. The manner in which those ledgers are kept will depend on whether an interlocking or integrated accounting system is used. These systems are examined in Chapter 6. In either case, control accounts are used to make the ledgers 'self-balancing'. One feature of the wages control account is that it highlights the separation of the posting of expenses (profit and loss items or assets when capitalized) from the posting of liabilities (balance sheet items). Example 4.6 is used to illustrate the postings in the form of journal entries.

EXAMPLE 4.6:
The posting of the expense element of wages is as follows:

	Dr.	*Cr.*
Wages control		10 000
(i) Work-in-progress control account	6 000	
(ii) Overhead control account	3 000	
(iii) Capital account	1 000	

(i) This value represents the amount of direct wages incurred during a period to bring a product or service to a completed state.
(ii) This value represents the indirect wages (supervisors, foremen, etc.), overtime premium, idle time, holiday pay, etc., incurred during a period.
(iii) This value represents the wages incurred in the making of a fixed asset.

The control accounts represent the total value of work-in-progress, overhead and capital. Detailed subsidiary records will also be maintained for each job, process, department and capital project, which should agree when totalled with the value of the relevant control account.

The posting of the liabilities element of wages is as follows:

	Dr.	*Cr.*
(i) Wages control	10 000	
(ii) National insurance (employers/employees)		2 000
(iii) Pay as you earn		1 000
(iv) Pension deductions		500
(v) Bank account		6 500

(i) The wages control posting is self-cancelling.
(ii/iii) The national insurance and PAYE values will be shown as a liability in the balance sheet at the end of the month and should be paid by the 15th of the following month.
(iv) Pension deductions will be paid to the pension fund on the appropriate date.
(v) Salaries are usually paid during the month earned whereas wages are paid a week in hand, for example, an employee works one week and is paid by the end of the following week. As regards the latter, the value of the week's wages in hand

will be represented as a credit balance on the wages control account.

4.8 THE COST OF LABOUR TURNOVER

The accounting process does not record the cost of labour turnover, which represents the value of human skills and the investments made by the firm in recruiting and training human resources subsequently lost as a result of employees moving to other firms. Although the cost of labour turnover is difficult to measure, firms have been concerned with obtaining an indication of labour turnover as a guide to management action in this area.

Labour turnover is expressed as follows:

$$\frac{\text{number of employees replaced in a period}}{\text{average number of employees in that period}}$$

Factors affecting labour turnover which may be influenced by management are as follows:

(a) terms and conditions of employment, pay rates, hours of work, unsocial hours, bonus and pension;
(b) low status work;
(c) lack of opportunity for advancement;
(d) poor working conditions, for example, filthy, smoky, dusty, toxic, cold or hot environments. (It should be noted that the Hawthorne experiments showed that these factors had little significance on labour turnover, if a significant amount of management time was devoted to employees.);
(e) poor amenities, such as medical facilities, family care, rest rooms, convalescent homes and beauty care;
(f) poor sports and recreational facilities, such as snooker, football, squash, cricket and pensioners' clubs.

Factors which are difficult for management to influence are:

(a) retirement;
(b) changes in family circumstances, for example, divorce, death and poor health;
(c) desire for a complete change of career;
(d) desire for promotion that cannot be satisfied within the organization;
(e) redundancy arising from decline of business.

Questions

1. What do you understand by 'effective labour cost control'?
2. What are the responsibilities of the personnel department?
3. Describe the timekeeping function.
4. What is a clock card? What information does it contain?

5. What is a job card? What is its accounting purpose?
6. Compare and contrast the time system and the output system of remuneration.
7. Do you consider it necessary for time records to be maintained for

   (a) pieceworkers;
   (b) outworkers?

8. What do you understand by the guaranteed time rate? What is the purpose of this method of remuneration?
9. Explain the premium bonus scheme. Illustrate some well-known examples of incentive schemes that are bonus related.
10. Describe the high day rate scheme. How is it different from the premium bonus scheme?
11. What is a group bonus scheme? How does it differ from other bonus schemes?
12. What problems exist with respect to the introduction of bonus schemes? How can such problems be avoided?
13. Explain the nature of profit sharing and co-partnership arrangements.
14. What items are included in the calculation of gross pay of pieceworkers?
15. Define net pay. Describe the deductions that enter into the calculation of net pay.
16. What procedures should be followed when paying out wages?
17. How can wages fraud occur?
18. Describe the accounting procedures involved in recording labour costs.
19. Define and explain the accounting treatment of the following:

   (a) idle time;
   (b) overtime;
   (c) holiday pay.

20. What do you understand by the cost of labour turnover? Explain how it is measured.

Problems

1. Elaine and Julie work in a bicycle factory making pedals. Details for the week ending 30 June are as follows:

	Number of pedals	*Time allowed*	*Time taken*
Elaine	100	100 hours	40 hours
Julie	50	50 hours	40 hours

Basic hourly rate for both: £2.00
Calculate their remuneration for the week and their effective hourly rate under:
(a) The Halsey 50/50 premium bonus scheme;
(b) The Rowan premium bonus scheme.

2. Traditional cost accounting assumes that the wages of direct workers are a variable cost; in practice, this assumption is frequently incorrect.

Required:
(a) Briefly describe a system of remuneration in which the wages of direct workers do vary directly with production activity. (2 marks)
(b) The following graphs show the cost characteristics of three different remuneration schemes:

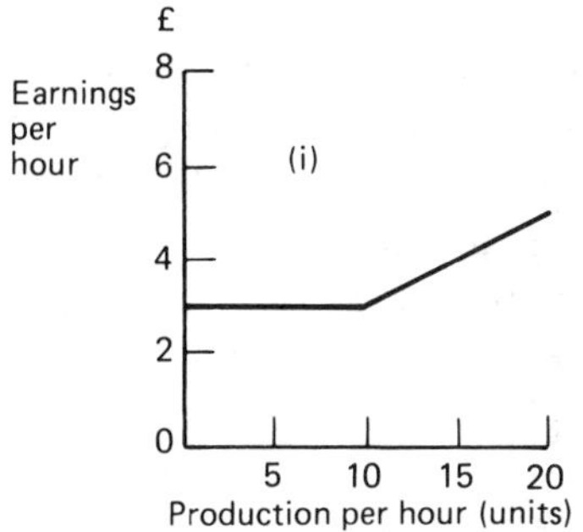

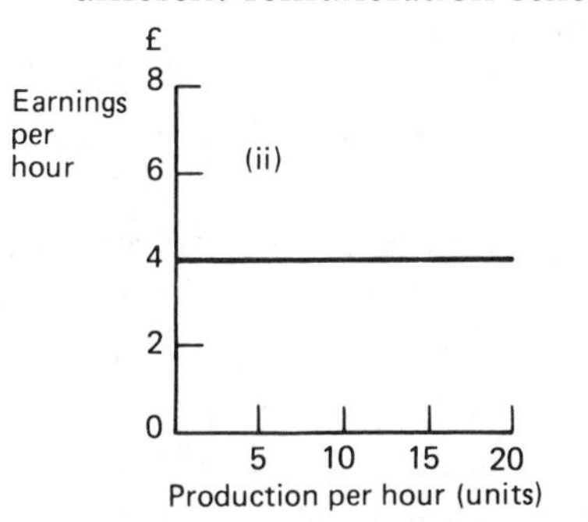

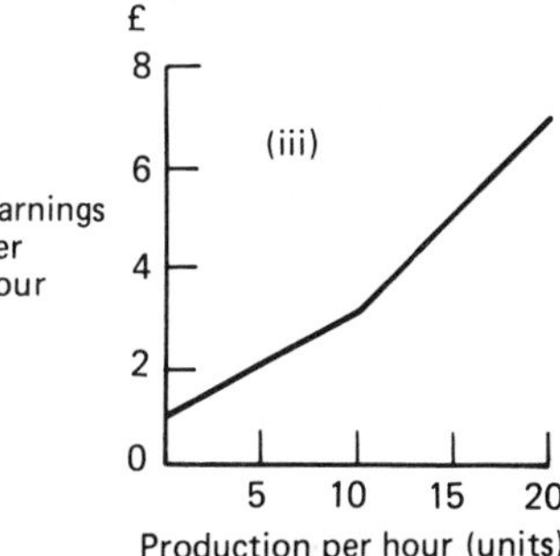

Briefly describe the significant features of each of the above remuneration schemes. (6 marks)
(c) Discuss the effect, on a company's profitability and product pricing policy, of a change in remuneration scheme and terms of employment for its direct workers which results in wages behaving and being treated, in the short to medium term, as a fixed instead of a variable cost. (9 marks)
(17 marks)

(*Chartered Association of Certified Accountants*)

3. A factory manufactures three components A, B and C. During week 26, the following was recorded:

Labour grade	*Number of employees*	*Rate per hour*	*Individual hours worked*
		£	
I	6	4.00	40
II	18	3.20	42
III	4	2.80	40
IV	1	1.60	44

Output and standard times during the same week were:

Component	*Output*	*Standard minutes (each)*
A	444	30
B	900	54
C	480	66

The normal working week is 38 hours, overtime is paid at a premium of 50 per cent of the normal hourly rate. A group incentive scheme is in operation. The time saved is expressed as a percentage of hours worked and is shared between the group as a proportion of the hours worked by each grade. The rate paid is 75 per cent of the normal hourly rate.

Required:

(a) Calculate the total payroll showing the basic pay, overtime premium and bonus pay as separate totals for each grade of labour. (18 marks)

(b) Journalize the payroll assuming: income tax deducted is £884.00; national insurance payable by employee is 6 per cent of gross pay; national insurance payable by employer is 5% of gross pay; twelve employees are members of the social club whose weekly subscription is 25p. (6 marks)

(c) Summarize two advantages and two disadvantages of group incentive schemes. (4 marks)

(Total 28 marks)

(*Association of Accounting Technicians*)

4. A small company classifies all its production overhead of £2400 per week as fixed. The company currently produces 150 components per week on a subcontracting basis and has been asked by its major customer to increase its output. Management is reluctant to operate for more than the normal 40 hours each week but in an attempt to meet its customer's wishes decides to offer an incentive scheme to its four direct operators whose current rates of pay are as follows:

	Hourly rate
	£
G Ahmed	3.00
A Brown	3.00
D Choudery	4.00
G Spencer (working foreman)	5.00

With the agreement of the employees, who are not members of a trade union, their basic hourly rates are to be reduced for a trial period of 4 weeks to those shown below but with *each* of them being given a bonus of £0.60 for every unit produced.

	Revised hourly rate
	£
G Ahmed	1.50
A Brown	1.50
D Choudery	2.50
G Spencer	3.50

After the first week of the trial period, production was 180 units. The production manager studied the results and believed the introduction of the bonus was too costly because the increase of 20 per cent in production had increased labour costs by 32 per cent. He is considering recommending changes to the newly introduced scheme.

Required:

(a) (i) Calculate how the increase in labour cost of 32 per cent was derived;

(ii) comment on whether the production manager was correct in assuming that the bonus scheme was too costly, showing your supporting calculations. (12 marks)

(b) List *eight* of the general principles which should be borne in mind when an incentive scheme for direct labour personnel is being considered. (8 marks)

(Total: 20 marks)

(*Chartered Institute of Management Accountants*)

5. The vehicle maintenance department of Largetown Corp. employs approximately 300 skilled and semi-skilled hourly paid operatives engaged in repairing and servicing the corporation's fleet of motor vehicles. The charges for repair and maintenance work undertaken by the department have increased significantly over the past 2 years, to the extent that it now appears to be cheaper to send the corporation's vehicles to local privately owned garages.

Mr Brusk the chief executive of Largetown Corp., has requested that a team of accountants should investigate the costs of operating the vehicle maintenance department and you have been appointed to the team with specific responsibility for investigating the wage preparation routine.

Operatives' wages are calculated and paid weekly.

Required:
Outline the internal checks and control procedures you would investigate to ensure that the risk of fraud is minimized in the payroll preparation and wage payment routines. (17 marks)

(*Association of Certified Accountants*)

6. (a) The following statement is an extract from an article about an electronics and telecommunications company. Turnover for the entire labour force is now stabilized at 23 per cent per annum, consisting of 4 per cent for management, and 30 per cent for hourly paid workers, one-third of whom are women.

    Explain what is meant by 'labour turnover' and list *five* cost implications.

   (b) The labour turnover of B Ltd has risen disturbingly and for the last six 4-weekly periods the figures are given below. State the further information desirable for the tabulation to be more useful as a basis for managerial action.

Period	*Average number employed*	*Number of leavers*
1	1000	60
2	1200	120
3	1100	100
4	1000	100
5	1000	110
6	1000	130

   (c) State *five* possible reasons for a company having a high labour turnover rate. (20 marks)

(*Chartered Institute of Management Accountants*)

7. The following totals were extracted from a weekly payroll for 400 employees at a production unit.

	£	£
Gross pay		32 000
Deductions:		
Employees' national insurance contributions	1 460	
Superannuation contributions	1 760	
Income tax	4 800	
Trade union dues	60	
Social club	40	
Total		8 120
Net pay		£23 880
Total of employees' and employer's national insurance contributions		£4 600

The wages analysis gave the following summary breakdown of the gross pay.

	Direct workers	Indirect workers
	£	£
Ordinary time	12 000	7 000
Overtime	3 200	2 000
Overtime premium	800	900
Shift allowance	1 600	800
Sick pay	800	200
Idle time	1 100	—
Capital items	1 600*	—

*This represented work on building a special purpose machine for the toolroom and the machine is not yet complete.

Required:
Show journal entries (narrations are *not* required) to indicate clearly how each item is dealt with in the accounts. (15 marks)

(*Chartered Institute of Management Accountants*)

5 Overhead Costs

This chapter deals with following topics:

5.1 The classification of overhead costs.
5.2 The purpose of production overhead cost allocation.
5.3 Ascertaining full production costs per unit.
5.4 Plant-wide and departmental overhead rates.
5.5 Product costs and levels of activity.
5.6 Product costs: the absorption of non-production overheads.
5.7 Limitations of full-product costs.

The purpose of this chapter is to examine the process of identifying overhead costs with individual products for the purpose of determining and recording the unit cost of production. Once that information is available, it may be used for product pricing and invoicing sales, as well as for stock valuations for balance sheet purposes.

5.1 THE CLASSIFICATION OF OVERHEAD COSTS

Overhead costs fall into two broad categories:

(a) production overhead costs;
(b) non-production overhead costs.

Production overhead costs consist of:

(a) indirect material costs, such as lubricants and supplies of materials needed for factory repairs and maintenance;
(b) indirect labour costs, such as the wages and salaries of workmen who do not work on specific product lines, foremen, timekeepers, inspectors and factory management staff:
(c) indirect expenses, such as factory heat, light, power, factory insurance and rates, as well as the depreciation of factory buildings, plant and machinery.

Non-production overhead costs consist of:

(a) selling and distribution expenses relating to the activities of the sales department;

(b) administrative expenses relating to management activities of head office;
(c) financial expenses relating to acquiring the funds needed to finance operations.

5.2 THE PURPOSE OF PRODUCTION OVERHEAD COST ALLOCATION

Production overhead costs are allocated to products for the following reasons:

5.2.1 Determining the cost of production

This is required for the purpose of establishing the cost of goods sold and the closing stocks of work-in-progress and finished goods, in the course of preparing periodic profit and loss accounts and balance sheets. As we noted in Chapter 3 SSAP 9 stocks and work-in-progress requires that production overhead costs are to be included with prime costs when preparing published accounts.

5.2.2 Making pricing decisions

Products costs are needed for making pricing decisions. Such pricing decisions may relate to setting unit product prices or preparing bids or quotes for jobs. This cost information allows the firm to make competitive pricing decisions based upon its own experience of production costs.

5.2.3 Determining the profitability of different products

Firms making different products seek to use limited resources to the most profitable end. When producing several different products, a firm will wish to make product mix decisions that combine the most profitable set of products. Hence, it will require information that relates to the cost of each product in order to evaluate profit margins and make decisions relating to products that are relatively unprofitable.

5.3 ASCERTAINING PRODUCTION COSTS PER UNIT

As mentioned earlier, the problem of ascertaining the cost of each unit of product is relatively simple when only one product is being made. All costs are direct to that product and it suffices to add all production costs and divide them by the number of units produced to ascertain the cost per unit.

EXAMPLE 5.1:
A firm produces only one product. During the accounting period, production costs totalled £2000 and 1000 units were made. The cost per unit is £2.

When more than one product is produced, direct material and direct labour costs can be traced to each product, but production overhead costs are common to all products. The cost per unit of each product necessitates a breakdown of production overheads to the different product lines, before there can be an allocation of such costs to each unit of different products.

The stages and problems involved in the breakdown of production overheads to the units of different products are as follows:

(a) classifying and coding production overheads;
(b) allotting overheads to service and production costs centres;
(c) apportioning service cost centre costs to production cost centres;
(d) absorbing production cost centres' overheads costs into products.

5.3.1 Classifying and coding production overhead costs

As we noted in Chapter 2, cost accounting is concerned with accumulating cost on the basis of cost centres, rather than units of product. Therefore, cost accounting procedures require that all source documents be coded by reference to cost centres, before they can be attached to individual products. For example, a requisition for stores must bear a reference number that identifies the cost centre making the requisition. Similarly, the time spent by inspectors, maintenance and supervisory staff in different cost centres will be recorded on their time cards by a code reference. In this way, indirect labour costs can also be traced to cost centres.

5.3.2 Allotting overhead costs to service and production cost centres

There are two types of cost centres:

(a) Service cost centres that are not involved in the actual manufacturing process, but provide services to the manufacturing cost centres, such as maintenance and stores, and facilities for the factory as a whole, such as the canteen.
(b) Manufacturing cost centres that are involved in the manufacturing process, such as machining and assembly cost centres.

Both types of cost centres have direct as well as overhead costs. Direct costs, such as direct material and direct labour, can be identified with both types of cost centres.

Accounting for overhead costs involves different procedures – cost allocations and cost apportionment:

(a) Cost allocation refers to the allotment of whole items of overhead costs to cost centres. The coding system used on source documents allows for the allocation of such overhead costs as indirect materials, indirect labour (such as inspectors and maintenance staff), and depreciation of machinery.
(b) Cost apportionment refers to the process of allocating to cost centres overhead costs that cannot be allotted to cost centres. For example, rates costs cannot be allotted to any particular cost centre and must be apportioned to all the cost centres found in the factory.

5.3.3 Apportioning service cost centre costs to production cost centres

Having accumulated both direct and overhead costs to both service and production cost centres, the next stage is to apportion service cost centre costs to production cost centres. This is effected by apportioning service cost centre costs to production cost centres on a usage basis. Exhibit 5.1 illustrates the case of a firm having three service cost and two production cost centres that requires the apportionment of the service cost centre costs to the two production cost centres.

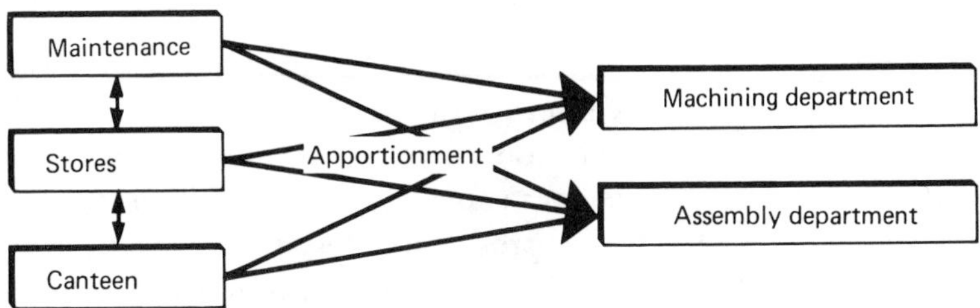

Exhibit 5.1 Apportionment of service cost centre costs.

EXAMPLE 5.2:

Evett Ltd is a manufacturing company having two production cost centres – machining and assembly; and two service cost centres – building and grounds maintenance, and general factory administration. The available cost information is as shown in Exhibit 5.2. This information shows that the first stage in the allocation of production overhead costs to products has been completed, since those costs that can be directly identified with cost centres have been allocated.

The next stage is to apportion the unallocated production overhead costs to the four cost centres. These unallocated production overhead costs are direct to the factory, but indirect to all four cost centres. The process of apportioning them to cost centres requires the use of bases of apportionment that should reflect the benefits that individual cost centres receive from such costs. Bases that reflect a usage benefit include surface area, kilowatt hours, number of employees.

Exhibit 5.2 Cost centre cost data.

	Total	*Machining*	*Assembly*	*Buildings and grounds*	*Factory administration*
	£	£	£	£	£
Allocated overheads:					
Indirect materials	15 700	4 000	10 000	500	1 200
Indirect labour	217 000	80 000	100 000	23 000	14 000
Depreciation of machinery	55 000	15 000	28 000	8 000	4 000
	287 700	99 000	138 000	31 500	19 200
Unallocated overheads:					
Rates	31 500				
Power	26 250				
Light, heat	15 750				
Total production overhead costs	361 200				

Evett Ltd has adopted the bases for apportioning unallocated overhead costs as shown in Exhibit 5.3. These bases are used to apportion the unallocated overhead costs to the four cost centres, as well as to apportion the resulting service cost centres' overhead costs to the production cost centres, as shown in Exhibit 5.4.

In this example, it is seen that the final stage in the apportionment of overhead costs to production cost centres was the apportionment of service cost centres' overhead costs, using bases of apportionment that reflect the usage of service cost centres by production cost centres. Thus, building and grounds maintenance was apportioned to

Exhibit 5.3 Bases of apportionment.

	Total	*Machining*	*Assembly*	*Buildings and grounds*	*Factory administration*
Number of employees	55	20	25	5	5
Square feet	10 500	3000	6000	500	1000
kW hours	13 125	3750	7500	625	1250

Exhibit 5.4 Apportionment of overhead costs.

	Basis	*Total*	*Machining*	*Assembly*	*Buildings and grounds*	*Factory administration*
		£	£	£	£	£
Overhead costs:						
Indirect materials	Direct	15 700	4 000	10 000	500	1 200
Indirect labour	Direct	217 000	80 000	100 000	23 000	14 000
Depreciation of machinery	Direct	55 000	15 000	28 000	8 000	4 000
Rates	Area	31 500	9 000	18 000	1 500	3 000
Power	kW hours	26 250	7 500	15 000	1 250	2 500
Light, heat	Area	15 750	4 500	9 000	750	1 500
		361 200	120 000	180 000	35 000	26 200
Service apportionment:						
Buildings and grounds	Area		10 500	21 000	(35 000)	3 500
Factory administration	Employees		13 200	16 500		(29 700)
		361 200	143 700	217 500	—	—

the production cost centres on the basis of their respective square footage, and factory administration was apportioned on the basis of their respective numbers of employees. In addition to the service cost centres mentioned above, other service cost centres may exist, requiring other bases of apportionment, as follows:

Service cost centres	*Basis of apportionment*
Purchasing	Cost of material purchased or number of orders placed
Stores	Cost of material used or number of stores requisitions
Personnel	Number of employees
Canteen	Number of employees
Depreciation	Capital equipment

The problem of reciprocal services

A further problem in apportioning service cost centre costs to production cost centres arises when service cost centres also use other service cost centres. In such cases, the service cost centres costs have to be apportioned between each other, before they can be apportioned to the production cost centres. Three methods are commonly used to deal with this problem – the elimination method, the repeated distribution method and the algebraic method.

The elimination method

This method is illustrated in Example 5.1 above. The costs of each service cost centre are apportioned in turn between users, but once they have been apportioned, they are eliminated from any subsequent apportionment. In Example 5.2, building and ground maintenance was the first to be apportioned between general factory (£3500), machining (£10 500) and assembly (£21 000). Following this apportionment, the building and ground maintenance cost centre is eliminated, leaving the overhead costs allocated to the general factory administration cost centre to be the next to be eliminated by apportionment to the production cost centres.

The elimination method allows for service cost centres to be eliminated in turn. It is usual to begin with the service cost centre serving the greatest number of other service cost centres. Where equal numbers of other service cost centres are involved, as in Example 5.2, it is usual to begin with the service cost centre carrying the largest costs. For this reason, the building and ground maintenance cost centre was the first to be apportioned.

The elimination method is not theoretically accurate for it does not take full account of reciprocal services. Thus, in Example 5.2, general factory administration renders services to buildings and ground maintenance that are ignored in the apportionment process. The repeated distribution and the algebraic methods have been devised to deal with this inadequacy of the elimination method.

Repeated distribution method

This method involves establishing the basis of the apportionment of service cost centre costs to all other service cost centres and production cost centres, as follows:

EXAMPLE 5.3:

Using the data provided for Evett Ltd, the basis of apportionment of cost centre costs given in Exhibit 5.3 is restated on a percentage basis:

	Services provided by			
	Buildings and grounds		*Factory administration*	
	£	%	£	%
Service cost centres				
Building and grounds	—	—	5	(10)
Factory administration	1 000	(10)	—	—
Production cost centres				
Machining	3 000	(30)	20	(40)
Assembly	6 000	(60)	25	(50)
	10 000	(100)	50	(100)

Using this method, the first service cost centre costs are apportioned between users of its services. This 'closes off' the first service cost centre. Next, the second service cost centre costs are apportioned between users. This procedure is followed for all other service cost centres.

After the first service cost centre has been 'closed off', the apportionment of the second service cost centre costs results in the first service cost centre receiving its share of the apportioned costs of the second service cost centre. Hence, it is required to 're-open' the first service cost centre, and to have a second round of apportionment of those costs to the second service cost centre and all other service cost centres. There will follow a third and subsequent rounds of apportionment until the amounts involved become insignificant.

Some savings in time can be achieved if the needed repeated apportionments are first settled between the service cost centres themselves. This is shown in Exhibit 5.5, where for ease of reference, buildings and ground maintenance and factory administration are denoted as X and Y, respectively. All apportionments are made in accordance with the percentages of services provided, as shown in Example 5.3.

The algebraic method

The problem with the repeated distribution method is the slowness resulting from making several rounds of apportionments. The use of

Exhibit 5.5 Service cost centre costs apportioned by the repeated distribution method.

	Buildings and grounds (X)	*Factory administration (Y)*	*Machining*	*Assembly*
	£	£	£	£
Original apportionments	35 000	26 200		
Allot *X* (10% to *Y*)	(35 000)	3 500		
Allot *Y* (10% tax)	2 970	(29 700)		
Allot *X*	(2 970)	297		
Allot *Y*	30	(297)		
Allot *X*	(30)	3		
Total positive figures	38 000	30 000		
Original apportionments	35 000	26 200	120 000	180 000
Apportion *X*	(38 000)	3 800	11 400	22 800
Apportion *Y*	3 000	(30 000)	12 000	15 000
	—	—	143 400	217 800

simultaneous equations affords a way of overcoming this problem, but the solution becomes increasingly complex as more service cost centres are involved.

EXAMPLE 5.4:

Using the data given for Evett Ltd, the apportionment of service cost centre costs to production cost centres is calculated as follows:

Costs to be apportioned to service cost centre X may be stated as X's costs (£35 000) plus 10 per cent of Y's costs. Stated algebraically, these costs amount to:

$$X = £35\,000 + 0.10Y$$

Costs to be apportioned to service cost centre Y may be stated as Y's costs (£26 200) plus 10 per cent of X's costs. Stated algebraically, these costs amount to:

$$Y = £26\,200 + 0.10X$$

Solving these equations simultaneously for either X or Y:

$$\begin{aligned} X &= £35\,000 + 0.10Y \\ X &= £35\,000 + 0.10\ (£26\,200 + 0.01X) \\ X &= £35\,000 + £2620 + 0.01X \\ 0.99X &= £37\,620 \\ X &= \underline{\underline{£38\,000}} \end{aligned}$$

Substituting X's costs in the calculation of Y's costs allows Y's costs to be calculated:

$$\begin{aligned} Y &= £26\,200 + 0.10\ (£38\,000) \\ &= £26\,200 + £3800 \\ &= \underline{\underline{£30\,000}} \end{aligned}$$

Once the service cost centre costs have been calculated, they are apportioned to the production cost centres, as shown in the repeated distribution method.

5.3.4 Absorption of production cost centre overhead costs by individual products

The apportionment of service cost centre costs to production cost centres results in the accumulation of all overhead costs into the production cost centre. Hence, the overhead costs now found in the production cost centres consist of:

(a) production cost centre overhead costs that have been allocated to them;
(b) service cost centre costs, both direct and overhead, that have been apportioned to them.

As mentioned earlier, where production is limited to only one product, all production cost centre overhead costs are direct to the one product, implying that total production costs consist of direct material, direct labour and production cost centre overhead costs.

Where a factory manufactures more than one product, the production cost centre overhead cost must be allocated to the different products. In effect, the total production costs of each product line in any one year will comprise direct costs such as direct materials and direct labour costs that are related to that product line in each separate production cost centre, plus the overhead costs accumulated in each production cost centre that are allocated to the product line.

The allocation of production cost centre overhead costs to products supposes that there exists a basis for attributing to each product line an equitable proportion of the overhead costs of each production cost centre. Bases usually used for this purpose are linked to one of the following:

(a) units of output;
(b) direct material costs;
(c) direct labour costs;
(d) prime costs;
(e) direct labour hours;
(f) machine hours.

They involve the calculation of 'overhead rates' for allocating costs to products that are designed to ensure that overheads are 'absorbed' or 'recovered' by products. Products vary in the manner in which they used the resources of different production cost centres. For this reason, there are alternative overhead bases for calculating an overhead rate that reflects the usage of resources. The selection of an appropriate 'overhead rate' is a prerequisite to the equitable allocation of production cost centre overhead costs.

EXAMPLE 5.5:

Having completed the allocation and apportionment of overhead costs to the two production cost centres – machining and assembly – Evett Ltd has now to select an appropriate overhead base for apportioning production cost centre overhead costs to products.

The following information relates to the machining cost centre:

Units produced	400 000
Direct material costs	£200 000
Direct labour costs	£50 000
Prime costs	£250 000
Direct labour hours	100 000
Machine hours	150 000

On the basis of this information, six alternative overhead bases may be used to calculate an overhead rate for absorbing production cost centre overhead costs into the full-product cost of each unit of the different products utilizing the machining cost centre, as follows:

overhead rate based on units produced;
overhead rate based on direct material costs;
overhead rate based on direct labour costs;
overhead rate based on prime costs;
overhead rate based on direct labour hours;
overhead rate based on machine hours.

Effect of using different overhead rates

Each of the foregoing overhead rates results in a different apportionment of product cost centre overhead costs into units of product, as may be seen in the calculation shown below:

Overhead rate based on units produced

The formula used is as follows:

$$\frac{\text{cost centre overhead costs}}{\text{cost centre units produced}} = \frac{£143\ 000}{400\ 000} = £0.36 \text{ per unit of product}$$

If all products are homogeneous, an overhead rate based on units produced is the simplest to use. However, most manufacturing operations involve heterogeneous products for which such a rate is unsuitable since different products absorb the same overhead cost per unit.

Overhead rate based on direct material costs

The formula used is as follows:

$$\frac{\text{cost centre overhead costs}}{\text{cost centre direct material costs}}\ \% = \frac{£143\ 000}{£200\ 000} \times 100 = 72\%$$

Thus, for each £1 of direct material cost that each unit of a product incurs in the machining cost centre, there will be absorbed in the product cost an additional 72 per cent or £0.72 in respect of overhead costs.

This base is also rarely used since there is usually little or no comparison between the direct material costs entering into different products. Therefore, although this base is also simple and easy to apply, it will lead to the following distortions in the apportionment of overhead costs to products:

(a) Products using the most expensive materials will absorb the greater proportion of production cost centre overhead costs.
(b) It ignores completely the fact the most production cost centre overhead costs, such as salaries, depreciation, rates, etc., accrue on a time basis.
(c) Raw materials are subject to price fluctuations that will not be reflected in movements in overheads costs.

Overhead rate based on direct labour costs
The formula used is as follows:

$$\frac{\text{cost centre overhead costs}}{\text{cost centre direct labour costs}}\,\% = \frac{£143\,000}{£50\,000} \times 100$$
$$= 286\%$$

Thus, for each £1 of direct labour cost that each unit of a product incurs in the machining cost centre, there will be absorbed in the product's cost an additional 286 per cent or £2.86 in respect of overhead costs. This base is easy to use since information regarding labour costs is usually readily available. It is an appropriate base for apportioning overhead costs to products for cost centres that are labour intensive, and workers are paid uniform hourly rates and have uniform productivity levels.

However, there may be no relationship between direct labour costs and overhead costs, as most overhead costs are incurred on a time basis and are not related to payroll costs. Distortions in the apportionment of overhead costs to different products will occur where rates of pay for similar work are not comparable.

Overhead rate based on prime cost
The formula used is as follows:

$$\frac{\text{cost centre overhead costs}}{\text{cost centre prime costs}}\,\% = \frac{£143\,000}{£250\,000} \times 100$$
$$= 57\%$$

This base is also simple to apply, since it relies on information that is readily available. However, it combines the disadvantages of both the direct material and direct labour cost bases. Moreover, it is suitable for use only where material and direct labour costs do not vary significantly, and any variation in costs is roughly the same for both. Since such conditions are unlikely to occur, this base is generally unsuitable for use in practice.

Overhead rate based on direct labour hours
The formula used is as follows:

$$\frac{\text{cost centre overhead costs}}{\text{cost centre direct labour hours}} = \frac{\pounds 143\ 000}{100\ 000}$$
$$= \pounds 1.43 \text{ per direct labour hour}$$

Thus, for every hour of direct labour spent on making a unit of a product, that unit will absorb overheads of £1.43. Hence, if product A needs 2 direct labour hours, overhead costs apportioned to it will be £2.86.

A major advantage of this base over other bases discussed above is that it reflects more accurately the incidence of production overhead costs, for as we have already noted, these costs tend to be incurred on a time basis. However, its use should be restricted to production cost centres that are labour intensive rather than machine intensive. Distortions will occur in labour intensive production cost centres using this base by the overcharge of overhead costs to products or jobs to which relatively inefficient workers have been assigned.

Overhead rate based on machine hours
The formula used is as follows:

$$\frac{\text{cost centre overhead costs}}{\text{cost centre machine hours}} = \frac{\pounds 143\ 000}{150\ 000}$$
$$= \pounds 0.96 \text{ per machine hour}$$

Thus, for every hour of machining that a unit of a product incurs in the machining cost centre, that unit will absorb £0.96 of overhead costs. Hence, if product A needs 3 hours of machining, the overhead costs apportioned to it will amount to £2.88 per unit. This base is most suitable for the apportionment of overhead costs of machine intensive production cost centres. Like the direct labour hour base, it reflects the incidence of many production overhead costs that are incurred over time. A disadvantage of this base is the need to maintain additional records relating to the hourly use of particular machines.

The choice of one particular overhead rate as against the others may substantially affect the amount of overhead costs apportioned to a unit of product, and lead to different product costs. Variations in product costs may result simply from the overhead rate used. The selection of the most appropriate rate to use is a matter of considering particular circumstances under which production is being conducted.

5.4 PLANT-WIDE AND DEPARTMENTAL OVERHEAD RATES

In Example 5.2 above, the allocation and apportionment of overhead costs was effected throughout by using overhead rates based on information relating to cost centres. Thus, in the case of the machining cost centre, overhead costs were allocated to products on the basis of machine hour overhead rate.

The use of departmental overhead rates that are specific to each cost centre involves developing several overhead rates. The use of plant-wide overhead rates simplifies the selection of an overhead rate, for a single rate is chosen for all overhead cost allocations. Departmental overhead rates that are specific to each cost centre produce more accurate overhead cost allocations, since they recognize the variation in the intensity of use of resources in different cost centres. For example, they recognize that different cost centres do not use proportionately the same number of labour or machine hours, nor do they incur the same direct material or direct labour costs.

The greater accuracy of departmental overhead rates over plant-wide rates is illustrated in Example 5.6.

EXAMPLE 5.6:
Eastlands Carburettors manufactures two types of carburettors, type X and type Y, both being processed in two cost centres – cost centre A and cost centre B. The following cost information is given:

	Type X	*Type Y*
	£	£
Direct production costs per unit	8	8
Direct labour hours	4 hours	1 hour
Cost centre A	1 hour	4 hours
Total hours	5 hours	5 hours

Overhead rates based on direct labour hours are given below:

Overhead rates	*Per direct labour hour*
	£
Cost centre basis	
Cost centre A	6
Cost centre B	1
Plant-wide basis	
Cost centre A	3
Cost centre B	3

This information allows the comparison of costs per unit that would result from the use of plant-wide as against cost centre overhead rates.

Unit costs using a plant-wide overhead rate

	Type A	*Type B*
	£	£
Direct production costs	8	8
Add: Overhead cost:		
(5 hours at £3)	15	15
Cost per unit	23	23

Unit costs using cost centre overhead rate

	Type A	*Type B*
	£	£
Direct production costs	8	8
Add: Overhead costs:		
Cost Centre A		
(at £6 per hour)	24	6
Cost centre B		
(at £1 per hour)	1	4
Cost per unit	33	18

The distortions that arise in the foregoing example as a result of using plant-wide rather than cost centre overhead rates are as follows:

(a) Product X that spends more processing time in cost centre A that has the higher overhead rate, is undercosted by £10 when plant-wide overhead rate is used.
(b) By contrast, product Y that spends more processing time in cost centre B that has the lower overhead rate, is overcosted by £5 when a plant-wide overhead rate is used.

These distortions indicate the danger of using overhead cost allocation bases, such as plant-wide overhead rates, that do not produce accurate calculations of unit product costs. The repercussions would be felt in the making of management decisions in such areas as pricing and production mix that require accurate cost data.

5.5 PRODUCT COSTS AND LEVELS OF ACTIVITY

The classification of production costs into direct and overhead costs has the objective of explaining the manner in which production costs are related to products for the purpose of determining their cost.

An alternative classification of production costs into fixed and variable costs, that we discussed in Chapter 2, seeks to explain the manner in which production costs vary according to different volumes of activity. Fixed costs are those that remain constant, irrespective of the volume of activity. Variable costs vary with the volume of activity.

The activity level has an important effect on product costs at the unit level. Given that overhead costs may be either fixed or variable in relation to activity levels, variations in activity levels will influence product costs as follows:

(a) Direct and overhead costs that are fixed in relation to activity levels will not vary as the volume of units produced increases or decreases.

But, expressed in terms of units of product, direct and overhead costs that are fixed in total will decrease as the number of units produced increases.

(b) Direct and overhead costs that are variable in relation to activity levels will increase in total as the volume of units produced increases. Likewise, they will decrease in total as the volume of units produced decreases.

But, expressed in terms of units of product, direct and overhead costs that are variable in total will remain constant, or fixed, irrespective of whether the volume of units produced increases or decreases.

EXAMPLE 5.7:

If fixed costs for the period are £10 000 and variable costs per unit are £10, product costs per unit will vary according to the number of units produced, as follows:

Activity level in units	*Fixed costs*	*Variable costs*	*Total costs*
	£	£	£
5 000	2	10	12
10 000	1	10	11
20 000	0.5	10	10.5

Exhibit 5.6 provides an expanded illustration of cost behaviour in relation to changes in activity levels.

Exhibit 5.6 Cost behaviour in relation to activity levels

Units produced	*Total fixed costs*	*Total variable costs*	*Total costs*	*Average fixed cost per unit*	*Average variable cost per unit*	*Average total cost per unit*
	£	£	£	£	£	£
1	300	100	400	300	100	400
2	300	200	500	150	100	250
3	300	300	600	100	100	200
4	300	400	700	75	100	175
5	300	500	800	60	100	160

Unit product costs for management decisions

The need for unit product cost information for management decisions arises in particular with regard to the following:

(a) pricing decisions;
(b) controlling costs;
(c) evaluating performance;
(d) stock valuation;
(e) profit measurement.

All these decisions require unit product cost information that is reasonably reliable in use. For example, pricing decisions require a more stable view of costs than those resulting from fluctuating output levels. Similarly, effective cost control implies comparisons of product costs of the current period against those of preceding periods. Such comparisons cannot be made if such costs reflect fluctuations resulting from varying output levels. This problem also applies to the evaluation of performance, where similar considerations apply. Even for stock valuation purposes, that are central to profit measurement, cost measurements based on actual product costs will produce distortions. Moreover, the normal process of recording actual costs at the end of accounting periods results in delays in making actual product cost data available. For these various reasons, product cost information derived from actual cost data is not suitable for management decision making.

The inadequacies of actual product cost data for decision making stem from the process of overhead cost allocations rather than from the recording of direct costs. Data relating to actual direct costs, such as materials and labour, generally may be obtained immediately. Data relating to the actual production overhead costs absorbed by any particular product can only be made available at the end of the accounting period, when the actual overhead costs incurred have been assigned to individual products in the manner explained in this chapter.

In short, there are two central problems that make the use of actual overhead costs impracticable for management decisions:

(a) the need to await end-period overhead cost allocations before overhead cost information relating to products can be known;
(b) the use of the actual level of activity for the purpose of determining the apportionment of fixed overhead costs to products.

The solution to these two problems is found by the following means.

(a) Actual direct costs are combined with predetermined overhead costs for obtaining product cost information. The delay in obtaining knowledge of end-period overhead costs is overcome simply by making a prior estimate using the formula:

$$\frac{\text{budgeted overheads for the period}}{\text{budgeted level of activity}}$$

(b) The instability found in the use of actual levels of activity in apportioning fixed overhead costs is solved by using a long-term estimate of the normal level of activity that smooths out short-term fluctuations in actual activity levels.

Selecting the normal level of activity

There are four alternative levels of activity that may be used for the purpose of deriving a stable fixed overhead rate:

(a) *Theoretical capacity*, which is the capacity of a particular cost centre to maintain output at 100 per cent capacity without interruption.
(b) *Practical capacity*, which is the theoretical capacity adjusted for allowances in respect of unavoidable interruptions, such as time lost for repairs, work stoppages and holidays.
(c) *Expected capacity*, which is the short-term forecast of the activity level expected in the immediate period.
(d) *Normal capacity*, which is a forecast of the activity level based on a time period that is sufficiently long to smooth out the peaks and troughs of cyclical fluctuations.

As defined above, normal capacity is the most suitable level of activity for use in determining fixed overhead rates that will be relatively stable over a period of years. Consequently, it provides the most reliable product cost information for management purposes. Nonetheless, there will invariably be some under- or over-absorption of fixed production overhead costs, whenever the actual level of activity differs from the normal capacity level. This problem will be discussed in detail in Chapter 16.

5.6 PRODUCT COSTS: THE ABSORPTION OF NON-PRODUCTION OVERHEADS

Non-production costs, such as selling, distribution, administrative and financial overhead costs, are not usually included in the definition of product costs for the purpose of measuring profit. Accordingly, these are not included in the cost of sales but are treated as period costs.

In order to establish the profitability of product lines, however, it may be useful for management to charge product lines with non-production overhead costs. Several methods of absorbing non-production overhead costs exist, as follows:

(a) as a percentage of selling price;
(b) as a percentage of full-product costs;
(c) as a percentage of conversion costs;
(d) as a rate per unit of product sold, in the case of single product firms.

5.7 LIMITATIONS OF FULL-PRODUCT COSTS

Full-product costing requires the absorption of overhead costs into production costs. This is achieved by the allocation of overhead costs to products using overhead rates that exhibit degrees of imperfection, making it difficult to obtain complete accuracy in the calculation of full-product costs. In a sense, all methods of apportioning overhead costs are arbitrary, and based on assumptions that are subjective to a degree.

The main criterion for allocating production overhead costs to products should be the 'benefit received' by products from the various cost centres in which they are processed. It is difficult to find bases of allocation that perfectly reflect this criterion. For example, the costs of the factory personnel department have to be apportioned to other service cost centres and to production cost centres. The use of the number of employees base for apportioning these costs assumes that all cost centres benefit equally from the factory personnel department. There is a gross simplification in that assumption for labour turnover and difference in skills between classes of employees will determine the time and effort expended by factory personnel staff in dealing with problems.

Subjectivity is an element that enters into many of the choices made in the selection of overhead rates. Even regarding the selection of the 'normal capacity level', that is crucial for establishing a reliable fixed overhead rate, two perfectly competent accountants may differ as to what constitutes normal capacity. It is evident that it is in the allocation of fixed overhead costs that the major problems lie, and for this reason, variable and fixed overhead rates require to be distinguished when providing full-product cost information.

Questions

1. Distinguish production and non-production overhead costs. What is the importance of this distinction for product costing?
2. List the purposes for which production overhead cost allocations are required.
3. What stages are involved in allocating production overhead costs to products?
4. Distinguish the process of cost allocation and the process of cost apportionment.
5. Give five examples of bases of apportionment for use in apportioning service cost centre costs to production cost centres.
6. What are the particular problems posed by the presence of reciprocal services when service cost centre costs are apportioned to production cost centres?
7. Describe the procedures involved in the following methods of dealing with the problem of reciprocal services:

    (a) the elimination method;
    (b) the repeated distribution method;
    (c) the algebraic method.

8. List seven allocation bases known to you for allocating production cost centre cost overheads to products.
9. Discuss briefly the problems involved in the selection of an overhead rate for allocating overhead costs to products.
10. What are the advantages or disadvantages of using departmental rather than plant-wide overhead rates?
11. Explain why you would expect overhead costs to be under- or over-absorbed when the level of activity changes.
12. List the purposes for which full-product costs are used in management decision making.
13. What do you understand by the term 'predetermined overhead rate'? What is the purpose of using such rates for allocating overhead costs to products?
14. What do you understand by 'normal activity level'? What is the relevance of this concept with respect to overhead cost allocations?
15. Given that non-production overhead costs are not included in

full-product costs, where are such overheads absorbed? What methods exist for dealing with such costs?

16. Discuss the advantages and disadvantages of full-product costing.

17. The chairman of your company has been studying the budgets for the next accounting period and has shown particular interest in the production cost budget. In this the production overhead will increase from the current absorption rate of 200 per cent of direct wages cost to 300 per cent. The production manager protests that this increase is unacceptable.

    As company cost accountant prepare a brief report for the chairman, explaining:

    (a) how the overhead absorption rate is calculated and used;
    (b) which factors may have contributed to the increase in the rate;
    (c) the circumstances in which such an increase can be acceptable.

    (20 marks)

    (*Chartered Association of Certified Accountants*)

18. The management of a company manufacturing special purpose industrial equipment is considering introducing an absorption job costing system.

    Required:
    (a) Explain how the information produced by the proposed costing system could be used and examine any weaknesses or inadequacies in the data provided by such a system (10 marks)
    (b) Consider how the effective utilization and the efficiency of the direct operatives may be measured in that company. (7 marks)

    (Total 17 marks)

    (*Chartered Association of Certified Accountants*)

19. (a) Explain why predetermined overhead absorption rates are preferred to overhead absorption rates calculated from factual information after the end of a financial period.
    (b) The production overhead absorption rates of factories X and Y are calculated using similar methods. However, the rate used by factory X is lower than that used by factory Y. Both factories produce the same type of product. You are required to discuss whether or not this can be taken to be a sign that factory X is more efficient than factory Y.

    (20 marks)

    (*Chartered Institute of Management Accountants*)

20. (a) Outline the procedures and information required in order to establish a set of predetermined production overhead absorption rates, for a company manufacturing a range of different products in a factory containing a number of production departments and several service departments. (12 marks)

(b) Critically examine the purpose of calculating overhead absorption rates. (5 marks)

(Total 17 marks)

(*Chartered Institute of Management Accountants*)

21. The power generating plant of Twingles Ltd is a service department supplying the power, heating and lighting requirements for all the production departments in the factory.

The total of the actual costs incurred by the power plant each month are apportioned over the production departments by using an engineer's technical estimate based upon the anticipated average power consumption in each department. The technical estimate, which is revised at the beginning of each year, also forms the basis for apportioning the budgeted power costs to each department.

Required:

(a) Briefly explain the purpose of charging service department costs to production departments. (4 marks)

(b) Carefully explain whether the existing method of charging the actual monthly power costs to the production departments of Twingles Ltd serves a useful purpose. (4 marks)

(c) Discuss the merits and the problems of charging the production departments for their actual monthly power consumption using, instead of actual costs, standard/budgeted costs calculated as follows:

A fixed annual charge (suitably apportioned over the year) calculated by apportioning the budgeted fixed costs of operating the power generating plant over the production departments according to their anticipated average power consumption during the year; plus a variable charge for each unit of power consumed based upon the budgeted variable costs of operating the power generating plant at standard efficiency. (9 marks)

(Total 17 marks)

(*Chartered Association of Certified Accountants*)

Problems

1. From the data given you are required to:
   (a) Prepare an 'overhead analysis sheet' showing the basis for apportionments made (calculated to the nearest £1).
   (b) Calculate (to two decimal places of £1) an overhead absorption rate based on direct labour hours for:
      (i) the assembly department;
      (ii) the finishing department;
   (c) State briefly, for each overhead item or group of items, why the basis of apportionment was chosen.
   (d) For purposes of apportioning costs, state what other information you would have preferred to have used for any of the items instead of the information given.

Data:

The information given relates to a 4-week accounting record. In addition to the cost centres listed there is an 'occupancy' cost centre which is charged with all the costs concerned with occupation of the building. The total of this cost centre should be apportioned before the stores costs are apportioned.

Department	*Machining*	*Assembly*	*Finishing*	*Stores*
Area occupied (ft^2)	24 000	36 000	16 000	4 000
Plant and equipment, at cost, in £000	1 400	200	60	10
Number of employees	400	800	200	20
Direct labour hours	16 000	32 000	4 000	—
Direct wages	£32 600	£67 200	£7 200	—
Number of requisitions on stores	400	1 212	200	—

Allocated costs:

	Total	*Machining*	*Assembly*	*Finishing*	*Stores*
	£	£	£	£	£
Indirect wages	34 000	9 000	15 000	4 000	6 000
Indirect materials	2 400	400	1 400	600	—
Maintenance	2 100	1 400	600	100	—
Power	2 200	1 600	400	200	—
Total	£40 700	£12 400	£17 400	£4 900	£6 000

Other costs:

	£
Rent	2 000
Rates	600
Insurance on building	200
Lighting and heating	400
Depreciation on plant and equipment	16 700
Wage related costs (holiday pay, graduated national insurance and company pension scheme)	28 200
Factory administration and personnel	7 100
Insurance on plant and equipment	1 670
Cleaning of factory premises by outside contract cleaners	800
	£57 670

(30 marks)

(Chartered Institute of Management Accountants)

2. The AAT company has two departments A and B engaged in manufacturing operations and they are serviced by a stores, maintenance department and tool room.

The following has been budgeted for the next financial period:

	Overheads (£000)					
	Total	*A*	*B*	*Stores*	*Maintenance*	*Tool room*
Indirect labour	1837	620	846	149	115	107
Supervision	140					
Power	160					
Rent	280					
Rates	112					
Plant insurance	40					
Plant depreciation	20					
	£2589					

Additional information available includes:

	A	B	Stores	Maintenance	Tool room
Floor area (m^2)	1 000	2 500	1 100	600	400
Number of employees	30	50	10	20	30
Power (kW hours)	60 000	30 000	3 000	15 000	12 000
Number of material requisitions	5 000	6 000	—	2 000	3 000
Maintenance hours	8 000	9 000	—	—	6 000
Plant valuation (£)	50 000	40 000	—	5 000	5 000
Tool room hours estimated	7 000	10 000	—	—	—
Machine hours estimated	55 200	99 000	—	—	—

Required:
Calculate appropriate machine hour overhead absorption rates for both manufacturing departments in which all overheads will be recovered, and show clearly the method of overhead allocation. (20 marks)

(*Association of Accounting Technicians*)

3. Shown below is an extract from next year's budget for a company manufacturing three different products in three production departments.

Product	A	B	C
Production	4000 units	3000 units	6000 units
Direct material cost	£7 per unit	£4 per unit	£9 per unit
Direct labour requirements:	hours per	hours per	hours per
Cutting department:	unit	unit	unit
Skilled operatives	3	5	2
Unskilled operatives	6	1	3
Machining department	$\frac{1}{2}$	$\frac{1}{4}$	$\frac{1}{3}$
Pressing department	2	3	4
Machine hour requirements:			
Machining department	2	$1\frac{1}{2}$	$2\frac{1}{2}$

The skilled operatives employed in the cutting department are paid £4 per hour and the unskilled operatives are paid £2.50 per hour. All the operatives in the machining and pressing departments are paid £3 per hour.

	Production departments			*Service departments*	
	Cutting	*Machining*	*Pressing*	*Engineering*	*Personnel*
Budgeted total overheads	£154 482	£64 316	£58 452	£56 000	£34 000
Service department costs are incurred for the benefit of other departments as follows:					
Engineering services	20%	45%	25%	—	10%
Personnel services	55%	10%	20%	15%	—

The company operates a full absorption costing system.

Required:

(a) Calculate, as equitably as possible, the total budgeted manufacturing cost of:
  (i) one completed unit of product A; and
  (ii) one incomplete unit of product B, which has been processed by the cutting and machining departments which has not yet been passed into the pressing department. (15 marks)

(b) At the end of the first month of the year for which the above budget was prepared the production overhead control account for the machining department showed a credit balance.

Explain the possible reasons for that credit balance. (7 marks)

(22 marks)

(*Chartered Association of Certified Accountants*)

Part 3 Costing Systems

Part III is concerned with the procedures required for product costing. It was noted in Part I that one of the major objectives of costing is the provision of product cost information.

Chapter 6 explains the structure of cost bookkeeping, and it will be seen that its basic objective is the accumulation of cost information for inclusion in the profit and loss account and balance sheet. Industrial activity takes different forms and uses different technologies. Accordingly, cost bookkeeping has to be adapted to the needs of the firm. Some firms work to specifications detailed by the client. Such firms use the job costing system for accumulating job costs. As explained in Chapter 7, in such cases the product is the completion of the job. Similarly, where jobs are very large and last for periods of longer than a year, the special nature of the large contracts involved require a form of cost bookkeeping, known as contract costing, that is explained in Chapter 8. The manufacture of a large category of goods takes place under mass production methods. The product is homogeneous and occurs in anticipation of demand. Chapter 9 explains cost accumulation for product costing under such conditions. Chapter 10 deals with the special cost bookkeeping methods required for service industries and similar industries.

6 Cost Bookkeeping

This chapter deals with the following topics:

6.1 Cost accounting and financial accounting.
6.2 Interlocking accounts.
6.3 Integrated accounts.

6.1 COST ACCOUNTING AND FINANCIAL ACCOUNTING

In Part II, the three elements of product costs, namely, materials, labour and overhead costs, were discussed and the basic records required for accumulating these costs in terms of cost units were described. The nature of these cost units depends on the method of production adopted by the firm. For example, if the firm is operating on a job order basis, the cost unit will be individual jobs for particular clients. If the firm is producing standardized and homogeneous products in a continuous production process, the cost unit will be a standardized quantity of output expressed in terms of units, weight or volume.

As explained in the introduction to this part, a manufacturing firm is maintaining, in effect, two accounting systems:

(a) A separate costing system maintained by the cost department for the purpose of accumulating and allocating production costs to cost units.
(b) A financial accounting system maintained to record the acquisition of resources appearing as costs in the costing system, such as the purchase of materials (materials cost in the costing system), wages and salaries expenses (labour costs in the costing system) and various other expenses, such as rates, electricity, etc. (overhead costs in the costing system).

These two separate systems are related to each other in the following important respects:

(a) The financial accounts record the financial obligations incurred by the firm in respect of the resources used in production and are recorded as costs in the cost accounts.

(b) Raw material, work-in-progress and finished goods stocks recorded in the cost accounts also represent asset values recorded in the stock account in the ledger.
(c) Finished goods recorded in the cost accounts are transferred out when sold, and appear in the cost of sales account at the value recorded in the cost accounts.
(d) Finally, as we shall see in Chapter 14, the control of product cost using standard costing methods relies on the supply of actual costs recorded in the financial accounting system as feedback information.

For the foregoing reasons, it is evident that these two accounting systems have to be reconciled. This may be achieved in two ways:

(a) Interlocking accounts, whereby separate ledgers are maintained for cost accounting and financial accounting. These separate ledgers are interlocked by a control account in each ledger, that acts as a link between the two ledgers.
(b) Integrated accounts, whereby a unified accounting system combines the cost and the financial accounts. Only one ledger is kept, and the information recorded therein is used to produce cost analyses for management and financial statements for financial reporting purposes.

6.2 INTERLOCKING ACCOUNTS

As explained above, under the system of an interlocking accounts system, separate cost accounting and financial accounting ledgers are maintained.

6.2.1 Cost ledger accounts

The following accounts are kept in the cost ledger:

(a) *Cost ledger control account* (or general ledger control account) that renders the cost ledger *self-balancing*.
(b) *Stores ledger control account* records purchases received and materials issued to work-in-progress, as follows:

Dr. stores ledger control	with materials purchases
Cr. cost ledger control	with materials purchases
Dr. work-in-progress	with direct materials issued
Dr. overhead control	with indirect materials issued
Cr. stores ledger control	with materials issued.

The balance remaining in the Stores ledger control account represents the cost value of materials held in stores.

(c) *Wages control account* records wages paid, as follows:

Dr. wages control
Cr. cost ledger control
with total wages paid.

At the end of each period, the balance in the wages control account is transferred as follows:

Dr. work-in-progress with the cost of direct labour
Dr. overhead control with the cost of indirect labour
Cr. wages control.

(d) *Production overhead control account* records production overhead expenses notified by the financial accountant, as well as indirect materials and indirect labour transferred from the stores ledger control and wages control accounts, as follows:

Dr. production overhead control
Cr. cost ledger control
with production overhead expenses notified
Dr. production overhead control
Cr. stores ledger control
with indirect material
Dr. production overhead control
Cr. wages control
with indirect labour.

Production overhead costs are absorbed *on an agreed basis* into work-in-progress, as follows:

Dr. work-in-progress
Cr. production overhead control
with the total production overheads for the period.

Where the *agreed basis* relies on using a *predetermined rate* (see Chapter 5), any resulting under- or over-recovery of production overhead costs will have to be debited or credited, as the case may be, to the profit and loss account.

(e) *Work-in-progress control account*, which records the cost of the work-in-progress, consisting of direct materials, direct labour and allocated production overhead costs that are transferred from those accounts, as follows:

Dr. work-in-progress control with direct materials, direct labour and allocated production overhead costs
Cr. stores ledger control with direct materials

Cr. wages control — with direct labour
Cr. production overhead control — with allocated production overhead costs.

On completion, finished cost units are transferred out of work-in-progress to finished goods, as follows:

Dr. finished goods control
Cr. work-in-progress control
with the cost of completed cost units.

The balance remaining in the work-in-progress control account represents the uncompleted cost units remaining in the factory.

(f) *Finished goods control account*, in which is recorded the cost of the completed cost units transferred from work-in-progress, as follows:

Dr. finished goods control account
Cr. work-in-progress control account
with the cost of completed cost units.

The balance shown in the finished goods control account represents the cost of completed cost units. Upon sales, the cost of the completed cost units sold is transferred to the cost of sales account as follows:

Dr. cost of sales
Cr. finished goods control account
with the cost of cost units sold.

(g) *Administrative overhead control account. Selling and distribution overhead control account.* These accounts record administrative, selling and distribution expenses notified by the financial accountant, as follows:

Dr. administrative overhead control
Cr. cost ledger control
Dr. selling and distribution overhead control
Cr. cost ledger control

These accounts are closed at the end of the period, and the balances transferred to the cost of sales account, as follows:

Dr. cost of sales with closing balance transferred
Cr. administrative overhead control
Cr. selling and distribution overhead control

(h) *Sales account* records total sales notified by the financial accountant, the entries being as follows:

Dr. cost ledger control   with the sales revenue
Cr. sales

At the end of the period, the balance on the sales account is transferred to the costing profit and loss account.

(i) *Costing profit and loss account* is debited with the closing balance on the cost of sales account, and credited with the closing balance on the sales account. The under- or over-absorbed balance on the production overhead control account is transferred to the costing profit and loss account.

The final balance appearing on the costing profit and loss account is transferred to the cost ledger control account to be reconciled with the balance shown on the profit and loss account prepared by the financial accountant.

Exhibit 6.1 illustrates the accounts that are maintained in the cost ledger.

EXAMPLE 6.1:

The following balances appear in the cost ledger of the Green Manufacturing Company at the beginning of the period:

	£	£
Stores control account	7 000	
Work-in-progress control account	6 000	
Finished goods control account	9 000	
Cost ledger control account		22 000
	22 000	22 000

The following transactions took place during the period:

		£
Purchases of raw materials	(a)	12 000
Direct wages paid	(b)	20 000
Administration costs incurred	(c)	5 000
Selling and distribution costs incurred	(d)	8 000
Raw materials issued	(e)	10 000
Production overhead incurred	(f)	10 000
Production overhead absorbed	(g)	9 000
Goods sold: At sales value	(h)	60 000
At cost	(i)	35 000
Transferred to finished goods	(j)	30 000

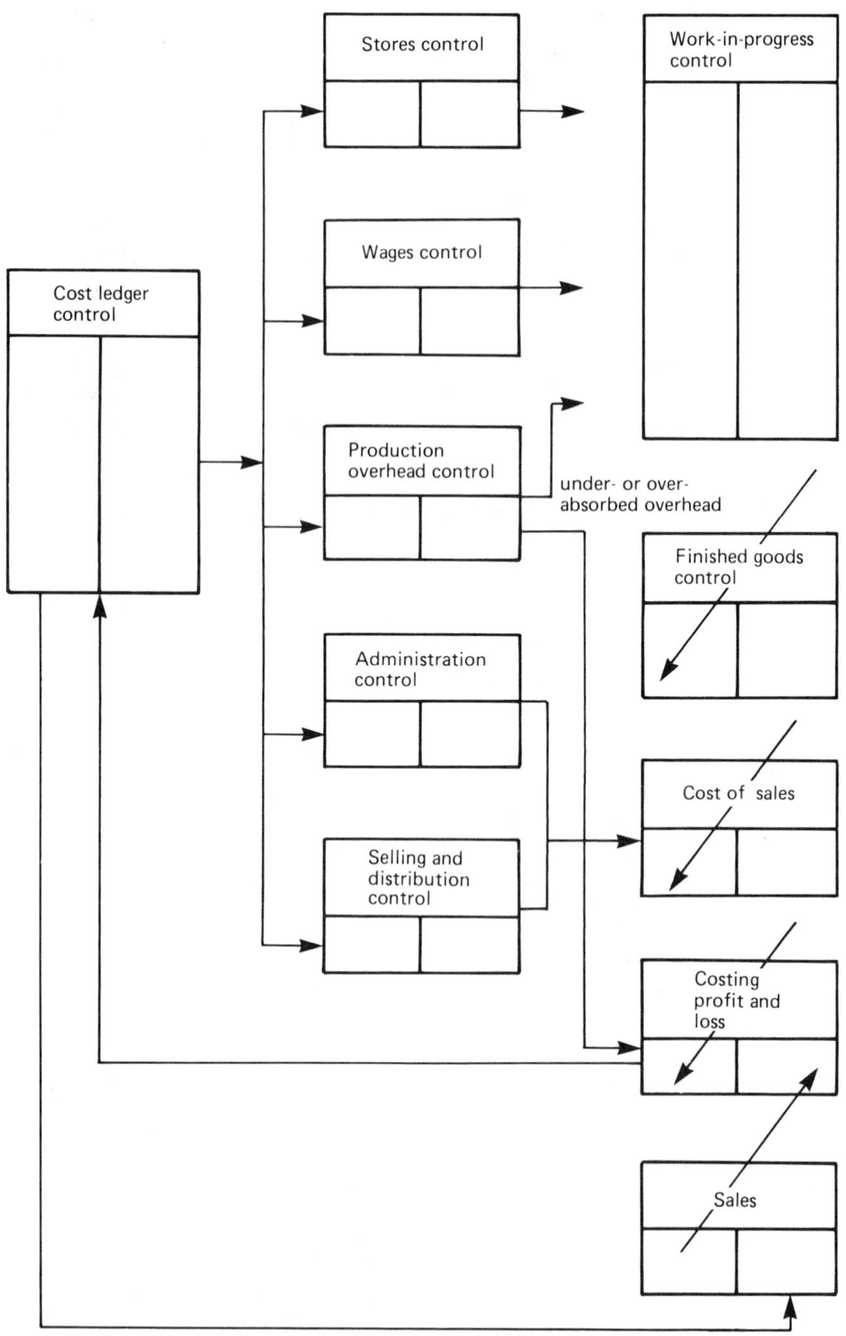

Exhibit 6.1 Flow chart showing accounting entries in an interlocking system

The entries required to record these transactions in the cost ledger, and the end of period trial balance are as follows:

Cost ledger of Green Manufacturing Co.

Stores control account

	£		£
Balance b/d	7 000	Work-in-progress control (e)	10 000
Cost ledger control (a)	12 000	Balance c/d	9 000
	19 000		19 000
Balance b/d	9 000		

Work-in-progress control account

	£		£
Balance b/d	6 000	Finished goods control (j)	30 000
Stores control (e)	10 000	Balance c/d	15 000
Wages control (b)	20 000		
Production overhead control (g)	9 000		
	45 000		45 000
Balance b/d	15 000		

Finished goods control account

	£		£
Balance b/d	9 000	Cost of sales (i)	35 000
Work-in-progress control (j)	30 000	Balanced c/d	4 000
	39 000		39 000
Balance b/d	4 000		

Wages control account

	£		£
Cost ledger control (b)	20 000	Work-in-progress control (b)	20 000

Administration overhead control account

	£		£
Cost ledger control (c)	5 000	Cost of sales	5 000

Selling and distribution overhead control account

	£		£
Cost ledger control (d)	8 000	Cost of sales	8 000

Production overhead control account

	£		£
Cost ledger control (f) (overhead cost incurred)	10 000	Work-in-progress control (g)	9 000
		Costing profit and loss (unabsorbed overhead)	1 000
	10 000		10 000

Cost ledger control account

	£		£
Sales costing (profit and loss) (h)	60 000	Balance b/d	22 000
		Stores control (a)	12 000
Balance c/d	28 000	Wages control (b)	20 000
		Administration overhead control (c)	5 000
		Selling and distribution overhead control (d)	8 000
		Factory overhead control (f)	10 000
		Profit and loss	11 000
	88 000		88 000
		Balance b/d	28 000

Cost of sales account

	£		£
Finished goods control	35 000	Transfer to costing profit and loss	48 000
Administrative overhead control	5 000		
Selling and distribution overhead control	8 000		
	48 000		48 000

Costing profit and loss acccount

	£		£
Cost of sales	48 000	Sales (cost ledger control)	60 000
Unabsorbed factory overhead	1 000		
Net profit – transferred to cost ledger control	11 000		
	60 000		60 000

Closing trial balance

	£		£
Stores control	9 000		
Work-in-progress	15 000		
Finished goods control	4 000		
		Cost ledger control	28 000
	28 000		28 000

6.2.2 Reconciliation of cost and financial accounting profits

Where separate cost and financial accounting records are maintained, the resulting two profit and loss accounts have to be reconciled. This is to ensure the reliability of the cost accounts, which purport to be a detailed analysis of financial expenditure.

Differences between the accounting systems occur for the following reasons:

(a) Some items appear only in the financial accounts, for example, taxation charges and provisions, dividends paid and proposed, interest received, profit on the sale of fixed assets, amounts written off goodwill.
(b) Some items appear only in the cost accounts. They are introduced in the cost accounts to improve the relevance of information for management purposes, for example, notional interest (interest on capital employed but not in fact paid), notional rent (charged in lieu of rent where premises are owned by the firm), depreciation on fully depreciated assets.
(c) Differences in stock valuation bases. Contrary to cost accounting, in which stock values are always recorded at cost, stock values in the financial accounts are reported at the lower of cost or market value.
(d) Varying charges for overhead expenses which result in the under- or over-recovery of overhead costs.

EXAMPLE 6.2:

Hamer Ltd has separate cost and financial accounting systems. Extracts from both sets of accounts for the year ended 31 December 19X0 are shown below:

Cost accounts

	£	£
Stock valuations	*Opening stock*	*Closing stock*
Raw materials	80 000	90 000
Work-in-progress	30 000	35 000
Finished goods	50 000	55 000
Notional rent		14 000
Notional interest on capital employed		12 000
Under-absorbed production overhead costs		8 000

Financial accounts

Stock valuations	*Opening stock*	*Closing stock*
Raw materials	75 000	94 000
Work-in-progress	34 000	38 000
Finished goods	55 000	58 000
Debenture interest		4 000
Interest received		2 000
Discount allowed		6 000
Discount received		3 000
Net profit before tax		25 000

The reconciliation of these different figures is as follows:

Reconciliation statement

	£	£	£
Financial account profit			25 000
Items appearing in the financial accounts only:			
Debenture interest	4 000		
Discounts allowed	6 000	10 000	
Interest received	(3 000)		
Discount received	(2 000)	(5 000)	5 000
			30 000

Reconciliation statement (contd)

		£	£	£
Total b/d				30 000
Differences in stock valuations:				
Raw materials:	Opening stock		(5 000)	
	Closing stock		(4 000)	
Work-in-progress:	Opening stock		4 000	
	Closing stock		(3 000)	
Finished goods:	Opening stock		3 000	
	Closing stock		(3 000)	(8 000)
Cost accounting profit				22 000

Notes:

(a) The notional rent and notional interest appearing in the cost accounts are self-adjusting. These items are debited to overhead costs and credited to the costing profit and loss account. Hence, they do not appear in the reconciliation statement.

(b) Under- and over-absorbed production overheads are also self-adjusting. They are shown on the costing profit and loss account and do not, therefore, appear on the reconciliation statement.

(c) If the value of opening stocks is lower in the financial accounts than that in the cost accounts, the financial accounting profit will be higher than the cost accounting profit. Therefore, the difference is *subtracted* from the financial accounting profit.

If the value of the closing stock is lower in the financial accounts than that in the cost accounts, the financial accounting profit is lower than the cost accounting profit. Therefore, the difference is *added* to the financial accounting profit.

6.3 INTEGRATED ACCOUNTS

Under the system of integrated accounts, there is only one accounting system that combines the cost accounts and the financial accounts.

6.3.1 The nature of integrated accounts

The features of integrated accounts are:

(a) There is only one ledger.
(b) There is only one profit and loss account, and one profit results.
(c) Information obtained for the ledger is used both for management and for financial reporting purposes.
(d) There is no necessity to reconcile cost accounts and financial accounts.

(e) The duplication of effort involved in maintaining separate accounting systems is avoided, and there is a consequent saving in clerical costs.
(f) Integrated accounts facilitate the use of computer applications.

Some disadvantage of integrated accounts are:

(a) Problems associated with difference in stock valuations. Thus, the financial accounts will record valuations based on the lower of cost and net realizable value, whereas cost valuations will be based on input cost only.
(b) Different treatments of items are required by the cost accounting system, for example, depreciation based on usage, the absorption of overheads using predetermined rates and the employment of notional charges.

6.3.2 Accounting entries

Where cost and financial accounts are integrated, control accounts are maintained in the general ledger for stores (or raw materials), wages, overhead expenses, work-in-progress and finished goods.

(a) Raw material purchases are recorded as follows:

    Dr. stores (or raw materials) control account
    Cr. trade creditors
    with the invoiced amount.

(b) Wages are recorded as follows:

    Dr. wages control account
    Cr. bank/wages payable
    with labour costs shown on the wages sheet.

(c) Overheads are recorded as follows:

    Dr. overhead cost control account
    Cr. trade creditors (or other control accounts, e.g. stores or wages control account).

(d) Work-in-progress is recorded as follows:

    Dr. work-in-progress control account
    Cr. stores control (with materials used), wages control and overhead control.

(e) Completed cost units are recorded as follows:

    Dr. finished goods control account

Cr. work-in-progress control account
with the production cost of the completed units.

(f) Sales are recorded as follows:

Dr. cost of sales control account
Cr. finished goods control account
with the production cost of the units sold.

Detailed manufacturing, trading and profit and loss accounts may be drawn up by analysing the various control accounts.

Exhibit 6.2 illustrates the accounting entries in an integrated system.

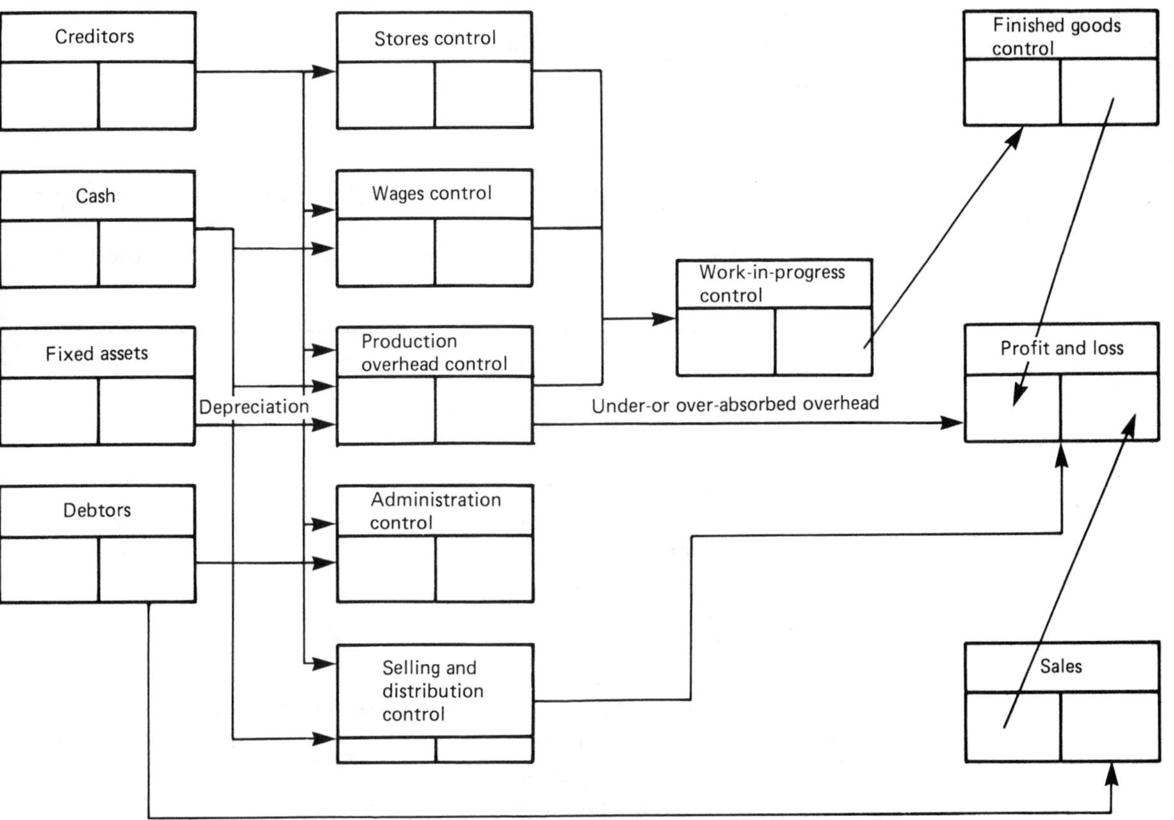

Exhibit 6.2 Flow chart showing accounting entries in an integrated system.

EXAMPLE 6.3:
Carefree Ltd operates an integrated accounting system.

The trial balance at 1 May 19X1 was as follows:

	£000	£000
Raw material stock	138	
Work-in-progress stock	34	
Finished goods stock	62	
Debtors	200	
Creditors		140
Expense creditors		58
Wages accrued		11
PAYE tax		45
Bank	40	
Freehold buildings	360	
Plant and machinery, at cost	240	
Provision for depreciation, plant and machinery		60
Issued share capital		600
Profit and loss account		160
	1074	1074

The following information is given of the transactions that took place in May 19X1:

	£000
Sales	320
Purchase of raw materials	92
Raw materials returned to supplier	4
Production overhead incurred	88
Selling and distribution costs incurred	42
Administration costs incurred	37
Direct wages incurred	42
Raw materials issued:	
To production	80
To production maintenance department	10
Raw materials returned to store from production	2
Abnormal loss in production	5
Cost of finished goods sold	210
Payment received in respect of sales	330
Payments made for raw materials purchased	101
Discounts allowed	11
Discounts received	3
Payments made to expense creditors	140
Direct wages paid	34
PAYE tax deducted from wages	16

Additional information is given as follows:

(a) depreciation of plant and machinery is provided for at 10 per cent per annum of cost;
(b) production overhead is absorbed on the basis of 250 per cent of direct wages incurred;
(c) selling and distribution costs incurred in May 19X1 are charged against the profit of May 19X1;
(d) work-in-progress was valued on 31 May 19X1 at £39 000.

The entries required to reflect this data are as follows:
(All figures in £000)

Stores control account

	£	19X0	£
Balance b/f	138	Creditors (returns)	4
Creditors (purchases)	92	Work-in-progress	80
Work-in-progress		Production overhead	10
(returns)	2	Balance c/f	138
	232		232
Balance b/f	138		

Work-in-progress control account

Balance b/f	34	Stores (returns)	2
Direct wages	42	Abnormal loss	5
Raw materials	80	Finished goods	215
Production overhead	105	Balance c/f	39
	261		261
Balance b/f	39		

Finished goods control account

Balance b/f	62	Cost of sales	210
Work-in-progress	215	Balance c/f	67
	277		277
Balance b/f	67		

Debtors account

Balance b/f	200	Cash	330
Sales	320	Discount allowed	11
		Balance c/f	179
	520		520
Balance b/f	179		

Creditors account

Raw material stock (returns)	4	Balance b/f	140
Cash	101	Raw material stock (purchases)	92
Discount received	3		
Balance c/f	124		
	232		232
		Balance b/f	124

Expense creditors account

Cash	140	Balance b/f	58
Balance c/f	85	Production overhead	88
		Selling and distribution expenses	42
		Administration expenses	37
	225		225
		Balance b/f	85

Wages control account

Cash	34	Balance b/f	11
PAYE deducted	16	Work-in-progress	42
Balance c/f	3		
	53		53
		Balance b/f	3

PAYE tax account

Balance c/f	61	Balance b/f	45
		Wages	16
	61		61
		Balance b/f	61

Bank account

Balance b/f	40	Creditors	101
Debtors	330	Expenses creditors	140
		Wages	34
		Balance c/f	95
	370		370
Balance b/f	95		

Freehold buildings account

Balance b/f	360	Balance c/f	360
Balance b/f	360		

Plant and machinery account

Balance of cost b/f	240	Depreciation to date b/f	60
Balance c/f	62	Depreciation for month (profit and loss account)	2
		Balance c/f	240
	302		302
Balance of cost b/f	240	Depreciation to date b/f	62

Share capital account

Balance c/f	600	Balance b/f	600
		Balance b/f	600

Profit and loss account

Balance c/f	176	Balance b/f	160
		Profit for month	16
	176		176
		Balance b/f	176

Sales account

Profit and loss	320	Debtors	320

Production overhead control account

Expense creditors	88	Work-in-progress	105
Stores	10		
Balance (over-absorption) c/f	7		
	105		105
		Balance b/f	7

Selling and distribution overhead control account

Expense creditors	42	Profit and loss account	42

Administration overhead control account

Expense creditors	37	Profit and loss account	37

Abnormal loss account

Work-in-progress account	5	Profit and loss account	5

Cost of sales account

Finished goods account	210	Profit and loss account	210

Discounts account

Allowed (debtors)	11	Received (creditors)	3
		Profit and loss account	8
	11		11

Profit and loss account for May 19X1

	£		£
Cost of sales	210	Sales	320
Discounts	8		
Depreciation: Plant and machinery	2		
Selling and distribution	42		
Administration	37		
Abnormal loss	5		
	304		
Profit and loss account	16		
	320		320

Notes:

(a) The balance of production overhead over-absorbed has been carried forward on the assumption that it would be written off at the end of the year.
(b) The abnormal loss has been written off.

Comment:
Having completed the accounts, students should take out a brief trial balance (for their own information) to prove their entries.

	Dr.	Cr.
	£	£
Raw material stock	138	
Work-in-progress	39	
Finished goods stock	67	
Debtors	179	
Creditors		124
Expense creditors		85
Wages accrued		3
PAYE tax		61
Bank	95	
Freehold buildings	360	
Plant and machinery at cost	240	
Plant and machinery depreciation		62
Issued share capital		600
Profit and loss account		176
Production overhead (over-absorption)		7
	£1118	£1118

Questions

1. Describe the nature of the records maintained by the financial and the cost accounting systems.
2. What is the relationship between the financial accounting and the cost accounting systems?
3. What do you understand by 'interlocking accounts'?
4. What is the difference between 'interlocking accounts' and 'integrated accounts'?
5. List the accounts that are kept in the cost ledger when interlocking accounts are maintained.
6. Under the interlocking accounts system, what is the purpose of the cost ledger control account?
7. Explain why non-production overhead costs, such as administrative, selling and distribution expenses have their own control accounts in the cost ledger when interlocking accounts are used.
8. What information appears in the costing profit and loss account under the interlocking accounting system?
9. What information appears in the financial profit and loss account under the interlocking accounting system?
10. What differences require to be reconciled between the costing profit and the financial accounting profit under the interlocking accounting system?
11. Under separate cost and financial accounting systems, why are

the following items charged in the costing profit and loss account:

(a) notional rent;
(b) notional interest on capital employed?

12. List the advantages and disadvantages of integrated accounts.
13. Describe briefly the cost accounting records that are maintained when cost and financial accounts are integrated.

Problems

1. *Required*:
   (a) Compare and contrast the operation of integrated accounts with a system where the financial and cost accounts are kept separately, stating *two* advantages and *two* disadvantages of a system of integrated accounts.
   (b) Draw a diagram or flowchart to show the flow of accounting entries within an integrated system, where standard costing is not used, for the following transactions:
      (i) purchase of raw materials, on credit terms;
      (ii) issue to production of part of the consignment received in (i) above;
      (iii) cash payment of wages to direct workers and to indirect workers associated with production:
      (iv) electricity for production purposes, obtained on credit;
      (v) depreciation of machinery used for production;
      (vi) absorption of production overhead, using a predetermined rate.

(20 marks)

(*Chartered Institute of Management Accountants*)

2. A repair workshop quotes its customers prices on the following basis: labour £5 per hour; materials, a price is extracted from a current price list; overhead 300 per cent on labour costs; profit 15 per cent on total cost.
   At the end of a 6-monthly period the following summary is extracted by the cost accountant.

	£
Direct labour: 16 000 hours	80 000
Material issues	92 460
Overheads	240 000
Profit	61 869
Sales	£474 329

The financial accountant extracts the following relating to the workshop for the same period of time.

	£	£	£
Sales			474 329
Less: Stock 1 Jan.	14 200		
Purchases	96 140		
	110 340		
Less: Stock 30 June	15 120		
		95 220	
Wages		87 372	
Factory expenses		8 528	
			191 120
Gross profit			283 209
Less: Administration costs		137 805	
Selling and distribution costs		103 004	
			240 809
Net profit			£42 400

Required:

(a) A statement reconciling the two profit figures. (14 marks)

(b) What steps would you recommend the cost accountant should take to minimize discrepancies between the two profit figures in the future.
Detail this by means of:
(i) investigations into costing matters; (4 marks)
(ii) analysis of actual costs. (4 marks)
(Total 22 marks)

(*Association of Accounting Technicians*)

3. C.D. Ltd, a company engaged in the manufacture of specialist marine engines, operates an historic job cost accounting system which is not integrated with the financial accounts.

At the beginning of May 19X0 the opening balances in the cost ledger were:

	£
Stores ledger control account	85 400
Work-in-progress control account	167 350
Finished goods control account	49 250
Cost ledger control account	302 000

During the month the following transactions took place:

		£
Materials: Purchases		42 700
Issues:	To production	63 400
	To general maintenance	1 450
	To construction of manufacturing equipment	7 650
Factory wages: Total gross wages paid		124 000

£12 500 of the above gross wages were incurred on the construction of manufacturing equipment, £35 750 were indirect wages and the balance were direct.

Production overheads:

Actual amount incurred, excluding items shown above, was £152 350; £30 000 was absorbed by the manufacturing equipment under construction and under absorbed overheads written off at the end of the month amounted to £7550.

Royalty payments:

One of the engines produced is manufactured under licence. £2150 is the amount which will be paid to the inventor for the month's production of that particular engine.

Selling overheads: £22 000

Sales: £410 000.

The company's gross profit margin is 25 per cent on factory cost.

At the end of May stocks of work-in-progress had increased by £12 000. The manufacturing equipment under construction was completed within the month, and transferred out of the cost ledger at the end of the month.

Required:

Prepare the relevant control accounts, costing profit and loss account, and any other accounts you consider necessary to record the above transactions in the cost ledger for May 19X0.

(22 marks)

(*Chartered Association of Certified Accountants*)

4. K Ltd operates separate cost accounting and financial accounting systems. The following manufacturing and trading statement has been prepared from the financial accounts for the *quarter* ended 31 March:

	£	£
Raw materials:		
Opening stock	48 000	
Purchases	108 800	
	156 800	
Closing stock	52 000	
Raw materials consumed		104 800
Direct wages		40 200
Production overhead		60 900
Production cost incurred		205 900
Work-in-progress:		
Opening stock	64 000	
Closing stock	58 000	
		6 000
Cost of goods produced carried down		211 900
Sales		440 000
Finished goods:		
Opening stock	120 000	
Cost of goods produced brought down	211 900	
	331 900	
Closing stock	121 900	
Cost of goods sold		210 000
Gross profit		230 000

From the cost accounts, the following information has been extracted:

Control account balances at 1 January:	£
Raw material stores	49 500
Work-in-progress	60 100
Finished goods	115 400
Transactions for the quarter:	£
Raw materials issued	104 800
Cost of goods produced	222 500
Cost of goods sold	212 100
Loss of materials damaged by flood (insurance claim pending)	2 400

A notional rent of £4000 *per month* has been charged in the cost accounts. Production overhead was absorbed at the rate of 185 per cent of direct wages.

Required:

(a) Prepare the following control accounts in the cost ledger:
raw materials stores;
work-in-progress;
finished goods;
production overhead.

(10 marks)

(b) Prepare a statement reconciling the gross profit as per the cost accounts and the financial accounts.

(11 marks)

(c) comment on the possible accounting treatment(s) of the under- or over-absorption of production overhead, assuming that the financial year of the company is 1 January to 31 December.

(4 marks)
(Total 25 marks)

(*Chartered Institute of Management Accountants*)

5. Shown below is 1 week's basic payroll data for the assembly department of Wooden Ltd, a manufacturer of a range of domestic furniture.

	Direct workers	*Indirect workers*
Total attendance time	800 hours	350 hours
Basic hourly rate of pay	£1.50	£1.00
Overtime hours worked	100 hours	40 hours
Shift premium	£150	£50
Group bonus	£160	£70
Employees' deductions:		
Income tax	£250	£100
National insurance	£75	£35
Employer's contributions:		
National insurance	£125	£55

Overtime, which is paid at basic time rate plus one-half, is used as a means of generally increasing the factory output. However, 20 per cent of the overtime shown above, for both direct and indirect workers, was incurred at the specific request of a special customer who requires, and is paying for, a particular batch of coffee tables to be completed quickly.

Analysis of the direct workers' time from returned work tickets shows:

Productive time		590 hours
Non-productive time:	Machine breakdown	50 hours
	Waiting for materials	40 hours
	Waiting for instructions	45 hours
	Idle time	75 hours

Required:

(a) Assuming the company operates an historical batch costing system, fully integrated with the financial accounts, write up the assembly department's wages, work-in-progress and production overhead control accounts, and other relevant accounts.

(14 marks)

(b) Explain the reasons for, and effect on product costs of, your treatment of the following items:

(i) employer's national insurance contributions;
(ii) group bonus;
(iii) overtime earnings.

(8 marks)
(Total 22 marks)

(*Chartered Association of Certified Accountants*)

6. In the absence of the accountant you have been asked to prepare a month's cost accounts for a company which operates a batch costing system fully integrated with the financial accounts. The cost clerk has provided you with the following information, which he thinks is relevant.

	£
Balances at beginning of month:	£
Stores ledger control account	24 175
Work-in-progress control account	19 210
Finished goods control account	34 164
Prepayments of production overheads brought forward from previous month	2 100
Transactions during the month:	£
Materials purchased	76 150
Materials issued: To production	26 350
For factory maintenance	3 280
Materials transferred between batches	1 450

		Direct workers		Indirect workers
		£		£
Total wages paid:	Net	17 646		3 342
	Employees deductions	4 364		890
			£	
Direct wages charged to batches from work tickets			15 236	
Recorded non-productive time of direct workers			5 230	
Direct wages incurred on production of capital equipment, for use in the factory			2 670	
Selling and distribution overheads incurred			5 240	
Other production overheads incurred			12 200	
Sales			75 400	
Cost of finished goods sold			59 830	
Cost of goods completed and transferred into finished goods store during the month			62 130	
Physical stock value of work-in-progress at end of month			24 360	

The production overhead absorption rate is 150 per cent of direct wages and it is the policy of the company to include a share of production overheads in the cost of capital equipment constructed in the factory.

Required:

(a) Prepare the following accounts for the month:
stores ledger control account;
work-in-progress control account;
finished goods control account;
production overhead control account;
profit and loss account.

(12 marks)

(b) Identify any aspects of the accounts which you consider should be investigated.

(4 marks)

(c) Explain why it is necessary to value a company's stocks at the end of each period and also why, in a manufacturing company, expense items such as factory rent, wages of direct operatives, power costs, etc. are included in the value of work-in-progress and finished goods stocks.

(6 marks)
(Total 22 marks)

(*Chartered Association of Certified Accountants*)

7. (a) A company operates a financial accounting system and a cost accounting system. Extracts from both final accounts for the year are shown below, from which you are required to prepare a reconciliation statement or account.

The final financial accounts included the following:

	£
Debenture interest	2 000
Interest received	1 000
Discount allowed	8 000
Discount received	3 000
Net profit	57 000

Stock valuations:

	Opening stock	*Closing stock*
	£	£
Raw materials	152 000	198 000
Work-in-progress	66 000	72 000
Finished goods	84 000	87 000

The final cost accounts included the following:

	£
Interest on capital	30 000
Notional rent	20 000
Administration overhead over-absorbed	10 000
Production overhead under-absorbed	15 000
Selling and distribution overhead over-absorbed	14 000

Stock valuations:

	Opening stock	*Closing stock*
	£	£
Raw materials	164 000	187 000
Work-in-progress	61 000	68 000
Finished goods	90 000	94 000

(b) Explain the meaning of:
   (i) interest on capital;
   (ii) notional rent.

Discuss briefly the reason why the cost accountant may choose to introduce these items into the cost accounts.

(30 marks)

(Chartered Institute of Management Accountants)

8. Using the information given below for the month of October 19X0 in respect of A Ltd, you are required to:

   (a) write up the integrated accounts;
   (b) prepare a trading and profit and loss account for October;
   (c) compile a trial balance as at 31 October;
   (d) comment on the difference in the level of stocks and state which administration cost will be increased following the changed levels of stocks.

1. List of balances at 1 October, 19X3:

	£000
Fixed assets: production	1000
Provision for depreciation of fixed assets	400
Material stores control	100
Work-in-progress stock	50
Finished goods stock	20
Debtors	600
Creditors	290
Creditor for PAYE and national insurance	85
Wages control: Credit balance (accrued direct wages)	20
Cash	5
Bank: Overdrawn	300
Share capital	600
Profit and loss appropriation: credit balance	80

2. Transactions for the month of October:

		£000
Received from debtors		380
Paid to creditors		170
Expenses paid by cheque:	Production	60
	Administration	40
	Selling	30
Bank interest on overdraft		10
Paid to creditor for PAYE and national insurance		60
Depreciation of fixed assets (for production)		25

Materials received and invoiced	110
Materials price variance, favourable, extracted as materials are received	10
Materials issued to production, at standard prices	80
Materials issued to production maintenance	20
Transfers from work-in-progress to finished goods	230
Sales on credit	310
Sales for cash	10
Production cost of goods sold	200

	Gross	*PAYE Nat. Ins.*	
	£000	£000	£000
Direct wages paid	86	20	66
Direct wages accrued	22	—	22
Indirect wages paid (production)	24	4	20
Administrative staff salaries paid	12	4	8
Selling staff salaries paid	20	4	16
Employer's contribution, national insurance:			
Production			9
Administration			3
Selling			2
Cash paid into bank			13

Production overhead is absorbed on the basis of 150 per cent on direct wages; any under- or over-absorption is transferred to the profit and loss account.

Administration and selling costs are not absorbed into product costs.

(35 marks)

(*Chartered Institute of Management Accountants*)

7 Job Costing

This chapter deals with the following topics:

7.1 The nature of job costing.
7.2 The job order.
7.3 The job cost sheet.
7.4 Recording the flow of costs.
7.5 Batch costing.
7.6 Managerial uses of job cost data.

The method of production employed by the firm determines the cost accounting system required for product costing. Manufacture according to specification determined by a customer placing an order retains its importance in the world of business, particularly in the field of specialized products. This necessitates treating every specific job order in the cost accounting system as a separate and distinct cost unit. This method of costing is also used for recording capital jobs, for example, the building of a furnace complex.

7.1 THE NATURE OF JOB COSTING

Job costing assigns production costs to individual units. It is the appropriate method of product costing when production is neither continuous nor stereotyped, and where each job requires different manufacturing specifications. It should be used whenever it is possible physically to distinguish each unit or groups of unit from all other units throughout the production process, for example, the making of foundry patterns and custom printing.

7.2 THE JOB ORDER

The procedures involved in handling job orders are as follows:

(a) An enquiry is received from a prospective customer.
(b) The precise details of the item required by the customer such as quantity, quality, size, colour, date of delivery, are discussed and agreed.

(c) Cost estimates are prepared and form the basis of the price quoted to the client. These cost estimates may be developed by an analysis of the firm's past experience with identical or similar jobs, taking into account cost changes that have taken place since and forecasts of future costs. Where the firm has no previous experience of the particular order, extensive studies will be required of the type and quantity of raw materials needed and the nature of the processes required.

(d) Upon receipt of a firm order, a production order is prepared for the factory. It contains information and instructions regarding product specifications, manufacturing schedule, route schedule, machines to be used, etc.

7.3 THE JOB COST SHEET

In job costing, product costs are accumulated for the individual job orders. Throughout the production process, therefore, raw materials, labour and overhead costs are collected on a separate form (or account) called the *job cost sheet.* Each separate job cost sheet records:

(a) the order number and the job number;
(b) the customer, description of the order and promised delivery date;
(c) materials used, with description, stock code, requisition number, quantity and price;
(d) labour employed, detailing cost centre operatives, hours worked and rates of pay;
(e) production overheads, detailing cost centre, basis of absorption, hours involved and the rate applied;
(f) administrative and selling and distribution overheads, detailing any allocations that have been made to the product;
(g) total costs;
(h) invoice price and number;
(i) profit recorded.

Exhibit 7.1 illustrates a job order cost sheet.

7.4 RECORDING THE FLOW OF COSTS

Job costing uses control accounts (explained in Chapter 6) in the process of recording job costs. In a job cost accounting system (interlocked or integrated), the job cost sheet constitutes a subsidiary ledger account with respect to the work-in-progress control account. At any time, the balance appearing in the work-in-progress control

JOB COST SHEET

Customer .... Job No. ....

Job description .... Order No. ....

Date ....

Date	Materials					Total cost		
						Actual	Estimated	Difference
	Description	Reference	Qty	Rate	Cost			
	Labour							
	Cost centre	Operative	Hrs.	Rate	Cost			
	Overhead							
	Cost centre	Basis	Hrs.	Rate	Cost			

Total production overhead
Administrative overhead
Selling and distribution overhead
Total cost
Invoice price
Estimated profit

Comments

Exhibit 7.1 Job cost sheet.

account is equal to the aggregate balances of the several job cost sheets recording the costs of uncompleted orders.

7.4.1 Recording materials cost

Materials issued to a specified job order by means of a requisition order (see Chapter 3) are recorded in the accounting system as follows:

Dr. work-in-progress control account
Cr. stores ledger control account
with the cost of the materials issued to the job.

At the same time, an entry will be made in the job cost sheet recording the quantity and the cost of the materials issued. At any time, the total of materials debited to the work-in-progress control account must correspond to the aggregate cost of materials charged to the several job cost sheets representing uncompleted orders.

7.4.2 Labour costs

As explained in Chapter 4, payroll accounting involves recording the hours worked and applying labour costs by means of a wages analysis sheet to cost units. In a job costing system, a job ticket records the following details in respect of each job:

(a) the name of each operative working on the job;
(b) the hours worked;
(c) the nature of the work.

The job ticket is sent to the cost office, where the hours worked will be costed and recorded on the job cost sheet, and posted as follows:

Dr. work-in-progress control account
Cr. wages control account
with the wages charged to each job.

At any time, the total of the work-in-progress control account will equal the aggregate labour costs on the job cost sheets.

7.4.3 Production overhead costs

As explained in Chapter 5, production overhead costs are allocated to cost centres, and those costs that cannot be directly allocated are apportioned to cost centres. In a job cost accounting system, production overhead costs accumulated in cost centres are applied to jobs on the basis of a predetermined rate. The entries are as follows:

Dr. work-in-progress control account
Cr. production overhead cost control account
with the production overhead costs applied to each job order.

The production overhead costs applied to each job are recorded in the job order cost sheets maintained for each job. The aggregate of production overhead costs recorded on the several job order cost sheets must equal the balance of overhead costs shown on work-in-progress account, and representing the aggregate of overhead costs applied to uncompleted orders.

At the end of the accounting period, the under- or over-applied overheads (i.e. the balance outstanding on the production overhead cost control account), will be debited or credited, as the case may be, to the profit and loss account.

7.4.4 Administrative, selling and distribution overheads

When the job is completed and put into the finished goods store it will not be valued at more than the sum of the cost of direct materials, direct labour and production overhead. This is the production, factory or works cost.

Later, when the job is sold and delivered the job cost sheet will be charged with the appropriate amount of administration, selling and distribution overhead, after which the total cost of the job can be ascertained. The difference between the agreed selling price and the total actual cost will be the supplier's profit or loss on the particular job.

As there may be a difference between the administrative, selling and distribution overheads incurred during the accounting period and the total applied, the under- or over-applied administrative, selling and distribution overhead cost will be debited or credited, as the case may be, in the profit and loss account.

EXAMPLE 7.1:

A small engineering works commenced business on 1 July 19X6 to manufacture parts to customers' specifications and instituted a job costing system in which the costs of each job are separately recorded. A summary of the job cost sheets for the year ended 30 June 19X7 is as follows:

	Completed orders	*Orders in progress*
	£	£
Materials used	210 000	23 000
Labour	92 000	8 400
Production overhead	31 000	3 600
	333 000	35 000

The following figures for the year ended 30 June 19X7 appear in the financial books as follows:

	£
Sales	486 000
Materials purchased	281 000
Wages	100 400
Production overhead	33 500
Selling and administrative expenses	41 000

Selling and administrative expenses are applied to the cost of finished jobs on the basis of a monthly charge of £3500. Work is invoiced to customers immediately on completion. Materials lost through wastage in storage amounted to £1500.

Required:
Write up the accounts in the cost ledger.

Solution

Stores control account

	£		£
Cost ledger control (a)	281 000	Work-in-progress control (b)	233 000
		Profit and loss (c)	1 500
		Balance c/d	46 500
	281 000		281 000
Balance b/d	46 500		

Wages control account

	£		£
Cost ledger control (d)	100 400	Work-in-progress control (e)	100 400

Production overhead control account

	£		£
Cost ledger control (f)	33 500	Work-in-progress control (g)	34 600
Profit and loss (h)	1 100		
	34 600		34 600

Work in progress control account

	£		£
Stores control (b)	233 000	Cost of sales (i)	333 000
Wages control (e)	100 400	Balance c/d	35 000
Production overhead control (g)	34 600		
	368 000		368 000
Balance b/d	35 000		

Selling and administrative overhead control account

	£		£
Cost ledger control (j)	41 000	Cost of sales (l)	42 000
Profit and loss (k)	1 000		
	42 000		42 000

Cost of sales account

	£		£
Work-in-progress (i)	333 000	Profit and loss (m)	375 000
Selling and administrative expenses (l)	42 000		
	375 000		375 000

Cost ledger control account

	£		£
Sales (n)	486 000	Stores control (a)	281 000
		Wages control (d)	100 400
		Production overhead control (f)	33 500
		Selling and administrative overhead (j)	41 000
		Balance c/d	30 100
	486 000		486 000
Balance b/d	30 100	Profit and loss	111 600
Balance c/d	81 500		
	111 600		111 600
		Balance b/d	81 500

Profit and loss account

	£		£
Cost of sales (m)	375 000	Sales	486 000
Material wastage (c)	1 500	Selling and administrative overhead (k)	1 000
Cost ledger control	111 600	Production overhead (h)	1 100
	488 100		488 100

Sales account

	£		£
Profit and loss	486 000	Cost and ledger control (a)	486 000

7.5 BATCH COSTING

This is a method of costing used when a number of identical cost units maintain their identity throughout one or more stages of production. Essentially, it is a variation of job costing. But whereas job costing identifies the specific order of a customer as the job, batch costing is concerned with making a quantity of objects which will often be placed in store and sold later.

Each batch is costed as a job and given an order number to which the costs incurred on producing the batch are assigned. Direct labour, material and expense which can be identified with the batch are recorded on the batch cost card and factory overhead is absorbed in similar manner to job costing. When production is complete, the costs are totalled, divided by the number of units produced in the batch to give the unit or average cost.

The size of the batch to be produced is highly critical in ensuring a least cost operation. The general principles that were discussed with respect to economic order quantity in Chapter 3, apply equally to the batch size of production. With each batch will be the attendant fixed costs of the time required for production of the batch, i.e. the setting-up time. As with all fixed costs, the greater the number of units produced, the smaller will be the individual unit's share of these fixed costs and, therefore, the larger the batch size the better. But opposing this is the cost of storage, the interest on the capital tied up, and the risk of obsolescence and deterioration when too large a stock is produced. The costs involved over a series of batch quantities may be tabulated and inserted on a graph as in Exhibit 7.2. The economic batch size is the point where the saving in production costs through utilizing the set-up machinery to produce one more unit, is just offset by the costs of storing an additional unit until it is

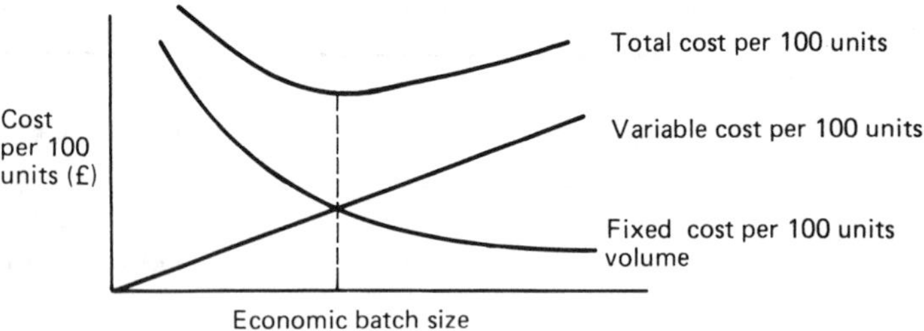

Exhibit 7.2 Economic batch size graph.

required. The economic batch size may also be found by applying the following formula:

$$\text{economic batch size} = \sqrt{\frac{2DS}{IC}}$$

where:

D = annual demand for the item;
S = set-up cost per batch;
I = annual storage and interest charges;
C = variable production cost per unit.

EXAMPLE 7.2:

The annual demand for a particular part is 5000;
the set-up cost per batch is £250;
the annual rate of interest is 15%;
the variable cost of manufacture is £10 per unit;
the economic batch quantity is:

$$\sqrt{\frac{2 \times 5000 \times 250}{0.15 \times 10}} = 1666$$

7.6 MANAGERIAL USES OF JOB COST DATA

Job cost sheets are an invaluable source of data for preparing the cost estimates needed for new job orders. As indicated earlier, past costing experience of similar jobs assists management in negotiating new orders. Exhibit 7.1 illustrates the need for 'comments' on the job cost sheet. For example: Was the material acceptable? Were there problems with its use? What grade of labour was used? Answers to questions of this type provide a guide to the preparation of future estimates. A limitation to the usefulness of data recorded in respect of earlier jobs is the extent of under- or over-applied overheads. Given that suitable correction is made in this respect, prior job cost sheets do provide reasonably accurate historical evidence.

Job cost sheets are also indicative of profitability, and may serve as a basis for analysing cost and pricing factors that have influenced profits.

Questions

1. What do you understand by *job costing*?
2. What accounting problems exist that are peculiar to job costing?
3. List the events involved in dealing with a job order.
4. Describe the data contained in the job cost sheet.
5. What is the cost accounting significance of the job cost sheet?
6. Describe the link between the job order cost sheet and work-in-progress control account.
7. Outline the entries required to record:
   (a) materials issued to a job;
   (b) labour costs applied to a job.
8. What problems arise when charging overhead costs to particular jobs?
9. Full-product costing limits product costs to direct and indirect production costs and treats non-production costs as periodic costs. Is this principle maintained for job costing? Explain.
10. When should job costing be utilized?
11. What is batch costing?
12. What factors determine the economic batch quantity? How is it calculated?
13. Discuss the managerial uses of job cost data.

Problems

1. Electronic equipment is manufactured and supplied to customers' special requirements. Job no. AB985 has been completed and supplied at the agreed price of £850 and the following cost details are on record:

Direct materials

Code	*Quantity*	*Price*
NB217	200 kg	£0.50 per kg
CL110	4 units	£21.00 each
X814	55 metres	£0.40 per metre
Paint	6 litres	£3.00 per litre

Direct labour			*Production overhead*
Dept	*Hours*	*Hourly rate*	*Rate per direct labour hour*
		£	£
1	30	3.20	2.50
2	20	3.50	2.75
3	10	3.10	2.90

Administration overhead is absorbed on the basis of 10 per cent of total production cost, whilst 4 per cent of the selling price is allowed for selling overhead. Delivery to the customer costs £48.00.

Required:
Prepare a job cost sheet showing prime cost, production cost, total cost and profit (or loss).

(20 marks)

(*London Chamber of Commerce and Industry*)

2. Equipment is manufactured to customers' special requirements by DEF Ltd. Job no. 171 was in progress on 31 March when accumulated costs were materials £900, wages £288 and overhead £258.

   The following costs were charged to jobs in April:

Job no.	*171*	*172*	*173*
	£	£	£
Materials	216	864	1242
Wages	720	1080	630

   Overhead expenditure in April amounted to £2250 but jobs were charged at the predetermined rate of 90 per cent of direct wages. The following two jobs were completed in April:

Job no.	*Contract price*
171	£3550
172	£3475

Required:

(a) Ascertain the cost of each job to 30 April.

(b) Ascertain the profit earned in April, taking under-absorbed overhead into account.

(20 marks)

(*London Chamber of Commerce and Industry*)

3. J. M. Daniels Company uses a job order cost system. On 1 January 19X1, the company had a work-in-progress stock balance of £44 000.

This account was made up of the following items:

Job no.	*Direct materials*	*Direct labour*	*Factory overheads*
	£	£	£
101	10 000	3 000	2 000
102	15 000	8 000	2 000
103	2 000	1 000	1 000

The following transactions were completed during the month:

(a) materials were requisitioned for production:

	£
Job no. 101	12 000
Job no. 102	6 000
Job no. 103	14 000
Indirect materials	8 000

(b) paid wages totalling £84 000. This was distributed as follows:

	Hours	*Amount*
Job no. 101	20 000	41 000
Job no. 102	12 000	25 000
Job no. 103	4 000	8 000
Indirect labour		10 000

(c) additional factory overheads incurred during January were £40 000;

(d) applied factory overheads to jobs at the rate of £1.50 per direct labour hour;

(e) completed jobs nos 101 and 102 which were despatched to the customer.

Required:

(a) Prepare job cost sheets for the three jobs.
(b) Complete the factory overheads account for January 19X1.
(c) Explain the reasons for the balance disclosed on the factory overheads account at the end of January 19X1.
(d) What is the value of work-in-progress stock?

4. CBA Ltd are manufacturers of jigs and tools to customers' special requirements. The business is not profitable and you, as a consultant, have been called upon to investigate the situation. You have already studied a number of quotations and job costs. The cost details of one of these jobs – no. 7512 – relate to a set of jigs recently supplied at a price of £400 and these details are given below:

				£
Direct materials				152.00
Direct wages:			£	
Department:	1	10 hours at £3.00	30.00	
	2	4 hours at £2.50	10.00	
	3	15 hours at £3.20	48.00	88.00
Overhead:		45% on prime cost		108.00
		Total cost		348.00
Profit margin	15%			52.00
		Selling price		400.00

You were also shown the current budget, in summary form, from which you noted the following figures:

		£000
Direct materials		782
Direct wages		390
Prime cost:		1172
Overhead:		
Production	373	
Administration, selling and distribution	155	528 (45% of prime cost)
Total Budgeted Cost		1700

Your investigations have disclosed the following facts:

(1) Only about half of the quotations submitted resulted in orders.
(2) The estimating of direct wages and materials was very accurate.

(3) A large debit for under-absorbed overhead appeared in the profit and loss account.

(4) Analyses of the budgeted wages and production overhead produced separate figures for the three departments as follows:

	Wages	*Overhead*
Department	£000	£000
1	130	143
2	160	80
3	100	150

Required:

(a) Briefly state why, in your opinion, profits have been too low.

(b) Using a sound costing method, re-assess the cost of job no. 7512 and state what price should have been quoted to yield a profit of 15 per cent of cost (to the nearest £1).

(*London Chamber of Commerce and Industry*)

8 Contract Costing

This chapter deals with the following topics:

8.1 The nature of contract costing.
8.2 Cost accumulation.
8.3 Progress payments.
8.4 Short-term contracts.
8.5 Long-term contracts.

8.1 THE NATURE OF CONTRACT COSTING

Contract costing is a form of job costing which applies to work undertaken in accordance with the specific requirements of customers, and where each order is of long duration. Contract costing is found in the construction industry among builders and contractors, and in shipbuilding and aircraft manufacture.

Contracts may be distinguished from job orders in the following respects:

(a) The money value of the contract is generally much larger than that of the job order.
(b) Correspondingly, the resources that are committed to the contract are significantly larger.
(c) The period of time taken to complete the contract generally spreads over more than one accounting year.
(d) Overhead costs are small in relation to direct costs.
(e) Special plant is often purchased for specific contracts.
(g) Progress payments are usually made.
(h) Where contracts take more than one year to complete, there is the problem of deciding what proportion of the profit or loss should be recognized in accounting periods preceding completion.

8.2 COST ACCUMULATION

A separate account is opened for each contract undertaken for the purpose of accumulating costs. As with job costing, all contract accounts are reflected in total in a contract control account. Usually, materials are purchased specifically for particular contracts and delivered to site. In some cases, certain items are held in central stores and sent to the site on requisition by the contract foreman. Material returned to stores from contracts are controlled along the same principles as those described in Chapter 3 relating to factory operations. Materials transferred from one site to another must be accompanied by a materials transfer note.

All labour costs related to a contract are usually classed as direct costs regardless of the nature of the work performed. On large contracts, resident timekeepers will be responsible for recording the attendance time of workers, preparing the payroll and payment of wages. Direct expenses incurred on specific contracts have to be charged to those contracts. This includes work done by subcontractors, which is treated as a purchase. Other direct expenses include architect and consultant's fees, plant hire, electricity and insurance.

The cost of plant owned by the firm and used on a contract may be charged in any one of the following ways:

(a) The full value is debited as a direct expense to the contract account. At the end of the contract, it may be returned to head office and the residual value is credited to the contract account. Maintenance and running costs are charged to the contract.
(b) The full value may be capitalized and depreciation charged against the contract on which it is used. Maintenance and running costs are charged to the contract.
(c) Depreciation and running costs are debited to a plant account. A notional hire charge is made against specified contracts at a daily rate.

Overhead costs are small compared to direct costs, consisting of management, selling, head office costs as well as costs relating to central stores. Often, they are apportioned periodically on an arbitrary basis, such as percentage of prime costs, or of the contract price. Alternatively, predetermined rates may be used for each functional cost, as shown in Exhibit 8.1.

Exhibit 8.1 Predetermined rates for apportioning contract overhead

Functional cost	*Apportionment basis*
Purchasing costs	% of materials and subcontracting
Personnel and training costs	% of direct labour
Estimating and planning	% of prime costs
Administration overhead	% of the contract price

8.3 PROGRESS PAYMENTS

Periodic payments are made to the contractor, as work progresses. These payments are made on the basis of work certified. Such certificates are issued to the contractor by the customer's agents. They state the money value of the work completed as a proportion of the total contract price, and authorize that money sum to be paid to the contractor.

A percentage of the payment due to the contractor made in respect of work-in-progress certified as completed is not paid to him immediately, but is retained. Such *retentions*, generally in the range of 5–10 per cent of the value of the work-in-progress certified is held as an insurance against defective work. It is paid over to the contractor after the lapse of a period of time that is stipulated in the contract. Retentions are a form of leverage on the contractor with respect to faulty work appearing subsequent to certification.

Progress payments are shown in the contractor's accounts as follows:

Dr. customer's account
Cr. contract account
with the value of the work certified.
Dr. cash
Cr. customer's account
with cash received.

The balance on the customer's account represents retentions.

8.4 SHORT-TERM CONTRACTS

Short-term contracts are defined as contracts that are commenced and completed during the accounting period.

EXAMPLE 8.1:
Ridgeway Builders obtained a contract to build a small block of flats for £800 000. Work was begun on 2 February 19X6 and was completed on 2 December 19X6. The following expenditure was incurred:

	£000
Materials	290
Wages	270
Expenses	30
Plant and tools	10
Overheads	50
	650

On 15 December 19X6, the client's architect issued the final certificate relating to the value of work done: at that date, the customer had already paid £720 000. The remaining £80 000 represents retentions outstanding at 31 December 19X6. The accounts appear as follows:

Contract account

	£000		£000
Materials	290	Cost of work done c/d	650
Wages	270		
Expenses	30		
Plant and tools	10		
Overheads	50		
	650		650
	£000		£000
Cost of work done b/d	650	Work certified	800
Profit and loss account	150		
	800		800

Customer (contractee) account

	£000		£000
Work certified	800	Cash	720
		Balance c/d	80
	800		800
Balance b/d	80		

Note that the contract account is divided into two parts. The first part shows the costs which have been allocated to the contract. The second part shows the profit or loss realized on the contract. The retentions of £80 000 shown as the balance on the customer's account will be included in the debtor's balances in the balance sheet.

8.5 LONG-TERM CONTRACTS

If contracts take more than 1 year to complete, there is the problem of deciding what profit, if any, should be recognized in the accounting periods prior to the period in which the contract is completed. The valuation of long-term contracts creates a conflict between two of the fundamental concepts of SSAP 2 Disclosure of Accounting Policies, namely prudence and accruals.

Prudence dictates that profit should not be taken until realized, which means at the satisfactory completion of the contract. Conversely, for a company that regularly undertakes long-term contracts, for example, in the construction industry, the accruals concept dictates that some profit be taken on contracts-in-progress. This ensures that profit measurement is related to effort expended rather than to the timing of the completion of contracts.

Two alternative accounting methods have been proposed for dealing with long-term contracts:

(a) The completed contract method, reflecting the concept of prudence by taking profit only on contract completion.
(b) The percentage of completion basis, reflecting the accruals concept by taking profit as it is considered to accrue during the contract period.

8.5.1 The completed contract method

Prior to SSAP 9 Stocks and Work-in-Progress issued in 1976, many companies engaged in long-term contracts utilized the completed contract method.

EXAMPLE 8.2:
Buxton Construction Co. Ltd obtained a contract to build a factory for £1 500 000. Work commenced on 1 January 19X6 and the following expenditure was incurred during the year:

	£
Plant and tools	70 000
Materials	275 000
Wages	236 000
Expenses	19 700
Overhead	46 200

Some of the materials costing £54 500 proved to be unsuited to the contract and were sold for £63 000. A portion of the plant was scrapped and sold for £10 800.

At 31 December 19X6, the value of the plant and tools on the site was £25 600, and that of materials was £16 200. The client's architect had certificates for work done valued at £630 000, and progress payments amounting to £500 000 had been received. The company had calculated that more work had been done since the last certificate had been issued, and estimated the cost of work done but not yet certified at £10 000.

The accounts appear as follows:

Contract account

	£		£
Plant and tools	70 000	Sale of materials	62 000
Materials	275 000	Sale of plant	10 800
Wages	236 000	Balance c/d:	
Expenses	19 700	Plant and tools	25 600
Overhead	46 200	Materials	16 200
Profit on sale of material	8 500	Cost of work done	539 800
	655 400		655 400
	£		
Balance b/d:			
Plant and tools	25 600		
Materials	16 200		
Cost of work done	539 800		

Customer (contractee) account

	£		£
Work certified	630 000	Cash	500 000
		Balance c/d	130 000
	630 000		630 000
	£		
Balance b/d	130 000		

Note:

(a) Under the completed contract method, none of the profit to date is taken. Profit to date may be estimated as follows:

	£
Work certified	630 000
Work done but not certified	10 000
	640 000
Cost of work done	539 800
Estimated profit	100 200

(b) The valuation of closing work-in-progress for balance sheet purposes will appear as follows:

	£
Cost of work done	539 800
Less: Cash received to date	500 000
Valuation of closing work-in-progress	39 800

(c) Retentions represent part of work-in-progress and should not be shown among debtors until the contract is completed. The following alternative method of calculating the value of closing work-in-progress illustrates this point:

	£
Cost of work done but not certified	10 000
Balance on client account (retentions)	130 000
	140 000
Estimated profit c/f	100 200
Valuation of closing work-in-progress	39 800

8.5.2 The percentage of completion method

Before the introduction of SSAP 9 in 1976, most of the companies that used the percentage on completion method calculated profit earned to date on the following basis:

> profit on contract for the period = value of work certified − cost of work certified.

The concept of prudence made it customary to take no more than two-thirds or three-quarters of the estimated profit to allow for contigencies before completion. Where retentions were involved, it was usual to further reduce the profits taken by reference to the proportion which the work certified bore to the actual cash received, as shown in the following formula:

$$\text{estimated profit} \times 2/3 \times \frac{\text{cash received}}{\text{work certified}}$$

EXAMPLE 8.3:

Using the information given in Example 8.2, the contract account appears as follows:

Contract account

	£		£
Plant and tools	70 000	Sale of materials	63 000
Materials	275 000	Sale of plant	10 800
Wages	236 000	Balance c/d	
Expenses	19 700	Plant and tools	25 600
Overhead	46 200	Materials	16 200
Profit on sale of material	8 500	Cost of work done c/d	539 800
	655 400		655 400

	£		£
Cost of work done b/d	539 800	Work certified to date	630 000
Profit and loss account	53 016	Work done but not yet certified c/d	10 000
Profit not yet claimed b/d	47 184		
	640 000		640 000
Plant and tools b/d	25 600	Profit not yet claimed b/d	47 184
materials b/d	16 200		
Work in progress b/d	10 000		

Note:

(a) The profit taken to the profit and loss account is calculated by the formula:

$$\text{estimated profit} \times 2/3 \times \frac{\text{cash received}}{\text{work certified}}$$

$$= £100\ 200 \times 2/3 \times \frac{£500\ 000}{£630\ 000}$$

$$= \underline{\underline{£53\ 016}}$$

(b) The valuation of closing work-in-progress for balance sheet purposes will appear as follows:

	£
Cost of work completed at 31 December 19X6	539 800
Add: Profit for which credit is taken	53 016
	592 816
Less: Cash received to date	500 000
Valuation of closing work-in-progress	92 816

An alternative method of calculating the value of closing work-in-progress is as follows:

	£
Cost of work done but not yet certified	10 000
Balance on client's account (retentions)	130 000
	140 000
Profit not yet claimed, carried forward	47 184
	92 816

8.5.3 The requirements of SSAP 9 Stocks and Work-in-Progress

SSAP 9 requires that long-term contract profit be valued by:

(a) the completed contract basis if the outcome of the contract cannot be foreseen with reasonable certainty; or by
(b) the percentage of completion basis if the outcome of the contract can be foreseen with reasonable certainty.

The standard further requires that as soon as estimates of total contract costs exceed those of total contract revenues a loss be recognized.

The standard states,

> 'In calculating the total estimated profit on the contract, it is necessary to take into account not only the total costs to date and the total estimated further costs to completion (calculated by reference to the same principles as were applied to cost to date) but also the estimated future costs of rectification and guarantee work, and any other work to be undertaken under the terms of the contract. These are then compared with the total sales value of the contract. In considering future costs it is necessary to have regard to likely increases in wages and salaries, to likely increases in the price of raw materials and to rises in general overheads so far as these items are not recoverable from the customer under the terms of the contract'.

An implication of the standard is that the traditional method of calculating the profit on an uncompleted contract does not comply with the requirements to take into account the estimated total profit (if any) on the contract as a whole. Therefore, the fact that some of the work has been certified does not necessarily mean some profit can be recognized. In accordance with the standard contract profit is calculated as follows:

		£
Total contract price		X
Costs to date	X	
Estimated future expenditure	X	
Estimated contract cost		X
Estimate profit		X

The estimated contract profit is then reduced to allow for contingencies as follows:

$$\text{profit taken} = \text{estimated profit} \times \frac{\text{value of work certified}}{\text{contract price}}$$

EXAMPLE 8.4:

In addition to the information given in Example 8.2 the following estimates of future expenditure to be included on the contract were made by the directors:

(a) the wages on the contract would amount to £246 750 for the ensuing period;

(b) the cost of materials required in addition to those in stock at 31 December would be £260 000 and further contract expenses would amount to £24 000;

(c) an additional amount of £89 000 would have to be paid out on plant and tools and the residual value of plant and tools at the completion of the contract would amount to no more than £11 000;

(d) overhead charges would cost the same per month as in the previous year;

(e) on the basis of past experience 2 per cent of the total cost would be due to defects, temporary maintenance and contingences.

The directors estimate that the contract would be completed by 30 September 19X7.

Required:

Prepare the contract account for the year ended 31 December 19X6 and show your calculation of the amount credited to the profit and loss account for that year. Show also how the contract would appear in the balance sheet at that date.

Solution:

Contract account

		£			£
Plant and tools		70 000	Sale of materials		63 000
Materials		275 000	Sale of plant		10 800
Wages		236 000	Balance c/d:		
Expenses		19 700	Plant and tools on site	25 600	
Overhead		46 200	Materials on site	16 200	41 800
Profit and loss account:					
Profit on sale of materials	8 500		Balance c/d (being cost of work completed to date including proportion of profit		644 800
Profit on contract to date	105 000	113 500			
		£760 400			£760 400
		£			
Balance b/d					
Plant and tools		25 600			
Materials		16 200			
Work completed		644 800			

Calculation of profit	£	£	£
Costs to date			539 800
Estimated future expenditure:			
Plant: In hand	25 600		
Additional	89 000		
	114 600		
Less: Scrap	11 000	103 600	
Wages		246 750	
Materials:			
In hand	16 200		
Additional	260 000	276 200	
Expenses		24 000	
Overhead		34 650	685 200
Add: Provision for defects and contingencies 2/98ths of £1 225 000			25 000
			1 250 000
Total contract price			1 500 000
Estimated contract profit			£250 000

Work certified to 31 December: £630 000

Proportion of profit to be taken to the profit and loss account:

$$\frac{£630\ 000}{£1\ 500\ 000} \times £250\ 000 = £105\ 000$$

The contract would appear on the balance sheet as follows:

	£
Work-in-progress on long-term contracts at cost plus attributable profit	644 800
Less: Progress payments received	500 000
Valuation of closing work in progress	£144 800

8.5.4 Proposed revision to SSAP 9

ED 40, Stocks and Long-Term Contracts, was issued in 1986 in order to remove a conflict between SSAP 9 and the 1985 Companies Act in regard to the balance sheet carrying value of long-term contracts. Whereas SSAP 9 requires that long-term contract work in progress is valued at cost plus attributable profit, the Companies Act provides that current assets shall be stated at cost (or net realizable value if lower).

For financial statement presentation purposes ED 40 distinguishes between value of work completed, cost of work completed and total costs incurred. The data given in Example 8.2 may be summarized as follows:

Value of work completed	£630 000
Cost of work completed	529 800
Total costs incurred	539 800
Payments on account	500 000

Assuming that the firm takes a profit £630 000 will be included in turnover and £529 800 in cost of sales, giving a profit of £100 200. The £130 000 excess of value of work completed over payments on account will be included in debtors. Work in progress (£10 000) is classified in the balance sheet as 'long-term contract balances' and separately disclosed within stocks.

Questions

1. What is contract costing?
2. Describe the information recorded in the contract control account.
3. State the procedure for dealing with materials returned to stores and materials transferred to other sites.
4. Describe three methods for recording plant used on a contract.

5. How are overheads allocated to contracts?
6. What are progress payments?
7. What are retentions?
8. State how retentions are recorded in the cost accounts?
9. Where do retentions appear in financial statements?
10. Compare and contrast the cost accounting implications of short- and long-term contracts.
11. Discuss, briefly, two accounting methods for accounting for long-term contracts.
12. Explain the implications of SSAP 2 Disclosure of Accounting Policies with regards to accounting policies for long-term contracts.
13. Discuss, briefly, the problems raised by SSAP 9 Stocks and Work-in-Progress with respect to accounting for long-term contracts.

Problems:

1. A public works company secures a contract to build a technical college at a fixed contract price of £5 million, completion must be in time to meet the start of the educational session starting 2 years hence.

   Work commenced on 1 July and at 31 December the following details had been recorded in the costing records:

	£
Materials purchased	620 000
Wages paid	140 000
Other direct charges	127 000
Plant sent to site at valuation, 1 July	180 000
Value of work measured (to 15 Dec.)	860 000
Cash received	774 000
Additionally you ascertain:	
Materials on site not used to date	14 000
Work completed, but not measured	74 000
Plant is depreciated at 20% per annum against valuation.	

   Required:

   (a) A contract account for the period showing the amount of profit or loss you consider should be taken to the profit and loss account. (12 marks)

   (b) Explain why the amount taken to the profit and loss account may differ from the normal profit. (6 marks)

   (c) Explain 'retention money' in connection with contract costing. (4 marks)

(d) Express your views as to the progress and profitability of this contract. (6 marks)

(Total 28 Marks)

(*Association of Accounting Technicians*)

2. EFG Constructions plc is building an office block for UK Developments plc, work having commenced in September 19X4. The financial year of EFG Constructions ended on 30 April 19X5, at which date the contract was still in progress and the following information appeared in the accounting records:

	£000
Direct materials:	
Issued to contract	400
Returned to central store	10
Transferred to other contracts	15
On site 30 April 19X5	25
Direct wages:	
Paid on site	250
Accrued at 30 April 19X5	10
Direct expenses:	
Paid on site	30
Accrued at 30 April 19X5	5
Cash received from contractee	840
Cost of work not yet certified	70
Invoice value of work certified	960
Plant installed (at cost)	120
Plant on site (revalued 30 April 19X5)	90
Allocation of company overhead	175

Required:

From the above information, prepare the contract account to 30 April 19X5 as it would appear in the books of EFG Constructions plc, clearly showing:

(a) the 'apparent' profit;

(b) the profit to be taken for the financial year;

(c) the opening entries for the year commencing 1 May 19X5.

(20 marks)

(*London Chamber of Commerce and Industry*)

3. On 3 January 19X8, B Construction Ltd started work on the construction of an office block for a contracted price of £750 000 with completion promised by 31 March 19X9. Budgeted cost of the contract was £600 000. The construction company's financial year end was 31 October 19X8 and on that date the accounts appropriate to the contract contained the following balances.

	£000
Materials issued to site	161
Materials returned from site	14
Wages paid	68
Own plant in use on site, at cost	96
Hire of plant and scaffolding	72
Supervisory staff: Direct	11
Indirect	12
Head office charges	63
Value of work certified to 31 October 19X8	400
Cost of work completed but not yet certified	40
Cash received related to work certified	330

Depreciation on own plant is to be provided at the rate of 12½ per cent per annum on cost.

£2000 is owing for wages.

Estimated value of materials on site is £24 000.

No difficulties are envisaged during the remaining time to complete the contract.

Required:

(a) Prepare the contract account for the period ended 31 October 19X8 showing the amount to be included in the construction company's profit and loss account.

(b) Explain the reason(s) for including the amount of profit to be shown in the profit and loss account.

(c) Show extracts from the construction company's balance sheet at 31 October 19X8 so far as the information provided will allow.

(20 marks)

(*Chartered Institute of Management Accountants*)

4. Jigantic Ltd is a building company engaged in the construction of hospitals and other major public buildings; most of the contracts undertaken extend over a 3- or 4-year period.

Shown below are the expenses incurred for the year ended 31 May 19X1, together with other operating details, for three of the contracts in which the company is currently engaged.

The agreed retention rate is 10 per cent of the value of work certified by the contractees' architects.

Contract C is nearing completion and the site manager estimates that costs, additional to those tabulated above, of £425 000 will be incurred in order to complete the contract. He also considers that the plant and equipment on site will be worthless by the time the contract is complete.

	Contract A	*Contract B*	*Contract C*
	£000	£000	£000
Contract price	4 000	10 200	12 000
Value of work certified by contractees' architects	2 350	7 500	11 000
Cash received from contractees	2 000	6 750	9 900
Work-in-progress at 1/6/19X0	—	2 400	6 700
Cost incurred during the year:			
Materials	1 100	1 600	1 050
Labour	700	1 150	975
Other expenses, excluding depreciation	350	475	775
Plant and equipment:			
Written down value at 1/6/19X0	300	800	700
Written down value at 30/5/19X1	600	525	175
Purchases during the year	725	400	125
Cost of work not yet certified	75	—	800

The nature of the work undertaken by Jigantic Ltd is such that it may be regarded as reasonable for the company to include in its annual accounts a prudent estimate for profit attributable to that part of the work on each contract certified as complete at the end of each accounting year.

The opening stock of work in progress shown above includes an estimated profit of £1 150 000 for contract C, but none for contract B as, at the beginning of the year, work on this project had only recently commenced.

The directors of Jigantic Ltd propose to incorporate into the company's profit and loss account for the year ended 31 May 19X1, the following amounts of profit/(loss) for each contract:

Contract A	Nil
Contract B	£720 000
Contract C	£2 400 000

Required:

(a) Making whatever calculations you consider necessary, carefully explain whether you agree with the proposed profit/(loss) figures for the above contracts. If you consider any of the proposed amounts are inappropriate suggest, with supporting explanations and calculations a more suitable figure. (15 marks)

(b) Show the relevant entries for each contract, incorporating any revised profit/(loss) figures, on the balance sheet of Jigantic Ltd as at 31 May 19X1.

(7 marks)
(Total 22 marks)

(Chartered Institute of Management Accountants)

5. (a) XY Constructions Ltd is building an extension to a college operated by the education authority. Work on the college extension commenced on 1 April 19X1 and after 1 year, on 31 March 19X2, the data shown below were available.

Required:

(a) Prepare the account for the contract for the year ended 31 March 19X2.

(b) Show in relation to the contract an extract from the balance sheet as at 31 March 19X2.

During the year:	£000
Plant sent to site	100
Direct materials received at site	460
Direct wages incurred	350
Direct expenses incurred	45
Hire of tower crane	40
Indirect labour costs	70
Supervision salaries	42
Surveyors fees	8
Service costs	18
Hire of scaffolding	20
Overhead incurred on site	60
Head office expenses apportioned to contract	70
Cash received from the education authority	1000

At 31 March, 19X2	£000
Value of plant on site	75
Work certified, valued at	1250
Cost of work not certified	250
Wages accrued	30
Service costs accrued	2
Materials unused on site	40

(b) Discuss the valuation of work-in-progress, with particular reference to contract building work.

(25 marks)

(Chartered Institute of Management Accountants)

9 Process Costing

This chapter deals with the following topics:

- **9.1 The nature of process costing.**
- **9.2 The measurement of output in equivalent completed units.**
- **9.3 Equivalent units and elements of cost.**
- **9.4 The valuation of work-in-process.**
- **9.5 Normal and abnormal process losses.**
- **9.6 Joint and by-products.**

9.1 THE NATURE OF PROCESS COSTING

Process costing is a method of product costing that assigns manufacturing costs to cost units under conditions of continuous production. It is used by manufacturing concerns that mass-produce standardized products. A special feature of such businesses is that they produce *in anticipation* of receiving orders from customers. Hence, production is stocked until sold.

Another feature of process costing is that, unlike job order costing, the cost unit is not a designated order from a named client, but a standard quantity of a homogeneous product expressed in quantity, weight or volume depending upon the product. For example, in the case of the steel industry the conventional cost unit is a tonne. It should also be noted that the cost unit for product costing purposes will generally be much larger than the conventional unit of quantity in which the product is marketed. For example, sugar costed on the basis of cost units measured in tonnes is sold at retail on the basis of a price per kilogramme.

Process costing is used in such industries as cement, flour, sugar, paper, tobacco, car, textile, steel, chemicals and oil refining. In addition, some public utilities such as electric power, gas and water use this method for product costing.

It was noted in Chapter 7 that job costing was used for costing specific job orders from customers. Where a business normally employs process costing for on-going production, special job production orders may well be costed on the job order method. Hence, the use of process costing in an industry does not preclude the use of alternative product costing methods, whenever the need arises.

9.1.1 Product costing

In continuous process production, the raw material is transformed into the final product as it moves through a designated sequence of production departments or cost centres. A production cost centre consists of one operation or a cluster of homogeneous operations involving the performance of a specific step in the making of the product.

Accordingly, production cost centres provide the basis for process costing. Costs are accumulated by cost centres in respect of standardized time periods, for example, 4-weekly periods, without any attempt to associate costs with individual cost units. At the end of the period, the accumulated total costs for each cost centre is divided by the volume of output in that period to establish the average product cost per cost unit.

The production measured and costed at the end of the period comprises two elements:

(a) completed cost units that will have been transferred out of the cost centre by the end of the period;
(b) end of period work-in-process that becomes the opening stock of work-in-process for the next period.

In the exceptional case where the product only requires processing through one cost centre, the completed cost units are transferred into the finished goods stock to await sale.

Generally, however, the product has to undergo processing through several cost centres before it reaches completion. Accordingly, from the viewpoint of the factory as a whole, work-in-process will comprise uncompleted cost units that will have been completed in one department, transferred out to the next cost centre in line, where they appear as 'transferred in' cost units.

It follows that process costing requires the following to be recorded for each cost centre.

(a) current period costs;
(b) current period production measured in the number of cost units that entered into process in that period;
(c) current period production transferred out, measured in terms of completed number of cost units valued at current period cost;

(d) end of current period work-in-process measured in terms of uncompleted cost units valued at current period cost.

Example 9.1 illustrates how process costing relates production costs to cost units in recording the flow of cost units through a sequence of three production cost centres. For simplification, it is assumed that there is no opening or closing work-in-process in any of the three production cost centres.

EXAMPLE 9.1:

Summerdrinks Ltd operates a soft drink bottling plant which has three processes – mixing (A), bottling (B) and packing (C). The following data were collected for the month of January 19X0:

			£
Materials used:		Process: A	10 000
		B	5 000
		C	2 000
Direct labour:		A	5 000
		B	2 000
		C	1 000
Factory overheads:	Direct	A	500
		B	1 000
		C	500
	Indirect (apportioned to process)		
		A	400
		B	200
		C	100

During the month of January, 100 000 gallons were produced and bottled. There were no opening or closing stocks of work-in-process. The process cost accounts will appear as follows:

Process A

	£		£
Materials	10 000	Transferred to process	
Direct labour	5 000	B (100 000 units at	
Direct overheads	500	£0.159)	15 900
Indirect overheads	400		
	15 900		15 900

Process B

	£		£
Transferred from process A (100 000 units at £0.159)	15 900	Transferred to process C (100 000 units at £0.241)	24 100
Materials	5 000		
Direct labour	2 000		
Direct overheads	1 000		
Indirect overheads	200		
	24 100		24 100

Process C

	£		£
Transferred from process B (100 000 units at £0.241)	24 100	Transferred to Finished Goods Stock (100 000 units at £0.277)	27 700
Materials	2 000		
Direct labour	1 000		
Direct overheads	500		
Indirect overheads	100		
	27 700		27 700

From the foregoing example, we may see not only how aggregate costs are built up through the consecutive processing departments, but also how the full-unit costs are accumulated.

9.2 THE MEASUREMENT OF OUTPUT IN EQUIVALENT COMPLETED UNITS

As indicated above, the output of any given period in respect of which current period costs are incurred consists of:

(a) completed cost units transferred out during the period;
(b) uncompleted cost units remaining as work-in-process at the end of the period.

The objective is to relate the costs incurred in the period with the output of the period, expressed as the work done in that period. In effect, the work done consists of:

(a) completing the cost units recorded as work-in-process at the beginning of the period;

(b) cost units started and completed during the period;
(c) cost units recorded as work-in-process at the end of the period.

The complicating factors that arise relate to:

(a) measuring the work done in the period on completing work-in-process at the beginning of the period;
(b) measuring the work done with respect to the cost units started during the period, but uncompleted at the end of the period and appearing as work-in-process.

The cost units recorded in both the opening and closing work-in-process will comprise cost units in states of completion ranging from 1 per cent to 99 per cent with respect to the particular cost centre involved. To overcome this problem, work-in-process is measured in terms of its equivalent in completed units. This requires uncompleted cost units at the end of the period to be estimated in terms of *equivalent completed units*. Thus, if at the end of the period the number of uncompleted cost units in a cost centre is found to be 1000 units, and it is estimated that, on average, these units are half-completed, the closing work-in-process is recorded as 500 equivalent units (1000 units half-completed).

The output for the period, expressed as work done, consists of:

(a) equivalent units of opening work-in-process to be completed during the period;
(b) the number of units started and completed during the period;
(c) equivalent units of work-in-process at the end of the period.

Having determined the output of the period in terms of *completed equivalent units*, it is possible to establish the product cost of the cost units produced during the period. Example 9.2 illustrates this procedure.

EXAMPLE 9.2:

Let us assume that the undermentioned data relates to the output of process A of Summerdrinks Ltd in the current accounting period:

20 000 units were one-quarter completed at the beginning of the period.
80 000 units were completed during the period.
40 000 units were half-completed at the end of the period.

The equivalent completed units of output for the current accounting period may be calculated as follows:

Completed units	80 000
Add: Half-completed units (40 000 × ½)	20 000
	100 000
Less: Opening inventory of work in progress (20 000 × ¼)	5 000
Equivalent units of output	95 000

9.3 EQUIVALENT UNITS AND ELEMENTS OF COST

In Example 9.2 it was assumed that equivalent units were simply those uncompleted units at the end of the period estimated at their extent of completion in a physical sense. For process costing purposes, however, costs are accumulated in terms of their defined classification. In this regard, it will be recalled that product costs are made up of three elements of costs, namely, direct materials, direct labour and production overhead costs. For this reason, equivalent units are expressed in terms of *equivalent units of cost elements*.

Example 9.3 illustrates the following key features of process costing:

(a) the accumulation of costs in terms of elements of costs;
(b) the calculation of physical output in terms of equivalent units;
(c) the valuation of cost units in terms of elements of costs.

EXAMPLE 9.3:
Walkley Ltd manufactures a single product that requires processing through three processes. For simplicity, it is assumed that there is no opening work-in-process. The following data relates to the operations of process 2 for the month of March 19X0:

		Materials	*Labour*	*Overheads*	*Total*
	£	£	£	£	£
Transferred in costs	60 000				60 000
Costs added	—	38 000	9 400	14 880	62 280
Total production costs incurred					122 280
Transferred in units	20 000				
Work done:					
Completed units transferred out	18 000	18 000	18 000	18 000	
Units in process	2 000	2 000	2 000	2 000	
% completed	100%	50%	40%	30%	

		Materials	Labour	Overheads	Total
	£	£	£	£	£
Equivalent completed units	2 000	1 000	800	600	
Total production in equivalent units	20 000	19 000	18 800	18 600	
	£	£	£	£	£
Cost per unit	3	2	0.50	0.80	6.30

Value of work completed and transferred out:

18 000 completed units at £6.30 = £113 400

Value of work-in-process at end of period:

	Units	Per unit	Value
		£	£
Transfers from process 1	2000	× 3 =	6000
Materials added	1000 (2000 × 50%)	× 2 =	2000
Labour	800 (2000 × 40%)	× 0.50 =	400
Overheads	600 (2000 × 30%)	× 0.80 =	480
			8880

It should be noted that process 2 records transferred-in costs as a cost element that is 100 per cent completed. The added costs incurred by processing further in process 2 are the three normal elements of product costs, namely, direct material, direct labour and production overhead costs.

The corresponding entries in the cost ledger are as follows:

Process 2 account

	Units	Value		Units	Value
		£			£
Transferred-in	20 000	60 000	Transferred-out	18 000	113 400
Materials added		38 000	Balance c/d	2 000	8 880
Labour		9 400			
Overheads		14 880			
	20 000	122 280		20 000	122 280
		£			
Balance b/d	2 000	8 880			

The closing balance of work-in-progress will be the opening balance for the beginning of the next month.

9.4 THE VALUATION OF WORK-IN-PROGRESS

From the foregoing example, it may be noted that the valuation of product costs per unit is made up of *two* costs:

(a) product costs per unit transferred-in during the current period, which represent the production costs of the transferror cost centre;
(b) current production costs of the processing cost centre.

It was assumed in the foregoing example that there was no opening work-in-progress. The presence of an opening balance of work-in-progress means that the valuation of product costs per unit is now composed of *three* costs:

(a) production costs of the *previous* period included in the opening balance of work-in-progress;
(b) product costs per unit transferred-in during the current period, which represent the production costs of the transferor cost centre;
(c) *current* production costs of the processing cost centre.

The production costs of the previous period included in the opening work-in-progress may well be different from the production costs of the current period. The manner in which the units comprised in the opening work-in-progress are treated will affect the unit product costs of those units.

EXAMPLE 9.4:
This example relates to the operations of process 2 for the month of April of Walkley Ltd. The closing stock values of the elements of cost for March became the opening values for April as follows:

Process costs	*Transfers from process 1*	*Materials added*	*Labour*	*Overheads*
	£	£	£	£
Opening stock	6 000	2 000	400	480
Process costs	70 800	38 320	12 800	18 960
Total cost	76 800	40 320	13 200	19 440

Units produced

Process costs	*Transfers from process 1*	*Materials added*	*Labour*	*Overheads*
Fully completed	20 000	20 000	20 000	20 000
Partly completed	4 000			
Percentage complete	100%	60%	50%	40%
Equivalent units of partially completed production	4 000	2 400	2 000	1 600

Unit costs

process costs	£76 800	£40 320	£13 200	£19 440
total equivalent production	£24 000	£22 400	£22 000	£21 600
= cost per unit	£3.20	£1.80	0.60	0.90

Value of closing stock comprises:

	Units	*Per unit*	*Value*
		£	£
Transfers from process 1	4000	× 3.20 =	12 800
Materials added	2400	× 1.80 =	4 320
Labour	2000	× 0.60 =	1 200
Overheads	1600	× 0.90 =	1 440
			£19 760

The process account for April appears as follows:

Process 2

	Units	*Value*		*Units*	*Value*
		£			£
Opening stock	2 000	8 880	Transfers to process 3	20 000	130 000
Transfers from process 1	22 000	70 800	Closing stock	4 000	19 760
Materials added		38 320			
Labour		12 800			
Overheads		18 960			
	24 000	49 760		24 000	149 760

The above method of calculating the unit cost values is the weighted-average cost method (WAC). The characteristic of this method is that the unit costs are identical for valuing transfers to the next process and valuing closing stock. Therefore, the unit cost of £3.20 for transfers from process 1 was used in the valuation of transfers to process 2 and the closing work-in-progress stocks.

An alternative method of valuing the output is on a first-in/first-out (FIFO) basis. This is similar to the method of valuing materials stock that was discussed in Chapter 3. An important difference between FIFO and WAC is that, under FIFO, the opening stock value is kept separate from the current period costs in calculating the average unit costs for the period. The following example is a recalculation of Example 9.3, based on the FIFO method of unit cost valuation.

EXAMPLE 9.5:

	Transfers from process 1	*Materials added*	*Labour*	*Overheads*	*Total*
	£	£	£	£	£
Opening stock	6 000	2 000	400	480	8880
Process costs	70 800	38 320	12 800	18 960	

Units produced

Fully complete	20 000	20 000	20 000	20 000
Partly complete	4 000	2 400	2 000	1 600
	24 000	22 400	22 000	21 600
Less: Opening stock	2 000	1 000	800	600
Equivalent units started and completed in April	22 000	21 400	21 200	21 000

Unit costs

process costs	£70 800	£38 320	£12 800	£18 960	
equivalent units	22 000	21 400	21 200	21 000	
= cost per unit	£3.218	£1.791	£0.604	£0.903	£6.516

The above unit costs are used to value the completion of the opening stock. Consider first materials added. 2000 units were only 50 per cent complete and, therefore, further expenses were incurred in April to bring them to the state of 100 per cent completion. Therefore, within the total of

21 400	equivalent units is
2 400	closing stock, and
19 000	
1 000	equivalent units to complete the opening stock
18 000	

This shows that 18 000 units have been started and completed in April. A similar calculation can be made for the other elements as follows:

	Labour		*Overheads*	
Equivalent units	21 200		21 000	
Less: Closing work-in-process	2 000		1 600	
	19 200		19 400	
Less: Equivalent units to complete	1 200	(2000 – 800)	1 400	(2000 – 600)
Units started and completed	18 000		18 000	

The process account can be prepared for April.

Process 2

	Units	*Value*		*Units*	*Value*
		£			£
Opening stock	2 000	8 880	Transfers to process 3	20 000	129 948
Transfers from process 1	22 000	70 800	Closing stock	4 000	19 812
Materials added		38 320			
Labour		12 800			
Overheads		18 960			
	24 000	149 760		24 000	149 760

The value of completed production transferred to process 3 is valued as follows:

	Units	Per unit	Value
		£	£
Opening stock			8 880
Plus expenses to complete:			
Materials added	1 000	× 1.791	1 791
Labour	1 200	× 0.604	725
Overheads	1 400	× 0.903	1 264
Plus started and completed	18 000	× 6.516	117 288
			129 948

The closing stock is valued as follows:

	Units	Per unit	Value
		£	£
Transfers from process 1	4000	× 3.218 =	12 872
Materials added	2400	× 1.791 =	4 298
Labour	2000	× 0.604 =	1 208
Overheads	1600	× 0.903 =	1 445
			19 823

The difference of £11 (£19 812 and £19 823) is due to rounding the unit costs.

The difference in the method has led to variations in both the transfer value and the closing stock value since the costs brought forward in opening stock varied from the current month costs. (per unit).

9.5 NORMAL AND ABNORMAL PROCESS LOSSES

Processing operations lead to losses of the following nature:

(a) Waste that arises naturally during processing. In the case of materials, normal waste arises during cutting, grinding and machining generally. In the case of liquids, normal waste in the form of evaporation occurs. Industries are concerned with reducing losses arising from waste. Whenever it is economically possible, waste is collected and sold.

(b) Normal losses also arise during processing in the form of reject work that is revealed on inspection. Tolerance levels are set in respect of material quality, machine settings, etc., and quality control procedures are adjusted to accept normal losses.

(c) Abnormal losses can occur, exceptionally, due to faulty materials and parts, bad machine settings, breakdowns, etc. They may result in serious financial losses, when entire batches of production have been affected.

These three categories of losses are treated in process costing as follows:

(a) Normal waste is built into material costs and is not recorded. Recoveries from the sale of scrap are set-off against normal losses, as shown in Example 9.6.
(b) Normal process losses are expensed into work-in-process and are reflected ultimately in the cost of sales.
(c) Abnormal losses are identified and recorded separately. They are not expensed into work-in-process, but are transferred to the profit and loss account after the cause has been investigated and corrected.

EXAMPLE 9.6:
The Chester Chemical Company produces a chemical compound from operations which take place in two departments – mixing and blending.

Data for the mixing department for the month of June when 10 000 gallons of materials were placed into production is given below:

Materials costs	£2500
Labour costs	£1600
Factory overhead	£2400
Units produced	8500 gallons
Normal loss of input	10%
Sales value of losses	5 pence per gallon

The mixing account appears as follows:

Mixing account

	Units	*Value*		*Units*	*Value*
		£			£
			Units transferred to		
Materials	10 000	2 350	blending	8 500	5 950
Labour		1 600	Normal loss	1 000	50
Overheads		2 400	Abnormal loss	500	350
	10 000	6 350		10 000	6 350

The calculation of the units transferred and the abnormal loss is:

(i)	Input cost	£6350
	Less: Scrap sales	£ 50
		£6300
(ii)	Units transferred	= 9000 (8500 + 500)
	Plus: Abnormal loss	
(iii)	Unit cost (i) ÷ (ii)	= 70 pence

The balance of the accounts in the cost ledger would be:

Mixing account

	Units	*Value*		*Units*	*Value*
		£			£
Materials	10 000	2 350	Units transferred to		
Labour		1 600	blending	9 500	6 650
Overheads		2 400	Normal loss	1 000	50
Abnormal gain	500	350			
	10 500	6 700		10 500	6 700

Normal process loss account

	Units	*Value*		*Units*	*Value*
		£			£
Mixing account	1000	50	Scrap sales account	1000	50

Abnormal process gain account

	Units	*Value*		*Units*	*Value*
		£			£
Scrap sales account	500	25	Mixing account	500	350
Profit and loss					
account		325			
		350			350

Scrap sales account

	Units	*Value*		*Units*	*Value*
		£			£
Normal process	1000	50	Abnormal process	500	25
loss account			gain account		
			Cash book		25
		50			50

The steps in the accounting records (assuming that only abnormal process losses occur are:

(a) Open a normal process loss account, debit the account with the units and value from the credit of the process account.
(b) Open an abnormal process loss account, debit the account with the units and value from the credit of the process account.
(c) Credit the normal and the abnormal process loss accounts with the value of scrap sales (5 p/gallon) and debit the relevant amounts in a scrap sales account.
(d) When the cash for the scrap sales is received, debit the cash book and credit the scrap sales account with the value.
(e) At a period end, calculate the balancing figure in the abnormal process account and post this value to the profit and loss account as an expense. Where abnormal gains occur they are treated the reverse of the treatment of process losses shown in Example 9.6.

9.6 JOINT AND BY-PRODUCTS

Process production generally involves the transformation of a basic raw material into the finished product. Frequently, however, the basic raw material input is used for producing several quite different products. Some of these products rank as being of equal importance to the business purpose and are treated as **joint products**. Others are not viewed as being the main business purpose, and are treated as **by-products**. For example, beef raised for slaughter produces two important *joint products*, namely meat for consumption and skins for leather. However, nothing is wasted for industrial and pharmaceutical uses are found for bones, hooves, various organs and offals. These are subsidiary business purposes to the two major purposes, and they are seen as *by-products*. Indeed, the success of modern technology is seen not only in reducing the net waste resulting from process production, but using waste for developing new and important by-products. Ultimately, such by-products are treated as joint products when their economic importance has become as significant as that of the already existing joint products.

Joint and by-products share the following common features:

(a) They have their original source in the same raw material.
(b) They are produced jointly for it is not possible to produce one of the products without the others.
(c) They appear at different stages of processing the raw material, when they are identified and can be separated. This is known as the *split-off point*.

(d) Until the split-off point, their individual processing costs cannot be identified. Further processing costs after the split-off point are easily ascertainable and allocated against the separate products.

For costing purposes, joint products and by-products are distinguished as follows:

9.6.1 Joint products

Production costs up to the split-off point have to be determined by *apportionment*, and an appropriate basis of apportionment has to be found. The following methods of apportioning joint costs illustrate the difficulties involved.

(a) *Market value at the split-off point.* Assume that products A and B are joint products. They are both saleable at the split-off point for £300 and £200 per tonne, respectively. Accordingly, the market value split-off point may be used to apportion the joint costs in the ratio of 3 : 2. The problems with this method of apportionment are as follows:

  (i) it does not reflect the relative benefits received by each product from the joint costs incurred in production;
  (ii) it depends entirely upon relative market values that may fluctuate, affecting product costs accordingly.

(b) *Physical measurement at the split-off point.* Assume that products A and B respectively weigh 40 tonnes and 20 tonnes at the split-off point. On a weight basis, joint costs may be apportioned in the ratio of 2 : 1. The problem with this method of apportionment arises from distortions that are introduced in the measurement of profit when the market value of the product differ substantially.

9.6.2 By-products

As defined above, a by-product is any product of value that is produced incidentally to the main product. They may consist of products of little value as well as those having significant importance. The accounting treatment of by-products varies as follows:

(a) By-products of little value can be treated in the same way as normal waste, and receipts from sales credited against normal losses.
(b) By-products of substantial value must be separately costed. The

main process account is then credited and the by-product account debited with the cost applicable to the by-product.

(c) By-products requiring further processing must be separated from the main product. The by-product account becomes, in effect, a new process account and is charged with all further expenses to bring the product to a saleable condition.

EXAMPLE 9.7:

A factory manufactures three products, A, B and C from a single basic raw material. The three products are 'split-off' from one another at the end of process 2. The following percentages of the three products are consistently obtained:

Product	*Percentage of the quantity of material put into process 2*
A	40%
B	30%
C	20%
Waste of no value	10%
	100%

(a) As a result of steam treatment the output weight at the end of process 1 is normally 5 per cent more than the input weight.

(b) At the end of process 2 product A is in its finished form ready for delivery in bulk to buyers, product C requires packaging at a cost equal to 25 per cent of the selling price and product B has to pass through a further process, No. 3, before completion, the cost of the process being £1 per 100 kg.

The selling prices of the finished products are as follows:

Product A	£3 per 100 kg
Product B	£4 per 100 kg
Product C	20p per 100 kg

Required:

State, giving reasons, what arrangements you would make for the costing of the various products.

Solution:

The net sales value of product C is negligible compared with that of A and B, the relative values for each 100 kg of input into process 2 being:

A	40 kg	at £3 per 100 kg	£1.20
B	30 kg	at £4 per 100 kg	£1.20
C	20 kg	at 20p per 100 kg	£0.04
Waste	10 kg	no value	
	100 kg		

The net return is:

		Selling price	Further costs	Net return
		£	£	£
A	40 kg	1.20		1.20
B	30 kg	1.20	0.30	0.90
C	20 kg	0.04	0.01	0.03
Waste	10 kg	—	—	—

It is evident from the foregoing that products A and B should be treated as joint products and product C should be treated as a by-product, the net sales value thereof going to reduce the total cost at the end of process 2.

The cost at this point should be apportioned to products A and B on some equitable basis. It is assumed that the basis in this case is to charge product A with 4/7ths and B with 3/7ths of the cost at the point of split-off, for both weight of products and net returns for the products are in these proportions. This is calculated as follows:

Process 1

	Weight kg
Input	100
Increase in weight	5
	105

Process 2

Input	105
Less: Waste (10%)	10.5
	94.5
Less: Product C (20%)	21.0
	73.5

Basis for allocating costs to joint products:

Product A (4/7)	42.0
Product B (3/7)	31.5
	73.5

Questions

1. What is process costing?
2. Explain the differences between job order and process costing?
3. State the basic procedures involved in process costing.
4. What is an 'equivalent completed unit'?
5. What valuation problems exist in process costing?
6. Explain the procedure for valuing closing work-in-process using the FIFO method.
7. How does the weighted-average cost method differ from the FIFO method insofar as closing work-in-process is valued?
8. Define the following:

   (a) normal waste;
   (b) normal losses;
   (c) abnormal losses.

9. Explain the accounting procedure for dealing with normal waste.
10. Explain the accounting procedure for dealing with normal losses.
11. What particular problems arise with respect to accounting for abnormal losses?
12. Define and distinguish joint products and by-products.
13. What is the split-off point?
14. Suggest ways in which joint costs should be apportioned.
15. Should joint costs be apportioned to by-products as well as to joint products?
16. How would we treat the sale of waste arising in processing?

Problems

1. (a) In a process costing system state what is meant by:
   (i) normal loss; and
   (ii) abnormal loss,
   and indicate how you would treat these items in the cost accounts.

   (b) A company makes one product which passes through two processes. From the data given below which relates to period 4, you are required to show the transactions which would appear in the two process accounts, finished goods account, abnormal loss account and the abnormal gain account.

Process no. 1
Material: 5000 kg at £0.5 per kg
Labour: £800
Production overhead 200% on labour

Process no. 2
Materials: 4000 kg at £0.8 per kg
Labour: £1753
Production overhead 100% on labour

Normal losses are 20 per cent of input in process 1 and 10 per cent of input in process 2 but without further processing any losses are able to be sold as scrap for £0.3 per kg from process 1 and £0.7 per kg from process 2.

The outputs for period 4 were:

3800 kg from process 1,
7270 kg from process 2.

There was no work in process at the beginning or end of period 4 and no finished goods stock at the beginning of the period. (20 marks)

(*Chartered Institute of Management Accountants*)

2. A manufacturing company makes a product by two processes and the data below relate to the second process for the month of April.

A work-in-progress balance of 1200 units brought forward from March was valued, at cost, as follows:

	£
Direct materials, complete	10 800
Direct wages, 60% complete	6 840
Production overhead, 60% complete	7 200

During April, 4000 units were transferred from the first process to the second process at a cost of £7.50 each, this input being treated as direct material within the second process.

Other costs incurred by the second process were:

	£
Additional direct materials	4 830
Direct wages	32 965
Production overhead	35 538

3200 completed units were transferred to finished goods store. A loss of 520 units, being normal, occurred during the process. The average method of pricing is used.

Work-in-progress at the end of April consisted of 500 completed units awaiting transfer to the finished goods store and a balance of unfinished units which were complete as regards direct material and 50 per cent complete as regards direct wages and production overhead.

Required:

(a) Prepare for the month of April the account for the second process.

(14 marks)

(b) Present a statement for management setting out the:

(i) cost per unit of the finished product, by element of cost and total;

(ii) cost of production transferred to finished goods;

(iii) cost of production of completed units awaiting transfer to finished goods;

(iv) cost of uncompleted units in closing work-in-progress, by element of cost and in total.

(6 marks)

(Total 20 marks)

(*Chartered Institute of Management Accountants*)

3. Shown below is the previous month's operating data for process 3, the final manufacturing operation in the production of standard sized insulation blocks.

Work-in-process:
Opening stock 400 blocks, total cost £1000.
Closing stock 500 blocks.

The degree of completion of both opening and closing stocks of work-in-process was:

Previous process costs	100%
Process 3 materials	80%
Conversion costs	60%

During the month 4500 blocks were transferred from process 2 at a total cost of £9000. Other costs charged to process 3 during the month were:

Materials	£4360
Labour and overhead	£2125

Process inspection occurs when process 3 materials are 60 per cent complete and conversion costs 30 per cent complete and normally no losses are expected at this stage. However during the month 300 blocks were rejected at inspection and sold as scrap for £1 each.

The company operates the FIFO method of charging opening stock to production.

Required:

(a) Prepare the process 3 account and an abnormal loss account recording the data shown above. Include a detailed working paper showing all your calculations.
(17 marks)

(b) Explain the reasons for valuing stocks of work-in-process.
(5 marks)
(Total 22 marks)

(*Chartered Association of Certified Accountants*)

4. Armor plc operates a process which produces an industrial cleansing chemical, and shown below are the costs incurred by the process during month 7 together with other relevant operating data.

Direct materials transferred into process:	
10 000 kg at £0.15 per kg	£1500
Conversion costs	£1330
Output:	
Finished production	8400 kg
By-product	500 kg
Toxic waste	800 kg

The toxic waste is the same chemical as the finished product except that it has been polluted at the final operation. The cost of disposing of the toxic waste is £0.80 per kg. The by-product is transferred to a subsidiary operation where it is packed at a cost of £0.25 per kg. These costs are not included in the direct materials and conversion costs tabulated above.

The selling price of the by-product is £0.75 per kg and the process is credited with the net realizable value of the by-product produced. During month 7, 30 kg of the by-product were sold.

The normal output from the process, per 1000 kg of direct material is:

Finished production	850 kg
By-product	50 kg
Toxic waste	60 kg
Loss as a result of evaporation	40 kg

Required:

(a) Prepare the following accounts recording month 7 transactions for the above process.

process account;
by-product account;
normal toxic waste account;
any relevant abnormal loss or gain accounts.

(15 marks)

(b) Explain the reasons for your treatment of the toxic waste including an explanation of how the total cost of abnormal toxic waste has been calculated.

(7 marks)
(Total 22 marks)

(*Chartered Association of Certified Accountants*)

5. Three joint products are produced by passing chemicals through two consecutive processes. Output from the first process is transferred into the second process, from which the three joint products are produced and immediately sold.

The previous month's operating data for the processes is tabulated below:

	Process 1	*Process 2*
Direct material (25 000 kg at £4 per kg)	£100 000	—
Direct labour	£62 500	£69 000
Overheads	£45 000	£69 000
Normal loss	10% of input	Nil
Scrap value of loss	£2 per kg	—
Output	23 000 kg	Joint product A 9000 kg Joint product B 8000 kg Joint product C 6000 kg

There were no opening or closing stocks in either process and the selling prices of the output from process 2 were:

Joint product A	£24 per kg
Joint product B	£18 per kg
Joint product C	£12 per kg

Required:

(a) Prepare an account for process 1, together with any loss or gain accounts you consider necessary to record the month's activities.

(8 marks)

(b) Calculate the profit attributable to each of the joint products by apportioning the total costs from process 2:
   (i) according to weight of output;
   (ii) by the market value of production.

(6 marks)

(c) Critically examine the purpose of apportioning process costs to joint products.

(8 marks)
(Total 22 marks)

(*Chartered Association of Certified Accountants*)

10 Service and Uniform Costing

This chapter deals with the following topics:

10.1 The nature of service costing.
10.2 Costing service operations.
10.3 The nature of uniform costing.

10.1 THE NATURE OF SERVICE COSTING

Manufacturing companies have many functions that are concerned with the provision of services, for example, maintenance, canteen, computer department and transport. With regard to its costing features, service costing is a special application of process costing, rather than a distinct type of costing system, and does not involve new principles. Its particular features lie in the following areas:

(a) selecting cost units;
(b) establishing cost centres;
(c) selecting an appropriate rate for charging customers.

10.1.1 Cost units

The selection of suitable cost units is not always easy. In most cases, the cost of services is related to several factors. For example, the transport of goods depends on two factors – weight and distance, which result in the need to use a composite cost unit, namely the ton-mile. If costs were calculated solely by reference to distance covered without regard to weight, service costing in the transport industry would produce the same costs whether the weight carried were one ton or one pound. Equally, the same results would obtain if weight were considered as the only cost factor.

Service cost units are intended to provide a basis for costing services on the same basis.

EXAMPLE 10.1:
Excel Transport Ltd is a haulage company. It has a tariff for haulage contracts of £1 per ton-mile. On 2 January, it undertook the following contracts, that were invoiced out on a ton-mile basis as follows:

20 tons carried a distance of 10 miles	= 200 ton-miles
6 tons carried a distance of 10 miles	= 60 ton-miles
10 tons carried a distance of 8 miles	= 80 ton-miles
4 tons carried a distance of 4 miles	= 16 tons-miles
Total	356 ton-miles

10.1.2 Cost centres

Appropriate service cost centres are established for the purpose of cost allocation and apportionment, using the same principles discussed in Part II.

10.1.3 Selecting a charging rate for services

As seen in earlier chapters, the purpose of apportioning service cost centre costs to factory production departments is to ensure the recovery of total factory costs for product costing purposes. The appropriate base for an apportionment rate will depend upon the nature of the services provided. In the case of a factory service cost centre, such as a canteen, the appropriate rate will be the number of meals served.

10.2 COSTING SERVICE OPERATIONS

The principles and methods of service costing may be best understood by reference to the typical examples discussed below:

(a) transport operations;
(b) canteens;
(c) computer services.

10.2.1 Transport operations

Many firms operate their own delivery fleet of lorries and vans for distributing their products. The size of the fleet will vary between firms. In addition to using its own fleet, external transport services also will be utilized.

At any time, management will need to compare their own operating costs with alternative forms of transport to determine the most efficient form of transportation and the size of their own fleet. In addition to operating efficiency, management will be concerned with reliability, which is partly a function of maintenance intended to avoid breakdown.

Cost accounting is concerned with two major routine functions:

devising a system for the control of transport costs; and
establishing procedures for recovering costs from users.

The control of transport costs

The control of transport costs requires procedures for cost collection and analysis and monthly cost reports that provide management with information for decision making.

i – Collection of cost centre data

Costs centres are established in respect of individual vehicles or groups of vehicle of identified categories. Costs are collected, analysed and apportioned on the basis of the following categories:
(*a*) *Operating costs*, which are variable costs and include such items as fuel, wages and oil. During the recent years of high fuel costs, these costs have had a preponderant weight in operating costs, and have replaced labour as the single most important cost. Log sheet records are a major source of data, that record only manning costs for each driver, for example, time started, and finished, journeys undertaken, mileage covered, weight carried, petrol and oil used. A driver's log sheet is illustrated in Exhibit 10.1.

DRIVER'S LOG SHEET

Date: ....
Vehicle no.: ....
Driver:....................
Route no.: ....

Time out: ....
Time in: ....

Trip no.	From	To	Tonnage		Mileage	Time
			Deliver	Collect		
1						
2						
3						
4						
5						

Supplies
Petrol: ....
Other: ....

Delays
Loading: ....
Repairs: ....
Traffic: ....
Accident: ....

Exhibit 10.1 Driver's log sheet.

(*b*) *Maintenance costs*, which include repairs and maintenance, including tyre replacement. Where a firm has its own vehicle maintenance department, it will usually be constituted as a separate cost centre. Costs incurred by the maintenance cost centre will be apportioned to vehicle operating cost centres. This will enable the cost of a particular repair or service to be compared with the cost of a similar job carried out by an outside garage.
(*c*) *Fixed costs*, which will include insurance, road tax and depreciation. For the purpose of calculating the unit operating rate, a proportion of fixed costs should be included in the total costs of vehicle operating cost centres.

ii – The monthly cost statement

The foregoing three cost elements are brought together in a *monthly cost statement*, from which the cost per ton-mile may be calculated. Exhibit 10.2 illustrates a monthly cost statement.

MONTHLY COST STATEMENT

Month ending: .... Mileage: ....
Vehicle no.: .... Tonnage: ....

Operating costs
Drivers
Mate
Fuel
Oil
£

Maintenance costs
Tyres
Repairs
Overheads
£

Fixed costs Annual
Insurance
Tax
Depreciation
Others

Cost per month	£
Total for month	£
Total ton/mile for month	£
Operating cost per ton mile	£

other performance data

Days operated: .... Days idle: ....
Hours operated: ....

Cost per mile	£
Cost per hour	£
Cost per day operated	£

Exhibit 10.2 Monthly cost statement.

The information contained in the monthly cost statement is essential for cost control purposes, allowing comparisons to be made between standard costs and actual costs (see Chapter 15), and costs over different periods and between different types of vehicles. It is also relevant to establishing charging out rates to users, which as discussed in Chapter 5 are usually calculated on a predetermined rather than on an actual basis.

The monthly cost statement illustrated in Exhibit 10.2 indicates the additional information in the form of cost per mile, cost per hour and cost per day that management requires for controlling vehicle operating costs.

10.2.2 Canteens

A feature of a company's canteen services is that they are usually subsidized to some extent. One of the objectives of canteen costing is to control the extent of the subsidy.

Main cost categories are as follows:

(a) food and drink;
(b) wages and salaries;
(c) services – gas and electricity;
(d) consumable stores – cleaning materials, crockery and cutlery;
(e) miscellaneous overheads – rent, rates and depreciation.

The extent of the subsidy is calculated by deducting revenue from canteen sales from total canteen expenses. Exhibit 10.3 illustrates a canteen cost statement, showing how budgeted income and expenses are compared to actual income and expenses.

The cost unit chosen is the meal, and canteen costs are apportioned to user cost centres on the basis of the number of meals consumed.

10.2.3 Computer Services

Investment by firms in computer services has grown at a rapid rate, and many companies now operate a central computer department.

(a) Cost centres

The Chartered Institute of Management Accountants has published recommendations with respect to charging computer services, suggesting that four cost centres be established to which related costs should be assigned (*Management Accounting Guidelines, Charging Computer Services*, CIMA, London, 1982). These are concerned with the following activities:

Exhibit 10.3 Canteen Cost Statement

Canteen Cost Statement
For the year ended 31 Dec. 19X7

	Total costs		*Cost per meal*		*Increase or decrease*
	Actual	*Budget*	*Actual*	*Budget*	
	£	£	£	£	£
Food and drink:					
Meats					
Fruit and veg					
Bread and cakes					
Sundries					
Tea and coffee					
Milk					
Wages and salaries:					
Supervisors					
Cooks					
Counter helpers					
Services:					
Gas					
Electricity					
Consumable stores					
Miscellaneous:					
Depreciation					
Rates, etc.					
Total expenses					
Income from sales					
Subsidy					

(*i*) *Development of systems and programs to be run on the computer*

staff salaries;
travelling expenses of analysts and programmers;
staff training;
cost of data preparation services or equipment used for converting written programs and text data into computer input;
cost of computer time used for compiling and testing programs;
rent and rates;
running cost of premises used;
security costs;
proportion of data processing management and office services.

(*ii*) *Data preparation at a central location*

staff salaries;
staff training;
equipment costs;
rent and rates;
materials – magnetic tapes and discs;
power and air conditioning;
insurance and security;
transport or other communication costs between the data preparation site and the data processing site;
proportion of data processing management and office services.

(*iii*) *Computer operations of the equipment at the central location.*

staff salaries;
staff training;
equipment costs;
operating system costs;
rent and rates;
magnetic tapes and discs;
power and air conditioning;
insurance and security;
communication costs between the computer site and the points to which output is delivered;
proportion of data processing management and office salaries.

(*iv*) *Terminal use*

equipment;
communication line to central computer;
running costs.

Exhibit 10.4 shows the budgeted costs for these four cost centres.

(b) Cost units

The following cost units may be used for charging the cost of computer services to users:

Cost centre	*Cost unit*
Development	Hours worked
Data preparation	Key depression per hour
Computer operation	Central processing unit (CPU) hours
Terminal use	Number of transactions

Exhibit 10.4 Budgeted Computer Services Costs.

Computer services cost budget
for year ending 31 December 19X8

Cost heading	*Development*	*Data preparation*	*Computer operation*	*Terminal use*	*Total cost*
	£	£	£	£	£
Salaries	10 000	4 000	15 000	—	29 000
Travelling	500	—	—	—	500
Training	400	—	400	—	800
Data preparation	200	—	—	—	200
Compiling and testing	12 000	—	—	—	12 000
Terminal use	—	—	—	60 000	60 000
Equipment	—	3 000	50 000	—	53 000
Maintenance	—	500	15 000	—	15 500
Operating	—	—	2 000	—	2 000
Materials	—	1 000	6 000	—	7 000
Power, air conditioning	—	300	8 000	—	8 300
Insurance, security	—	400	2 000	—	2 400
Transport, communications	—	200	1 000	—	1 200
Accommodation	2 000	2 000	10 000	—	14 000
General charges	400	400	2 000	—	2 800
	25 500	11 800	111 400	60 000	208 700

The charge rates for the cost centres is determined by dividing the estimated costs given in Exhibit 10.4 by the planned activity level for each cost centre, as follows:

Cost centre	*Budgeted costs*	*Budgeted level of activity*	*Recovery rate*
	£		
Development	25 500	15 000 hours	£1.7 per hour
Data preparation	11 800	10 million key depressions	£1.18 per thousand key depressions
Computer operations	111 400	9 000 CPU hours	£12.38 per CPU hours
Terminal use	60 000	5 million transactions	£0.12 per transaction

10.3 THE NATURE OF UNIFORM COSTING

In earlier chapters, many alternative methods of cost analysis, cost allotment and cost absorption were described. For many individual firms, the principles and procedures adopted for devising a cost accounting system will reflect the accountant's view of the particular circumstances and conditions of his firm. Given the existence of many alternative methods, different accountants could apply different principles and adopt different procedures for the same costing system, which would result in different cost calculations. If reliable cost comparisons are needed, it is essential to establish uniform costing for all the separate activities whose costs are required to be compared.

Uniform costing is necessary in the following circumstances:

(a) Where a parent company controls several activities. The costs of producing identical products or providing similar services need to be compared.
(b) Where a number of businesses are members of a trade association, one of whose objectives is the fixing of common prices for the whole industry. In this case, it is essential that cost information provided by members should be comparable and consistent.
(c) Where private sector firms submit tenders for government contracts. In the United States, the Cost Accounting Standards Board was established in 1970 with the objective of promulgating cost accounting standards designed to achieve uniformity and consistency with respect to cost accounting principles used in all negotiated defence contracts and subcontracts in excess of $100 000.

10.3.1 The objectives of uniform costing

The aims and objectives of uniform costing are:

(a) To improve the operating efficiency of individual undertakings by providing uniform information of the most efficient methods of manufacture and control.
(b) Where it is used to fix prices, competitive conditions can be improved by the provision of cost information which is based on sound principles.
(c) To provide members of an industry with reliable information as to the best means of preparing cost statements and reports most suitable for the needs of each member.
(d) To eradicate the evil of spurious low-cost producers, thereby promoting greater stability within an industry.

(e) To inspire confidence in the public by showing that prices charged are based on reliable information carefully sifted by the whole industry.
(f) To provide information which the industry can confidently place before government bodies, as being representative of the industry as a whole.
(g) To convince the less knowledgeable members of the industry of the advantages of a good accounting system.

10.3.2 Requirements for uniform costing

The fundamental costing principles which need agreement for the introduction of uniform costing methods are:

(a) The method of cost accounting which is to be used, for instance, job costing, process costing or variations of these systems, standard costing or historical costing;
(b) Details of the items to be included in product costs, for example, whether interest on capital is to be included and on what basis;
(c) The departments and cost centres which are to be used for the purpose of assembling costs;
(d) The classification, coding and issue price methods which are to be applied to materials;
(e) The classification, coding and the basis on which wages are paid;
(f) Basis for classifying, allocating, apportionment and absorption of production overheads;
(g) Basis for applying administrative, distribution and selling expenses to prime costs;
(h) Basis for treating expenses incurred in connection with buying, storing, issuing and handling stores materials;
(i) Depreciation rates to be applied to plant and machinery;
(j) Methods and forms to be used for cost statements and reports.

10.3.3 Inter-firm comparisons

A natural outcome of uniform costing systems are inter-firm comparisons. These depend on the acceptance of standard terms, definitions and methods of cost accounting, which form the foundation stone of any basis for inter-firm comparison.

A scheme for inter-comparison for many industries, which is run along national and, to some extent, international lines is organized by the Centre for Inter-Firm Comparison. In addition, there are many schemes run by trade associations. Participants to such schemes submit their own performance statistics to the organizing body. These are prepared to standard formulae and, together with statistics of other firms, are used to calculate average performances and individual firm performance. Selected ratios are circulated to all participants, but each firm is given a code number to preserve anonymity and confidentiality. This exchange of information provides companies with significant comparisons, against which to judge their own performance and indicate possible areas for improvements in efficiency.

Questions

1. What is service costing?
2. Describe possible areas of application of service costing.
3. Distinguish service costing from other forms of product costing.
4. What problems exist with respect to selecting cost units in service costing?
5. What is a charging rate?
6. Describe the elements of a service cost system used in one of the following:

   (a) transport;
   (b) canteen;
   (c) computer services.

7. Describe the content of the monthly cost statement used for cost reporting.
8. Outline the cost centre structure proposed by the CIMA for computer services.
9. Define uniform costing.
10. State the objectives of uniform costing.
11. List the requirement for uniform costing.
12. Explain the basis on which inter-firm comparisons could be made.

Problems

1. CDE (Transport) Ltd, who have a contract to deliver bricks to customers of Middleton Brickworks Ltd, have now been invited by the latter to tender for a contract to convey clay from nearby quarries to the brickworks.

   The clay is available from two alternative sources: (1) Weston Quarry which is 10 km distance; or (2) Easton Quarry which is 12½ km distant. At Weston, loading time averages 30 minutes, but at Easton there are better loading facilities and the average loading time is 10 minutes. The route to and from Weston is congested and road speed for the double trip averages 15 km per hour, whereas Easton can be reached by motorway and an average speed of 25 km per hour can be maintained. Unloading at the brickworks takes 10 minutes.

Drivers' wages, state insurance, vehicle insurance, licences and depreciation cost £6.00 per man-hour. Fuel, oil, tyres and repairs are related to kilometres run and the cost per kilometre is £0.40.

The garage of CDE (Transport) Ltd adjoins the brickworks and the lorries have a carrying capacity of 10 tonnes.

To the operating costs detailed above, 25 per cent is added for general administration and 20 per cent is added to the total cost for profit.

Required:

Calculate a charge per tonne for conveying clay:

(a) from Weston Quarry to the brickworks;
(b) from Easton Quarry to the brickworks.

(*London Chamber of Commerce and Industry*)

2. (a) Write a brief note to show clearly the distinction between service (or operating) costing and uniform costing.
   (b) As assistant to the accountant of a public passenger transport authority, you have been asked to:
      (i) prepare a statement showing the profitability of routes R1, R2 and R3 including the contribution per vehicle and contribution per mile *after deducting all direct costs*;
      (ii) comment on a proposal that route R3 be discontinued;
      (iii) comment on a proposal to reduce the service on route R3 by half on the assumption that only four vehicles would be used, operating for a total of 100 000 miles per annum and that the estimated revenue from passengers would be reduced by £40 000 per annum. (You may assume that any surplus vehicles could be readily sold for their written down values.)

The latest information available for the last 12 months is as follows:

Routes	*R1*	*R2*	*R3*	*Total*
Number of vehicles used	12	16	8	36
Total mileage on each route (000)	300	400	200	900
	£000	£000	£000	£000
Revenue from passengers	210	296	116	622
Direct costs:				
Variable	150	200	100	450
Fixed (specific to vehicles)	36	48	24	108
Fixed costs:				
Apportioned (garage maintenance and administration)	24	32	16	72

(20 marks)

(*Chartered Institute of Management Accountants*)

Part 4 Planning and Control Techniques

It was explained in Part I that the original and the predominant objective of cost accounting is product costing. The elements of cost analysis required to meet this objective, and the different forms of product costing systems, formed the substance of Parts II and III.

Other and equally urgent cost accounting objectives have appeared in response to the need for information for a more complete range of management decisions. These decisions require cost analysis which have their own specific cost classifications. These were briefly introduced and explained in Chapter 2.

Management decisions requiring their own cost classifications fall into the following categories:

(a) Short-run output planning decisions, in respect of which the relationship between cost–volume–profit is critical to determining the output level that will make the most profitable use of existing production capacity. The cost classification required in this context distinguishes fixed and variable costs. This is discussed in Chapters 11 and 12.

(b) Various one-off decisions for which relevant cost information is needed, for example, the acceptance of a special order, a decision to make or buy a component, etc. The cost classification needed for the various decisions of this category emphasizes 'relevant costs', defined as future and differential costs. These are discussed in Chapter 13.

(c) Decisions relating to the efficient control of operations. These decisions are at two levels. First, the control of expenditure at the enterprise level through an annual budget that defines the total amount allowed to support the operations of the coming period. This budget is broken down into spending limits at each management level. Expenditure determined in advance is known as 'budgeted expenditure' and the costs foreseen in this context are known as 'budgeted costs'. Second, the control of product costs is designed to ensure that production takes place under the most cost efficient conditions. This requires that costs be standardized to acceptable levels of efficient resource use and resource cost. Costs defined in this sense are known as 'standard costs'. These problems are discussed in Chapter 14.

Finally, management decisions have two aspects. First, to impose a direction on future events through planning. Second, to ensure that decisions throughout the firm are carried out according to plan. At the expenditure level, budget report procedures must function to highlight expenditures that vary from budget. At the product cost level, this means that cost reporting procedures must exist that highlight divergences from 'standard costs' and 'actual costs'. Such divergences, known as variances, require to be investigated. This is examined in Chapter 15.

The presentation of information in the form needed for management effectively to control and to evaluate performance today constitutes a major problem area. This is discussed in Chapter 16.

11 Cost–Volume–Profit Analysis

This chapter deals with the following topics:

Cost–volume–profit analysis examines the relationship between activity and costs at different levels of activity with a view to establishing the most profitable level of operations in the short-term. It is a basic tool of analysis for planning studies that precede a management decision regarding the annual operating plan or budget for the coming period, which will be discussed in Chapter 14. This chapter introduces important concepts underlying the management use of cost information essentially in the context of profit planning studies.

11.1 THE NATURE OF COST–VOLUME–PROFIT ANALYSIS

Cost–volume–profit (hereinafter referred to as c–v–p) analysis has its roots in the analysis of cost behaviour that distinguishes costs as between fixed cost and variable costs. These were discussed in Chapter 2 and defined as activity level costs.

It is important to stress that c–v–p analysis is concerned with the behaviour of *aggregate costs* at different activity levels. For this purpose, *fixed costs* are those that remain constant in aggregate *irrespective* of the level of activity, and *variable costs* are those that vary in aggregate *in response to changes* in the level of activity. It assumes that *semi-variable costs* have been split into their *fixed* and *variable* elements.

It is also important to stress that c–v–p analysis is *not concerned* with the impact of changes in activity levels on product costs. As explained in the introduction to this part, c–v–p analysis is based on activity costs, as defined in Chapter 2 and not on product costs.

The impact on profits of changes in aggregate costs at different activity levels leads management to view 'volume' as a key profitability factor. This is because a substantial proportion of a firm's fixed costs may be fixed in the long-term, as in the case, for example, of an industrial company that is heavily capitalized and has substantial depreciation to write off as fixed costs each year.

Since a significant proportion of total costs may be fixed in respect of any particular accounting period, the focus of c–v–p analysis is on the *break-even point*. This is the level of activity where profits are just sufficient to cover costs. It is not unusual to find manufacturing firms with fixed costs constituting over 50 per cent of total costs. It is for this reason that such firms tend to 'push for volume' as a means of 'getting into profit'.

Cost–volume–profit analysis assists in profit planning studies in a variety of ways. The following are examples of classical application of c–v–p analysis:

(a) product mix studies, aimed at determining the most profitable mix of different products, having regard to their product costs and market prices;
(b) sales mix studies, aimed to defining a marketing strategy for the best sales mix under changing market conditions;
(c) pricing strategies for dealing with special orders;
(d) alternative product studies for considering changes in the product lines;
(e) selecting channels of distribution;
(f) changing plant lay-out;
(g) strategies for entering foreign markets.

11.2 SEPARATING SEMI-VARIABLE COSTS INTO FIXED AND VARIABLE COST ELEMENTS

It is a basic requirement for c–v–p analysis that costs should have been separated into fixed costs and variable costs. Semi-variable costs, sometimes referred to as semi-fixed costs or mixed costs, will always be present in the firm's cost structure. Such costs do not vary directly with changes in the level of activity, as is the characteristic feature of variable costs. Examples of semi-variable costs are:

(a) electricity expenses made up of two elements – a standard periodic charge and a charge that relates to the rate of consumption;
(b) salary expenses in respect of foremen and supervisory staff, that will be constant for a given range of production, but beyond which will increase as added staff is needed;

(c) plant repairs and maintenance that will tend to increase sharply beyond a certain degree of intensity of plant usage.

Three techniques have been developed for separating semi-variable costs into their fixed and variable costs elements, as follows:

(a) the high/low method;
(b) the scatter graph method;
(c) the least square method.

11.2.1 The high/low method

This method compares total costs at two activity levels as a means of identifying variable costs, as those costs that change as the activity level changes.

EXAMPLE 11.1:

The following activity levels expressed in machine hours are reported as incurring costs varying under:

Activity	*Costs*
hours	£
7540	3008
7000	2900
6400	2780
5900	2680
5300	2560
4750	2450

By definition, only variable costs vary with changes in the level of activity. They may be calculated by comparing total costs at one activity level (high level) with total costs at another activity level (low level), as follows:

	Difference in activity	*Difference in total costs*
	hours	£
High level	7540	3008
Low level	4750	2450
	2790	558

The variable costs per unit of activity is as follows:

$$\frac{£558}{2790} = \underline{\underline{£0.20 \text{ per machine hour.}}}$$

Since total fixed costs at any level of activity are fixed costs + variable costs at that level, it follows that fixed costs may be calculated by reference to any activity level by extracting total variable costs at that point from total costs. Taking total cost of £3008 at the high level of activity of 7540, the fixed costs present in the cost structure are:

$$\begin{aligned} \text{fixed cost} &= \text{total costs} - \text{variable costs} \\ &= £3008 - (£0.20 \times 7540) \\ &= \underline{\underline{£1500}} \end{aligned}$$

The high/low method assumes that variable costs are linear over the range of output. It requires that the two points of reference selected for the calculations should be sufficiently apart.

11.2.2 The scatter graph method

A graph is drawn on standard graph paper. Costs are shown on the vertical axis, and activity levels are shown on the horizontal axis.

EXAMPLE 11.2:
Assume the same data as given in Example 11.1, as follows:

Activity	*Costs*
hours	£
7540	3008
7000	2900
6400	2780
5900	2680
5300	2560
4750	2450

These various points are plotted on the scatter graph, costs being shown on the *x*-axis and activity level on the *y*-axis, as in Exhibit 11.1.

The variable cost and the fixed cost lines are identified as follows:

(a) Draw a line A ensuring that it passes through the middle of the different scattered point. This line is known as the '*line of best fit*'. This line will represent variable costs.
(b) From the point where the variable cost curve meets the *y*-axis, draw a horizontal line B. This line will represent fixed costs.

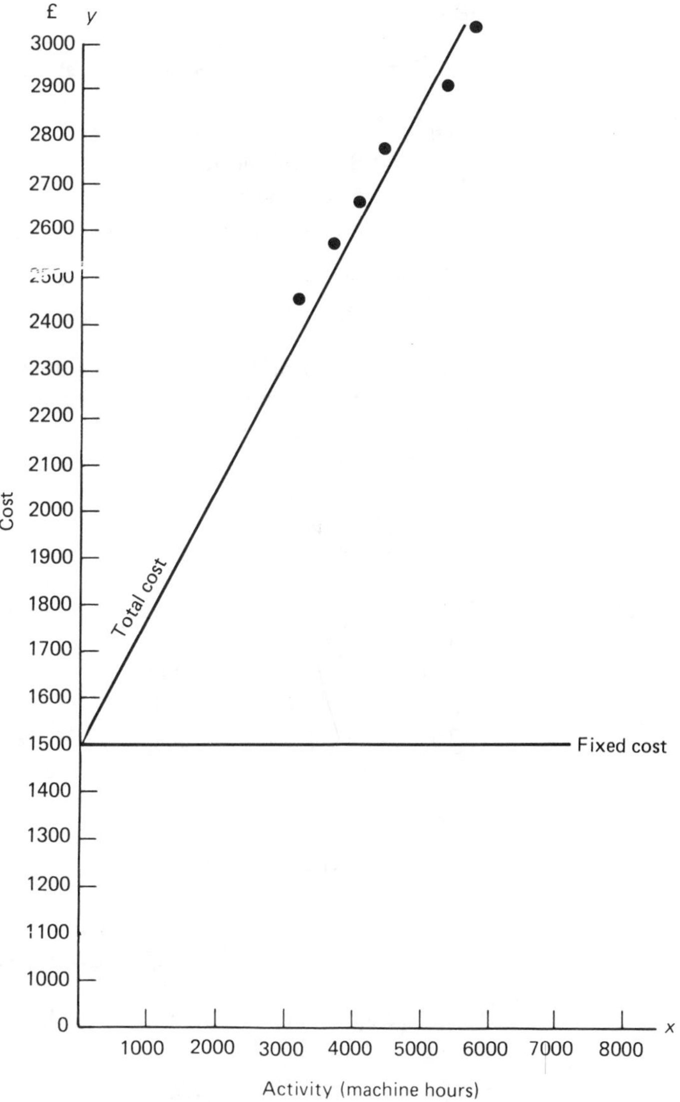

Exhibit 11.1 The scatter graph.

The variable costs and fixed costs at any activity level may be read off directly from the scatter graph.

11.2.3 The least square method

This method involves the use of simple regression analysis for determining the line of best fit. Instead of the visual approximation used in the scatter graph, the line of best fit is calculated mathematically. It is derived from the following formula:

$$y = a + bx$$

where:

y = total costs at a specified activity level, that is, the average costs at a specified point;
a = y intercept, that is, the level of fixed costs;
b = slope of the total cost curve, from which variable costs are determined;
x = the average activity level.

The line of best fit, or regression line, is calculated as shown in Exhibit 11.2.

Exhibit 11.2 Calculation of regression line using the least squares method.

(1) Activity hours	(2) Difference from average	(3) Costs £	(4) Difference from average	(5) (Column 2)^2	(6) Column 2 × Column 4
7 540	+1 392	3 008	+278	1 937 664	386 976
7 000	+ 851	2 900	+170	724 201	144 670
6 400	+ 251	2 780	+ 50	63 001	12 550
5 900	− 248	2 680	− 50	61 504	12 400
5 300	− 848	2 560	− 170	719 104	144 160
4 750	− 1 398	2 450	− 280	1 954 404	391 440
36 890		16 378		5 459 878	1 092 196
6 148 average		2 730 average			

Therefore, $\frac{\text{Column 6}}{\text{Column 5}}$ = variable cost 'b'

$$= \frac{£1\ 092\ 196}{5\ 459\ 878} = £0.20 \text{ per machine hour}$$

At the average hours of 6148, total variable cost is £1230 (6148 × £0.20) and fixed cost is £1500 (£2730 – £1230).

Substituting these figures into the formula:

$$y = a + bx$$
$$£2730 = a + £1230$$
$$a = £2730 - £1230$$
$$a = £1500$$

11.3 PROFIT PLANNING AND COST ANALYSIS

As indicated above, the most widespread use of c–v–p analysis is in the context of budgeting for profitability. In the perspective of the manual operating plan (budget), the firm's cost structure is already defined and it is assumed that costs have been classified as either fixed costs or variable costs.

As its name implies, c–v–p analysis focuses on the relationship of costs and volume of activity and its impact on profits. Price per unit is assumed to remain constant. The question that c–v–p analysis poses is – What will be the effect on a projected change in the volume of activity on the following variables:

(a) total costs;
(b) profit?

EXAMPLE 11.3:
Simplex Ltd manufactures a product that is sold for £10 per unit. Annual fixed costs total £150 000, and variable costs are £4 per unit. The actual annual sale volume is running at 40 000 units. It is proposed to increase sales to 50 000 units for the next year. The impact of the proposed change in the sales volume is shown below:

Unit sales	40 000		50 000	
	Total	*Unit*	*Total*	*Unit*
		£		£
Revenue	400 000	10.0	500 000	10.0
Variable costs	160 000	4.0	200 000	4.0
Contribution margin	240 000	6.0	300 000	6.0
Fixed costs	150 000	3.8	150 000	3.0
Net profit	90 000	2.2	150 000	3.0

It is seen that fixed costs remain at £150 000 *irrespective* of the volume of sales, and that variable costs will increase directly with the increase in the number of units sold in a constant proportion of £4 per unit. The impact of increased volume on profits is seen in the *increased contribution margin* of £60 000, enabling net profit to rise from £90 000 to £150 000.

Alternatively, Example 11.4 also shows the impact of changes in sales in terms of profit per unit sold. In this respect, the *contribution margin per unit* remains constant at £6 per unit, but fixed cost per unit falls from £3.8 to £3 per unit. This is because total fixed costs of £150 000 are spread over 50 000 units instead of 40 000.

11.3.1 The contribution margin

The contribution margin is an important concept in all profit planning studies. It is defined as *the excess of the sales revenue over variable costs.* The contribution margin is first used to cover fixed costs and any surplus remaining is profit. In Example 11.3, the contribution margin is smaller at the lower volume of sales, but increases as sales rise. Given that fixed costs remain constant, the net result is an increase in profits that corresponds to the increase in the contribution margin.

11.3.2 The break-even point

The contribution margin is the excess of revenue over variable costs that is available, first, to cover fixed costs, and then to leave a surplus as profit. It suggests that the first concern in profit analysis is to cover fixed costs, that is, *to break-even*. The break-even point is defined as *the volume of activity at which the contribution margin is equal to total fixed costs*.

Exhibit 11.3 illustrates the relationship between the contribution margin and fixed costs. It depicts fixed costs as a horizontal straight line, indicating that they are constant over the total possible volume of activity. The contribution margin is shown as rising linearly from zero at zero output. The slope of the contribution margin curve will be a function of the size of the contribution margin per unit – the greater the contribution margin per unit, the steeper will be the slope of the contribution margin curve.

Exhibit 11.3 shows the break-even point x as the point of intersection between the fixed costs and the contribution margin curves. The break-even volume of output required to reach the break-even point is shown as OA. The contribution margin required to break-even is shown as OB.

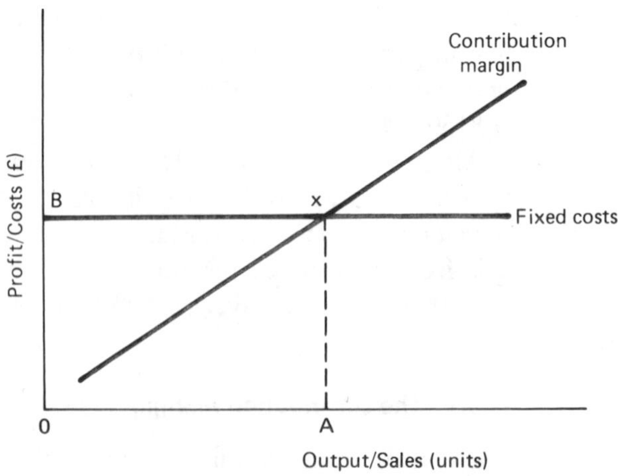

Exhibit 11.3 Revenue, costs, contribution margin and break-even.

11.4 BREAK-EVEN ANALYSIS

Break-even analysis, as applied to annual budgeting, is based on a number of simplifying assumptions as follows:

(a) price per unit remains constant during the budget period irrespective of the level of output;
(b) total costs have been classified into fixed cost and variable costs;
(c) fixed costs remain fixed over the range of possible output during the budget period;
(d) variable costs per unit will remain constant over the range of possible output during the budget period;
(e) volume of output is the only factor affecting total costs during the budget period.

Used for short-term profit analysis, c–v–p analysis assumes also that other factors, such as the technology employed and the efficiency of production, will remain unchanged.

The usefulness of break-even analysis as a management decision model is that it highlights the inter-relationship between the factors affecting profits, allowing management to make certain assumptions about these factors for the purpose of considering the likely effects of changes in these assumptions.

11.4.1 Calculating the break-even point

Three methods are commonly used for calculating the break-even point:

(a) the equation method;
(b) the contribution margin method;
(c) the graph method.

In all three cases, the following two questions are posed:

(a) What is the break-even point of output volume?
(b) What is the break-even point in sales revenue?

(a) The equation method

The equation method is based on the expression of the relationship between sales, variable costs, fixed costs and profits as the following equation:

sales = variable costs + fixed costs + net profit

EXAMPLE 11.4:

Assume the same facts as in Example 11.3, namely that the unit sale price is £10 per unit, that variable costs per unit are £4, and that fixed costs are £150 000 per annum.

(i) Calculation of break-even point in activity level

Let x be the required volume in units, so that

$$\begin{aligned} £10x &= £4x + £150\ 000 + £0 \\ £10x - £4x &= £150\ 000 + £0 \\ x &= \frac{£150\ 000}{6} \\ &= \underline{25\ 000 \text{ units}} \end{aligned}$$

(ii) Calculation of break-even point in sales revenue

Since the net profit at break-even is zero, break-even revenue is:

sales = variable costs + fixed costs

Let x be the required sales revenue, and knowing that variable costs are $\frac{4}{10}$th of x, we can substitute as follows:

$$\begin{aligned} x &= \tfrac{4}{10}x + £150\ 000 \\ x - \tfrac{4}{10}x &= £150\ 000 \\ \tfrac{6}{10}x &= £150\ 000 \\ x &= \underline{£250\ 000} \end{aligned}$$

Note: The break-even sales revenue can also be derived as follows:

$$\begin{aligned} \text{break-even sales} &= \text{break-even volume of sales} \times \text{sales revenue per unit} \\ &= 25\ 000 \text{ units} \times £10 \\ &= \underline{\underline{£250\ 000.}} \end{aligned}$$

(b) The contribution margin method

This method uses the unit contribution margin for calculating the break-even point in output volume and in revenue as follows:

(i) Calculation of break-even point in activity level

Let x be the required volume as follows:

$$\begin{aligned} x &= \frac{\text{fixed costs} + \text{net profit}}{\text{unit contribution margin}} \\ x &= \frac{£150\ 000 + £0}{£(10 - 4)} \\ x &= \frac{£150\ 000}{£6} \\ x &= \underline{\underline{25\ 000 \text{ units}}} \end{aligned}$$

(ii) Calculation of break-even point in sales revenue

The contribution margin ratio is used instead of the unit contribution margin to calculate the break-even sales revenue. The contribution margin ratio is calculated as follows:

$$\text{contribution margin ratio} = \frac{\text{unit contribution margin}}{\text{revenue per unit}}\ \%$$
$$= \frac{£(10 - 4)}{£10}\ \%$$
$$= \underline{60\%}$$

Let x be the required break-even revenue as follows:

$$x = \frac{\text{fixed costs} + \text{net profit}}{\text{contribution margin ratio}}$$
$$x = \frac{£150\ 000 + £0}{60\%}$$
$$x = \underline{\underline{£250\ 000}}$$

(c) The graph method

This method involves using plotting a break-even chart using normal graph paper, as shown in Exhibit 11.4. The vertical axis is used to

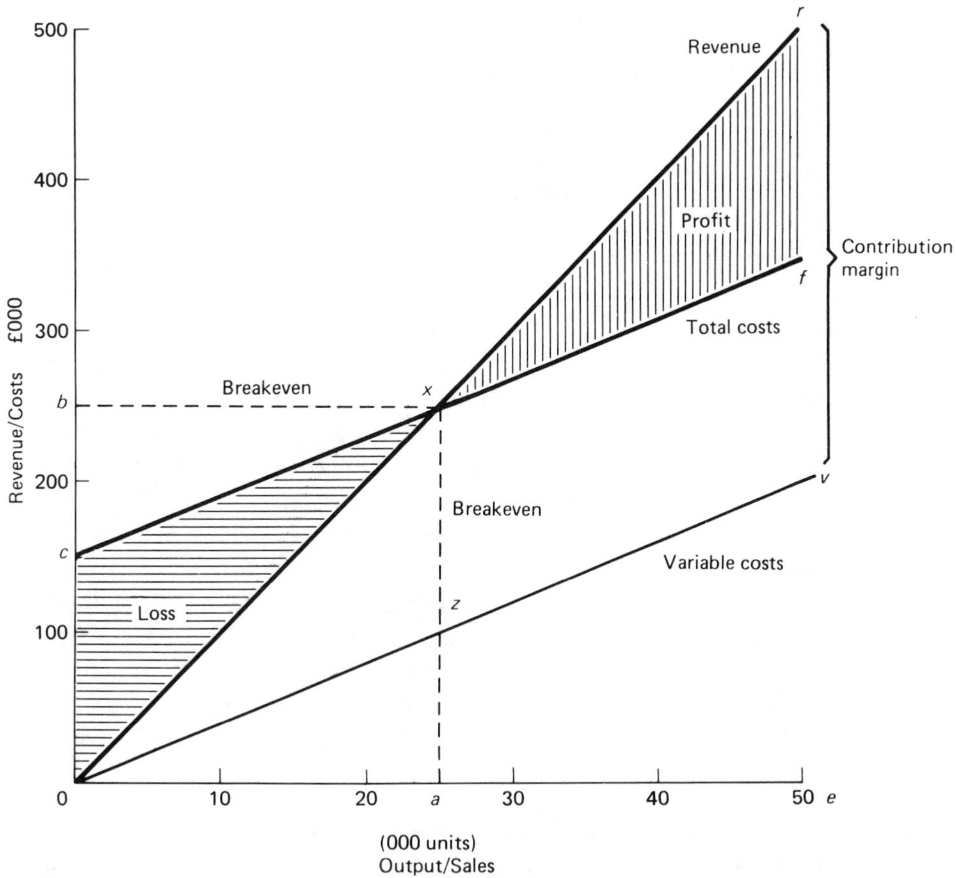

Exhibit 11.4 The break-even chart.

show money values, and the horizontal axis is used to show sales in units. The break-even point is found at the intersection of the total revenue and total cost curves associated with different volumes of activity. The sales volume and the sales revenue required to break even is read directly from the break-even point.

The procedure for preparing the break-even chart for the data given in Example 11.4 is as follows:

(a) Using suitable graph paper, draw a horizontal axis to measure total output range in units (50 000 units) and a vertical axis to represent the revenue to be derived from selling this output at £10 per unit.
(b) Draw the variable cost curve as a straight line to represent the range of variable costs from zero to £200 000 at 50 000 units of output (50 000 × £4).
(c) Draw the fixed cost curve parallel to the variable cost curve but at a value of £150 000 greater at all points of the variable cost curve. Total costs (fixed costs + variable costs) will be represented by the area below the fixed cost curve.

The break-even chart provides the following information:

(a) The break-even point is at *x* which is the intersection of the total revenue curve or and the total cost curve *cf*. The break-even volume of output reads 25 000 units and the break-even revenue reads £250 000.
(b) The contribution margin is the area overlying between the total revenue curve and the variable cost curve.
(c) The area of loss below the break-even point lies in the triangle 0*cx*. It is at maximum at zero output, and at that point is equal to total fixed costs of £150 000. It is progressively reduced as output rises by an amount equal to the contribution margin per unit of output. In effect, the area of loss 0*cx* is reduced *at a rate equal to the contribution margin per unit.* This may be seen by comparing the progressive reduction in the loss-making area 0*cx* with the increasing total contribution margin depicted by the area 0*xz*, so that at *x*, the break-even point the loss area 0*cx* is exactly equal to the contribution margin 0*xz*.
(d) The area of profit lies between *xrf* which is above the break-even point *x*. The rate at which profit increases is a function of the relative slopes of the revenue and variable costs curves.

11.5 APPLICATIONS OF BREAK-EVEN ANALYSIS

Among the several applications made of conventional break-even analysis, the following especially should be noted:

(a) the margin of safety ratio;
(b) the profit–volume chart.

11.5.1 The margin of safety ratio

The margin of safety is the extent to which sales revenues may fall before the break-even point is reached and losses are subsequently incurred. It is expressed as a percentage ratio as follows:

$$\text{margin of safety ratio} = \frac{\text{margin of safety revenue}}{\text{actual sales}}$$

where the margin of safety revenue is the sales revenue required to break-even.

EXAMPLE 11.5:
If sales revenue required to break-even is £250 000, and the actual sales revenue is £500 000 (50 000 units at £10), the margin of safety ratio *at that level of sales* is:

$$\begin{aligned}\text{margin of safety ratio} &= \frac{£250\ 000}{£500\ 000}\\ &= 50\%\end{aligned}$$

The higher is the margin of safety ratio, the stronger are the firm's prospects of remaining profitable.

11.5.2 The profit–volume chart

The profit–volume chart is an adaptation of the break-even chart that focuses more sharply on the relative profit or loss at different levels of activity. The profit–volume chart is less detailed than the break-even chart and only illustrates the following:

(a) fixed costs;
(b) break-even point;
(c) the profit or loss associated with relative levels of activity.

Exhibit 11.5 shows the profit–volume chart in respect of the data given in Example 11.4, namely, fixed costs £150 000, break-even revenues £250 000, and the profit of £150 000 at the assumed level of activity of 50 000 units.

Exhibit 11.5 has the advantage of sharply revealing the loss and profit areas about the break-even point x and the rate of change of profitability relative to activity levels. The curve DA represents, in effect, the contribution margin at the different levels of output that is applied first to cover fixed costs and beyond the break-even point x results in profits.

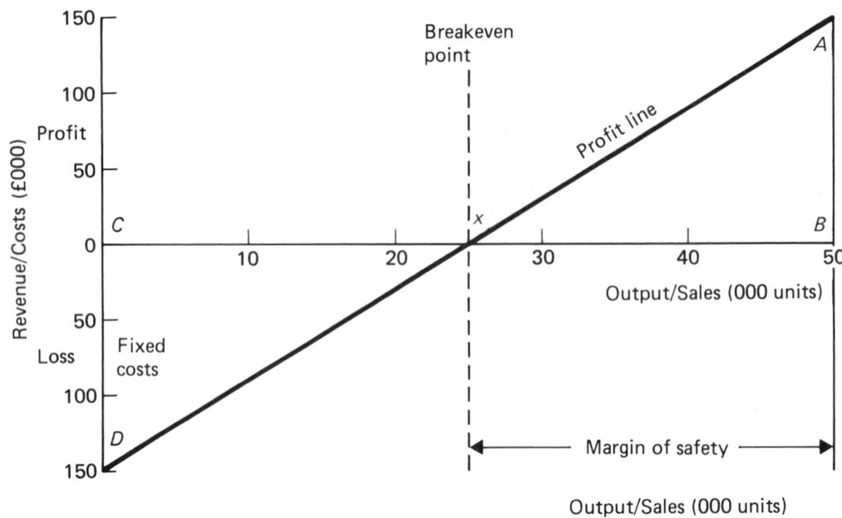

Exhibit 11.5 The profit-volume chart.

The slope of the curve *DA* reflects the contribution margin ratio. The steeper the slope of the curve *DA*, the larger is the contribution margin ratio and the more rapid is the rate of recovery of fixed costs. Consequently, the smaller is the increase in volume required to reach break-even. Correspondingly, the shorter is the margin of safety when volume recedes. Exhibit 11.6 illustrates the impact of different contribution margin ratios on the break-even point and on the margin of safety.

11.6 PROFIT IMPROVEMENT

The approach of profit analysis on which c–v–p analysis is based is concerned with four principal factors that affect profitability, namely, sale price and sales volume, fixed cost and variable costs. Since c–v–p analysis is essentially a management tool for short-term profit planning, factors that affect long-term profitability, such as changes in taste and technology, are excluded from consideration. In the short-term, the possibilities for profit improvement are assumed to be limited to changes in the aforementioned four principal factors that are regarded as susceptible to change in the short-term. Susceptibility to change is evident as regards sale price, sales volume and variable cost, it is less evident with regard to some elements of fixed costs, such as depreciation. Nonetheless, short-term variations in other fixed costs can occur, for example, a decision to lease a building for a short-period or to hire additional managerial staff would increase fixed costs, as they are defined.

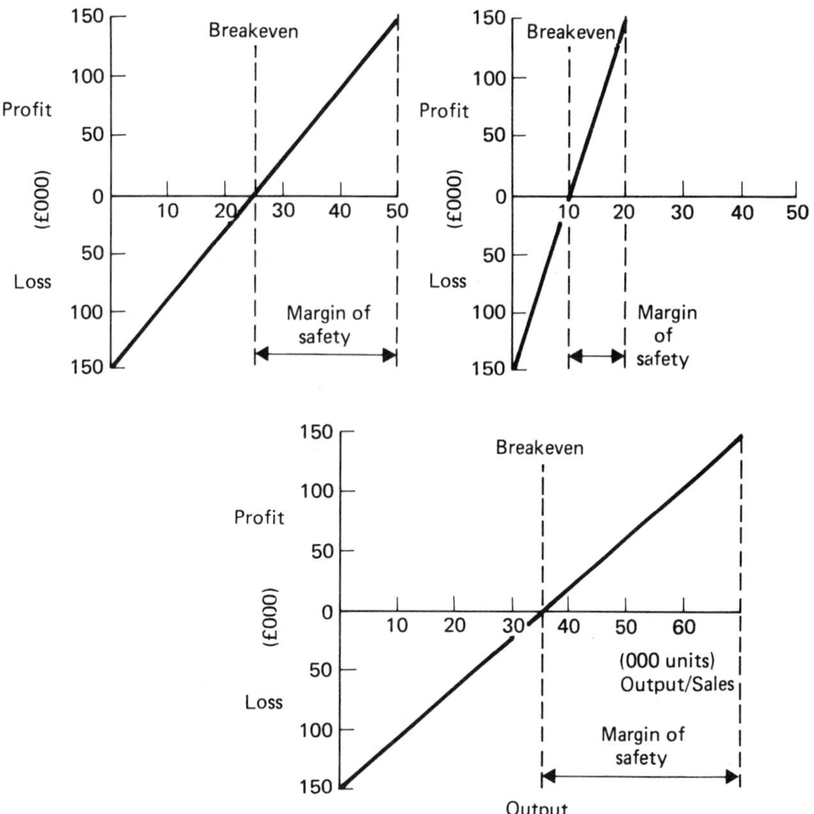

Exhibit 11.6 The impact of changes in the contribution margin ratio.

So far, it has been assumed that the bottom line to profit analysis is the break-even point. Break-even analysis can easily be adapted to allow management to consider the implications of a profit target simply by substituting the profit target for the zero profit that occurs at the break-even point.

Profit improvement does not occur simply as a result of a decision to seek a particular profit target measured as a percentage above costs. On the contrary, profit improvement involves looking at the current level of profitability indicated by the break-even chart, and considering the following:

(a) the feasibility of changing one or several of the key profitability factors, namely, sale price, sales volume, variable costs and fixed costs;
(b) the impact of a proposed change in one or several of these factors on current profitability;
(c) finally, choosing that factor which appears as most suitable for seeking the desired profit improvement.

The possibility for profit improvement is examined in terms of:

(a) changes in sale price;
(b) changes in sales volume;
(c) changes in variable costs;
(d) changes in fixed costs.

11.6.1 Changes in sale price

The impact of changes in selling price on sales revenues is seen in the relative change in demand for the product. If demand is price elastic, a decrease in price will lead to a proportionately larger increase in demand, resulting in higher total revenue. If demand is inelastic, it is better to seek higher total revenue by price increases, since the level of demand will not fall proportionately to the price increase.

EXAMPLE 11.6:
Assume, as in Example 11.4, that the sale price is £10 per unit, variable costs are £4 per unit, fixed costs are £150 000. Current sales volume is 50 000, and the break-even point in volume is 25 000 units. The price elasticity of demand is unity, that is, a change in price will lead to the same proportionate change in demand. Hence, a 10 per cent increase in the sale price will result in a 10 per cent fall in demand.

The change in sale price will have the following consequences:

(a) an increase in profits;
(b) a reduction in the break-even point.

The changes are measured as follows:

(a) Net profit will increase by £15 000, and at the same time, the contribution margin ratio will rise from 60 per cent to 63.6 per cent as shown below:

	Original	*After increase in selling price*	
Sales in units	50 000	45 000	
Sales revenue	£500 000	£495 000	(45 000 at £11)
Variable costs	200 000	180 000	(45 000 at £4)
Contribution margin	300 000	315 000	
Fixed costs	150 000	150 000	
Net profit	150 000	165 000	
Contribution margin ratio	60%	63.6%	

Effect of changes in sale price

(b) The break-even point will fall from 25 000 units to 21 429 units as the result of the increased contribution margin, as follows:

$$\text{Break-even point in volume} = \frac{\text{fixed costs}}{\text{unit contribution margin}} = \frac{\text{£}150\ 000}{\text{£}7} = \underline{\underline{21\ 429 \text{ units}}}$$

It is very important for management to know the nature of the price elasticity of demand for the firm's products, shown in the relative slope in the demand curve. The impact on profits of price changes under differing elasticities of demand is illustrated in Example 11.7.

EXAMPLE 11.7:
Consider the same data as given above, namely, that the sale price is £10 per unit, variable costs are £4 per unit, fixed costs are £150 000. Current sales volume is 50 000, and the break-even point in volume is 25 000 unit.

A price increase of 10 per cent is proposed under the following different conditions of price elasticity of demand:

(a) where demand is elastic, so that a 10% price increase is assumed to lead to a 20 per cent reduction in sales;
(b) where the elasticity is unity (as in Example 11.6), so that a 10 per cent price increase leads to a 10 per cent reduction in sales;
(c) where demand is inelastic, so that a 10 per cent price increase is assumed to lead to only a 5 per cent reduction in sales.

The resulting profits associated with these differing elasticities are as follows:

	Elastic	*Unity*	*Inelastic*
Sales units	40 000	45 000	47 500
Sales revenue (£11)	£440 000	£495 000	£522 500
Variable costs (£4)	160 000	180 000	190 000
Contribution margin	280 000	315 000	332 500
Fixed costs	150 000	150 000	150 000
Net profit	£130 000	£165 000	£182 500

Changes in sale price under different states of demand elasticity

It is noted from these results, that where demand is price elastic, a 10 per cent price increase results in a *fall of £20 000 in profits* (from £150 000 to £130 000). By contrast, where demand in price inelastic, a 10 per cent price increase results in an *increase of £32 500 in profits* (from £150 000 to £182 500).

11.6.2 Changes in sales volume

Assuming that the price elasticity of demand is constant, that fixed costs remain fixed, and that variable costs per unit remain unchanged, the impact of changes in sales volume on the net profit is measured by multiplying the contribution margin per unit by the increase or decrease in the number of units sold.

EXAMPLE 11.8:
In Example 11.4, the contribution margin is £6 per unit (sale price £10 – variable costs per unit £4). At any point starting at or above break-even, an increase in volume will result in an increase in net profits corresponding to the increased total contribution margin.

11.6.3 Changes in variable costs

A change in variable costs will result in the following:

(a) a change in the contribution margin;
(b) a change in the break-even point.

EXAMPLE 11.9:
Assume the same facts as above, namely that the sale price is £10 per unit, variable costs are £4 per unit, fixed costs are £150 000. Current sales volume is 50 000, and the break-even point in volume is 25 000 units. It is decided to improve the attractiveness of the product by improved packaging at an additional cost of 10 per cent, with the consequences shown below:

	Original	*After increase in variable costs*
	£	£
Sales revenue	500 000	500 000
Variable costs	200 000	220 000
Contribution margin	300 000	280 000
Fixed costs	150 000	150 000
Net profit	150 000	130 000
Contribution margin ratio	60%	56%

Effect of changes in variable costs

The new break-even point will be:

$$\frac{\text{fixed costs}}{\text{contribution margin per unit}} = \frac{\pounds 150\ 000}{\pounds 5.6} = \underline{\underline{26\ 786}} \text{ units}$$

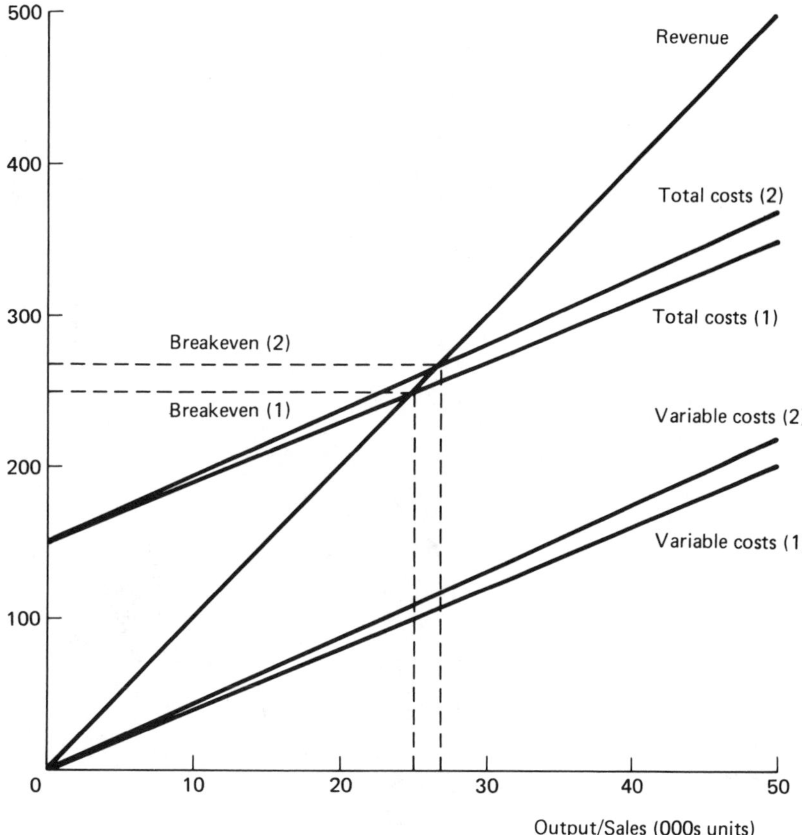

Exhibit 11.7 Changes in variable costs.

Note that profits have fallen by £20 000, that the contribution margin has fallen by 4 per cent, and that the break-even point has risen from 25 000 units to 26 786.

11.6.4 Changes in fixed costs

Changes in fixed costs have more limited effects than changes in variable cost. In particular, changes in fixed costs do affect net profits and the break-even point but it is important to note that they do not affect the contribution margin.

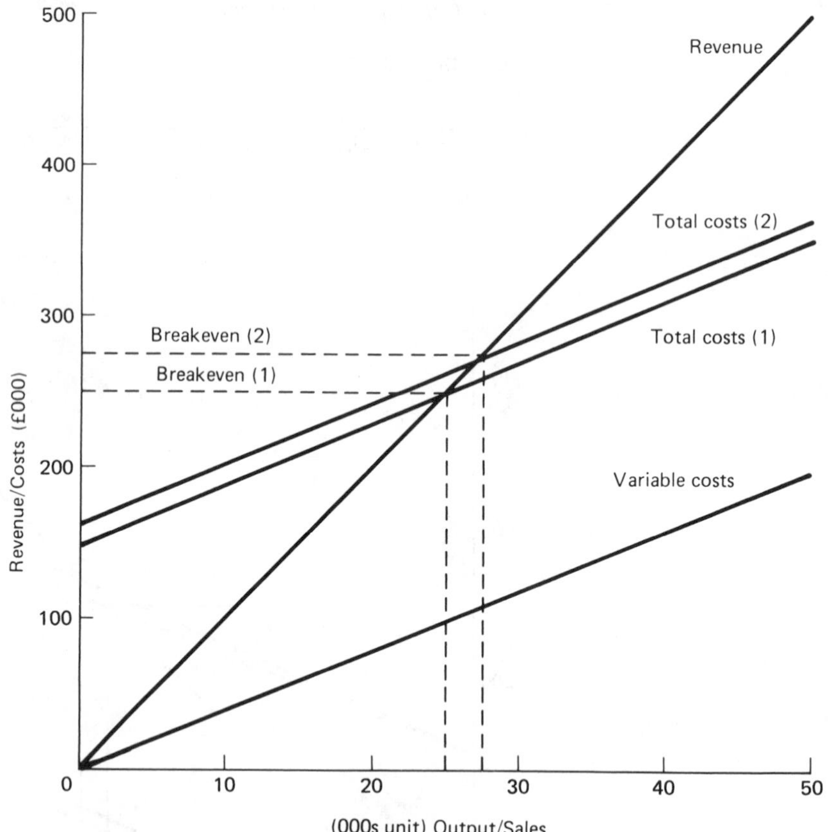

Exhibit 11.8 Changes in fixed costs.

EXAMPLE 11.10

A firm is faced with an increase of £15 000 in head office costs, all other facts remaining constant. Assuming the same data as above, profit falls by £15 000, the contribution margin remains constant, and the break-even point increases to 27 500 units, as under:

	Original	*After increase in fixed costs*
	£	£
Sales revenue	500 000	500 000
Variable costs	200 000	200 000
Contribution margin	300 000	300 000
Fixed costs	150 000	165 000
Net profit	150 000	135 000
Contribution margin ratio	60%	60%

Effects of changes in fixed costs

The new break-even point is:

$$\frac{\text{fixed costs}}{\text{unit contribution margin}} = \frac{£165\ 000}{£6} = \underline{\underline{27\ 500}} \text{ units}$$

These effects are illustrated in Exhibit 11.8.

11.7 COST-VOLUME-PROFIT ANALYSIS AND CONTRIBUTION MARGIN ANALYSIS

Cost–volume–profit analysis pays special importance to the contribution margin as the path to profitability. As discussed above, profit improvement is discussed in terms of altering the four central factors involved in c–v–p analysis, and in particular in seeing how changes in these factors result in an increase in the contribution margin. The discussion of profit improvements leads to the search for optimal profits, defined as the highest profit level that the firm can achieve within existing market constraints. Where the firm sells several products, an alteration of the sales mix may result in improving the overall contribution margin, increasing net profit and reducing the break-even point.

EXAMPLE 11.11:

Assume that Maximix Ltd has data concerning the three products which it markets as follows:

Product	*A*	*B*	*C*	*Total*
	£	£	£	£
Sales revenue	100 000	100 000	50 000	250 000
Variable costs	50 000	30 000	20 000	100 000
Contribution margin	50 000	70 000	30 000	150 000
Fixed costs				150 000
Net profit				Nil
Contribution margin ratio	50%	70%	60%	60%

If the firm could switch its sales so as to sell more of product B, which has a higher contribution margin ratio than the other two, it will succeed in improving its profitability. At the present moment, the firm is just breaking even. Let us assume that it maintains the present total sales of £250 000, but that the sales mix is altered as shown below:

Product	*A*	*B*	*C*	*Total*
	£	£	£	£
Sales revenue	50 000	175 000	25 000	250 000
Variable costs	25 000	52 500	10 000	87 500
Contribution margin	25 000	122 500	15 000	162 500
Fixed costs				150 000
Net profit				12 500
Contribution margin ratio	50%	70%	60%	65%

Hence the new product mix has raised the contribution margin ratio by 5 per cent leading to a profit of £12 500 and a lowering of the break-even point from £250 000 to £230 769 as follows:

$$\frac{\text{fixed costs}}{\text{contribution margin ratio}} = \frac{£150\ 000}{65\%} = \underline{\underline{£230\ 769}}$$

The effect of the change in the product mix may be depicted graphically as in Exhibit 11.9.

The foregoing example indicates that, given the relative market demand for its products and its ability to alter the sales mix, the firm should seek to optimize profit by selecting the sales mix that will lead to the best profit position, and the lowest break-even point.

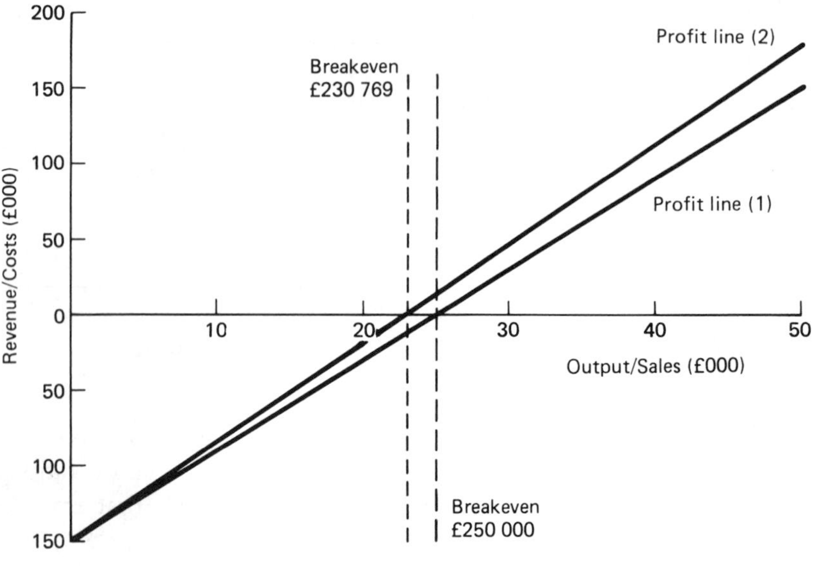

Exhibit 11.9 Change in sales mix.

11.8 LIMITATIONS OF COST–VOLUME–PROFIT ANALYSIS

Cost–volume–profit analysis has been shown in this chapter to have a particular relevance to short-term profit planning. In that context, it focuses upon a number of key factors, such as the behaviour of fixed and variable costs, the break-even point and the importance of the contribution margin for profit improvement. The conclusions to which c–v–p analysis points are correct, for as long as the assumption on which c–v–p analysis is based holds good, for example:

(a) that fixed costs are constant and will not change with the level of output;
(b) that variable costs vary linearly, that is, that the price per unit of cost will remain unchanged in the face of change in market supply;
(c) that revenue will vary linearly, that is, that the price per unit will remain unchanged in the face of changes in market demand;
(d) that the activity level (volume) is the only factor affecting cost and profits;
(e) that stock levels are constant.

All these assumptions can be challenged, as follows:

(a) fixed costs may be constant over a range of output, but may then rise sharply as illustrated in Exhibit 11.10;
(b) variable costs per unit are unlikely to remain constant (linear) and may suffer the effects of changes in the market supply price, as the demand level changes;
(c) equally, revenue is unlikely to remain constant for the price per unit may have to be adjusted in the face of market demand.

The usefulness and relevance of c–v–p analysis is limited, therefore, as follows:

(a) its conclusions are reliable only to the extent that its assumptions hold. In particular, these assumptions are reliable only for a limited range of activity in the short-term;

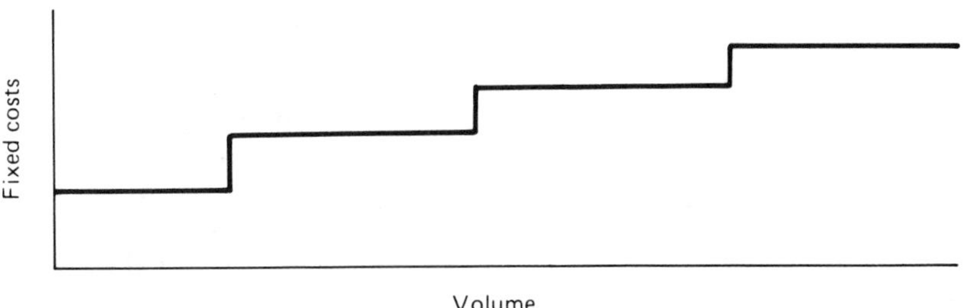

Exhibit 11.10 Likely behaviour of fixed costs over volume.

(b) it is a simplified picture of the key factors that affect short-term profits.

Its strength lies as a framework in which short-term profit planning decisions can be examined, and likely consequences can be discussed.

Questions

1. What is c–v–p analysis?
2. State the cost classification on which c–v–p analysis relies.
3. Define fixed costs for the purposes of c–v–p analysis.
4. Give two examples of semi-variable costs, and explain how they should be classified for c–v–p analysis.
5. Explain the importance of volume in c–v–p analysis.
6. Define the break-even point.
7. Give five examples of applications of c–v–p analysis.
8. Describe briefly the high/low method.
9. What is the 'line of best fit'?
10. State the mathematical formula used in the least squares method of calculating the 'line of best fit'.
11. Define the contribution margin.
12. Explain the importance of the contribution margin in c–v–p analysis.
13. State the equations for calculating the break-even level of activity in volume terms and in revenue terms. Refer your answer to the so-called equation method.
14. State the equations for calculating the break-even level of activity in volume and in value using the contribution margin method.
15. Define and distinguish the following:

    (a) the break-even chart;
    (b) the profit–volume chart.

16. Explain what is meant by the margin of safety ratio, and state how it may be calculated.
17. Explain how the following changes will affect the net profit (assume in each case that all other factors remain constant):

    (a) an increase in the selling price;
    (b) a decrease in fixed costs;
    (c) an increase in variable costs;
    (d) an increase in the level of sales.

18. Explain how the following changes will affect the break-even point (assume in each case that all other factors remains constant):

    (a) a decrease in the selling price;
    (b) a decrease in fixed costs;

(c) a decrease in variable costs;
(d) an increase in the level of sales.

19. What is the sales-mix? Describe a change in the sales-mix that would increase profits. State also how the break-even point might be affected by such a change.
20. List the advantages and limits of c–v–p analysis.

Problems

1. The following standard cost statement relates to a product which sells for £100 per tonne:

	per tonne	
	£	
Direct materials	30.00	
Direct wages	20.00	
Variable overhead	10.00	
	60.00	
Fixed overhead	20.00	(based on output
Total cost	80.00	of 3000 tonnes)

Required:
(a) Calculate the break-even point (a graph is not required).
(b) Calculate the contribution to sales ratio.
(c) Calculate the margin of safety.
(d) Calculate the percentage increase in profit if sales volume is increased by 10 per cent.
(e) Calculate the extra tonnes to be sold in order to maintain the existing profit level if the selling price is reduced by 10 per cent.

(*London Chamber of Commerce and Industry*)

2. Two businesses, AB Ltd and CD Ltd, sell the same type of product in the same type of market.

Their budgeted profit and loss accounts for the year ended 30 June are as follows:

	AB Limited		*CD Limited*	
	£	£	£	£
Sales		150 000		150 000
Less: Variable costs	120 000		100 000	
Fixed costs	15 000	135 000	35 000	135 000
Budgeted net profit		15 000		15 000

Required:

(a) Calculate the break-even point of each business.

(b) State which business is likely to earn greater profits in conditions of:

  (i) heavy demand for the product;

  (ii) low demand for the product.

Give your reasons.

3. An electrical component manufacturer budgets to sell 36 000 units although the factory has the capacity to produce 40 000 units in normal circumstances.

Direct costs per unit are:

Wages	£2.00
Materials	£8.00
Overheads	£4.00
	£14.00

Fixed costs for the period are expected to be £201 600. The selling price is £20 per unit.

Required:

(a) Calculate how many units must be made and sold in order to break-even during the period. Express the information on a break-even chart for presentation to the management. (6 marks)

(b) Ascertain the budgeted profit for the period assuming opening and closing stocks are the same. (4 marks)

(c) State the number of units to be manufactured when the amount of capital invested in this production is £330 000 and the directors require a 15 per cent return on this. (6 marks)

(d) Advise the management on the results calculated in item (c) above stating any reservations you may have. (6 marks)

(Total 22 marks)

(*Association of Accounting Technicians*)

4. Shown below is a typical c–v–p analysis chart:

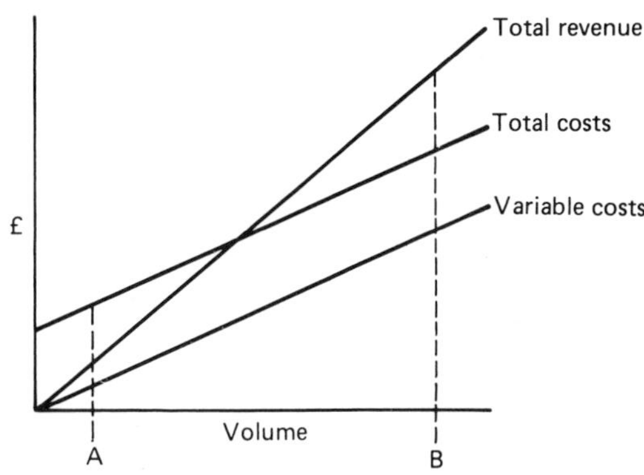

Required:

(a) Explain to a colleague who is not an accountant the reasons for the change in result on the above c–v–p analysis chart from a loss at point A to a profit at point B.

(3 marks)

(b) Identify and critically examine the underlying assumptions of the above type of c–v–p analysis and consider whether such analyses are useful to the management of an organization.

(14 marks)
(Total 17 marks)

(*Chartered Association of Certified Accountants*)

5. The following data relate to a company:

Sales	*Delivery costs*
£000	£000
80	16
85	11
115	21
160	16
205	23
280	18
290	27
330	32
390	30
450	37
470	25
550	35

Required:

(a) (i) Plot these costs on a graph;
(ii) draw on the graph the 'line of best fit';
(iii) state the approximate level of fixed costs.

(15 marks)

(b) State and explain a formula which may be used for predicting future delivery costs for any level of sales. (*Note*: figures are not required.)

(5 marks)
(Total 20 marks)

(*Chartered Institute of Management Accountants*)

6. Shown below are the previous 2 years' summarized trading results of Soafit Ltd, a company manufacturing a single product.

		19X0		*19X1*
	£000	£000	£000	£000
Sales		6000		7920
Cost of sales:				
Direct materials	2000		3000	
Direct labour	1000		1150	
Overheads	2000	5000	2420	6570
Profit		£1000		£1350

Throughout 19X1 the selling price of the product was £6 per unit and variable overheads, which vary with the number of units produced, amounted to £0.50 per unit.

At the beginning of 19X2 the selling price increased by 10 per cent, the purchase price of direct materials by 20 per cent, and direct wage rates by 15 per cent. During 19X2 expenditure on overheads also increased, in the case of fixed overheads this amounted to £200 000.

The number of direct workers employed in the manufacturing process is constant, they remain unaffected by any change in the volume of output.

Stock levels remained unchanged throughout the above 2-year period.

Required:

(a) Present a statement to management analysing the reasons for the increase in profit in 19X2. All your workings and any assumptions must be shown.

(17 marks)

(b) Calculate the sales volume, in units, necessary to achieve a profit of £1 500 000 in 19X3 if, at the beginning of the year the selling price had been reduced by £0.50 per unit, and the cost structure remains unchanged from 19X2.

(5 marks)

(Total 22 marks)

(*Association of Certified Accountants*)

12 Marginal Costing

This chapter deals with the following topics:

12.1 The nature of marginal costing.
12.2 The significance of marginal costing for profit planning.
12.3 Absorption and marginal costing compared.
12.4 Marginal costing and variable non-production expenses.
12.5 Advantages and disadvantages of marginal costing.

12.1 THE NATURE OF MARGINAL COSTING

Cost bookkeeping methods discussed in Part II record product costs on the basis of absorption costing. It will be recalled that absorption costing is a method of accumulating production costs that requires costs to be identified either as direct or indirect costs. For product costing purposes, direct costs are recorded directly as product costs: indirect costs, defined as costs that cannot be traced directly to one particular product, have to be allocated or apportioned to the various products. In this way, absorption costing results in measuring product cost on a 'full-cost' basis. Accountants have traditionally adopted costing systems that record product costs on a 'full-cost' basis in order to meet the regulations that govern external financial reports.

Marginal costing is a radically different approach to cost accumulation. Its objective is to identify 'relevant' product costs. In this sense, it adopts the definition of relevant costs explained in Chapter 2 and discussed in greater depth in Chapter 11. Relevant product costs are those that would be affected by a decision to vary the output level. Since fixed costs are constant irrespective of the output level, the costs that change are the variable costs. Variable costs are 'differential costs' – costs that result from a decision to increase or decrease the output level. The terms 'variable costing' and 'marginal costing' are used synonymously to refer to product costing methods that exclude fixed costs from product costs.

12.2 THE SIGNIFICANCE OF MARGINAL COSTING FOR PROFIT PLANNING

As noted in Chapter 11, the analysis of cost behaviour at different activity levels is crucial to understanding the nature of short-term profitability. It was also noted that the distinction between fixed and variable costs has a usefulness that extends to the possibility of improving profits by changing such key profitability factors as the sales price, the sales volume or the cost structure itself. In the latter regard, it was seen that changes that affected variable costs had a direct impact on profits through a corresponding change in the contribution margin. By contrast, changes in fixed costs were seen as having no effect on the contribution margin.

The relationship between variable costs, the contribution margin and profits is crucial for decision making. This has led some to argue that costing systems should be based on marginal rather than absorption costing principles for cost accumulation and for product costing purposes. According to advocates of marginal costing, cost book-keeping should accumulate cost data in a manner that would be more relevant to decision making. They assert that accumulating product costs on the basis of variable costs only would make relevant product cost information immediately available. In particular, it would allow management to adopt more aggressive pricing policies. Since fixed production expenses are not affected by a decision to vary the output level, such expenses should not influence short-term pricing decisions. For financial reporting purposes, marginal costing implies that balance sheet stock valuations and cost of sales on profit and loss accounts be based on variable costs. Unlike conventional accounting practice that is based on absorption costing, the contribution margin and fixed production costs would be shown separately on profit and loss accounts.

12.3 ABSORPTION AND MARGINAL COSTING COMPARED

Product cost data, accumulated under absorption and marginal costing principles, differs as a result of the exclusion of fixed production expenses from product costs. Cost of sales and stock valuations under absorption costing includes allocated fixed production expenses: under marginal costing, cost of sales and stock valuations include only direct material, direct labour and variable indirect costs. Under marginal costing, fixed production expenses appear as period costs. Therefore, they are charged against the profit of the period in which production occurs. They are not carried forward in stock valuations to the period when sales are realized.

The differences in cost of sales and stock variations shown under the two alternative costing methods affect net profit in the following circumstances:

(a) when the output level is greater than the volume of sales;
(b) when the volume of sales is greater than the output level.

12.3.1 Profit results with constant stock levels

It is only in the exceptional case when opening and closing stocks remain the same that the net profit under absorption and marginal costing are the same. However, even in this case, the formats of the profit and loss accounts are different in that marginal costing identifies the contribution margin, whereas absorption costing shows the gross margin. Example 12.1 illustrates this situation.

EXAMPLE 12.1

Fastrack plc is a manufacturing company that uses latest management techniques. The board of directors is considering adopting marginal costing for product costing purposes, and wishes to compare the effects of this method of cost accumulation and product costing on profit results over the last 4 years. The company is able to sell all its output and maintain a constant stock level as a safety buffer between production and sales. The following data is given:

Total sales and production over 4 years (500 units per year)	2000 units
Direct material costs per unit	£1
Direct labour cots per unit	£1
Variable proportion overhead costs per unit	£0.5
Fixed proportion overhead costs	£1000 p.a.
Sales price per unit	£6

The volume of production, sales and the level of stocks in units is as follows:

Year	*1*	*2*	*3*	*4*	*Total*
Opening stock (units)	40	40	40	40	40
Production (units)	500	500	500	500	2000
Sales (units)	500	500	500	500	2000
Closing stock (units)	40	40	40	40	40

The results under the two forms of costing would appear as follows:

Year	*1*	*2*	*3*	*4*	*Total*
Marginal costing	£	£	£	£	£
Sales revenue	3000	3000	3000	3000	12 000
Costs of goods produced	1250	1250	1250	1250	5 000
Add: Opening stock	100	100	100	100	100
Available for sale	1350	1350	1350	1350	5 100
Less: Closing stock	100	100	100	100	100
Cost of goods sold	1250	1250	1250	1250	5 000
Contribution margin	1750	1750	1750	1750	7 000
Fixed overheads	1000	1000	1000	1000	4 000
Net profit	750	750	750	750	3 000
Absorption costing					
Sales revenue	3000	3000	3000	3000	12 000
Cost of goods produced	2250	2250	2250	2250	9 000
Add: Opening stock	180	180	180	180	180
Available for sale	2430	2430	2430	2430	9 180
Less: Closing stock	180	180	180	180	180
Cost of goods sold	2250	2250	2250	2250	9 000
Net profit	750	750	750	750	3 000

Under the conditions assumed in Example 12.1, the net profit figure remains the same under both methods of product costing.

12.3.2 Profit results under changing stock levels

The reality of industrial production is that stock levels do not remain constant. For example, process production that involves producing in anticipation of market demand results in a production cycle in which stock level fluctuations absorb variations in market demand.

Process production can be severely affected by material shortages that affect production, and changes in indirect taxation and credit squeezes that affect demand levels. Moreover, efficiency of operations and cost economies generally require that fluctuations in output be avoided. As a result, fluctuations in stock levels are commonplace. The effects of fluctuations in stock levels take two forms:

(a) sales fluctuate but production remains constant;
(b) sales are constant but production fluctuates.

The resulting net profit results under these conditions are considered below.

(a) Sales fluctuate, but production remains constant

As soon as sales fluctuate, the use of alternative methods of stock valuations results in differences in net profit figures.

EXAMPLE 12.2:

Fastrack plc keeps production levels constant in the face of fluctuations in market demand. The following figures cover a 4-year period during which stock levels varied, as a result of sales fluctuating and production remaining constant.

Year	*1*	*2*	*3*	*4*	*Total*
Opening stock (units)	40	140	340	240	40
Production (units)	500	500	500	500	2000
Sales (units)	400	300	600	700	2000
Closing stock (units)	140	340	240	40	40

The results under the two methods of costing would appear as follows:

Year	*1*	*2*	*3*	*4*	*Total*
Marginal costing	£	£	£	£	£
Sales revenue	2400	1800	3600	4200	12 000
Cost of goods produced	1250	1250	1250	1250	5 000
Add: Opening stock	100	350	850	600	100
Available for sale	1350	1600	2100	1850	5 100
Less: Closing stock	350	850	600	100	100
Cost of goods sold	1000	750	1500	1750	5 000
Contribution margin	1400	1050	2100	2450	7 000
Fixed overheads	1000	1000	1000	1000	4 000
Net profit	400	50	1100	1450	3 000
Absorption costing					
Sales revenue	2400	1800	3600	4200	12 000
Costs of goods produced	2250	2250	2250	2250	9 000
Add: Opening stock	180	630	1530	1080	180
Available for sale	2430	2880	3780	3330	9 180
Less: Closing stock	630	1530	1080	180	180
Cost of goods sold	1800	1350	2700	3150	9 000
Net profit	600	450	900	1050	3 000

These differences may be illustrated graphically (Exhibit 12.1), and it may be seen that profit profile fluctuates more widely when fixed

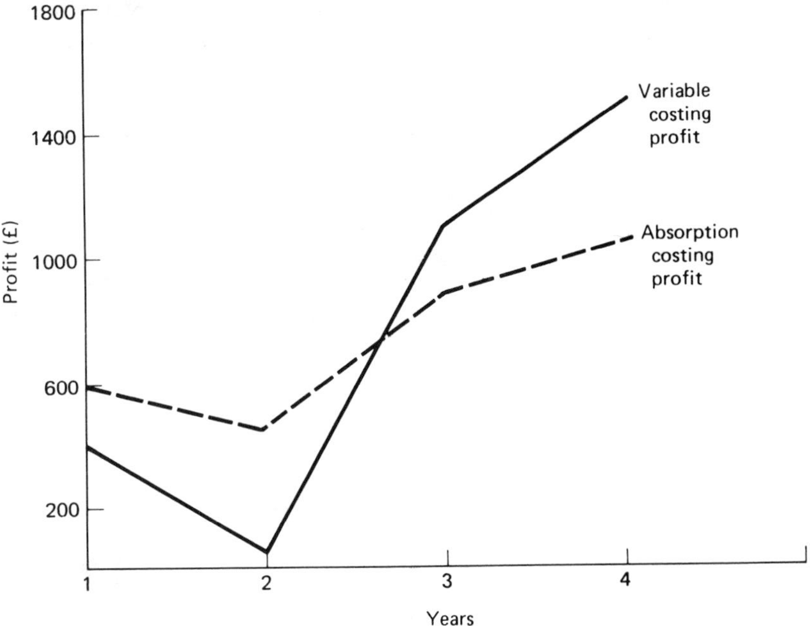

Exhibit 12.1

costs are excluded, as they are under marginal costing, than when they are included as under absorption costing.

The differences in the net profit figures result from fluctuations between sales and production. For example, in year 1, sales fell below production by 100 units. Under absorption costing, fixed costs totalling £200 (100 units at £2) are absorbed into closing stock and transferred to the next period. Under marginal costing, these costs are treated as period costs and set off against the profits of year 1. Therefore, the net profit under marginal costing is £200 less.

(b) Sales are constant but production fluctuates

As explained in Chapter 5, the absorption of fixed overhead costs into product costs requires an overhead recovery rate based on a normal production level. Hence, production fluctuations will lead to over- or under-absorption of fixed overhead costs when the output level changes. This added complication is considered below.

EXAMPLE 12.3:

Fastrack plc experiences a steady demand for its products, but is unable to maintain a regular output. For the purpose of considering the impact of production fluctuations in the face of stable market demand, let the following be assumed:

(a) the normal production level is 500 units per year;
(b) the fixed overhead recovery rate is £2 per unit.

Data relating to production and sales is given below.

Year	*1*	*2*	*3*	*4*	*Total*
Opening stock (units)	40	140	340	240	40
Production (units)	600	700	400	300	2000
Sales (units)	500	500	500	500	2000
Closing stock (units)	140	340	240	40	40

The results under the two methods would be calculated as follows:

Year	*1*	*2*	*3*	*4*	*Total*
Marginal costing	£	£	£	£	£
Sales revenue	3000	3000	3000	3000	12 000
Cost of goods produced	1500	1750	1000	750	5 000
Add: Opening stock	100	350	850	600	100
Available for sales	1600	2100	1850	1350	5 100
Less: Closing stock	350	850	600	100	100
Cost of goods sold	1250	1250	1250	1250	5 000
Contribution margin	1750	1750	1750	1750	7 000
Fixed overheads	1000	1000	1000	1000	4 000
Net profit	750	750	750	750	3 000
Absorption costing					
Sales revenue	3000	3000	3000	3000	12 000
Costs of goods produced	2700	3150	1800	1350	9 000
Add: Opening stock	180	630	1530	1080	180
Available for sale	2880	3780	3330	2430	9 180
Less: Closing stock	630	1530	1080	180	180
Cost of goods sold	2250	2250	2250	2250	9 000
Over or (under) absorbed overhead	200	400	(200)	(400)	—
Total cost of goods sold	2050	1850	2450	2650	9 000
Net profit	950	1150	550	350	3 000

The opening and closing stock per unit remains constant at £4.50 (variable costs per unit £2.50 + fixed overhead recovery rate of £2 per unit). In year 1 and 2, actual output exceeds the normal production level of 500 by 100 and 200 units, respectively, whereas in years 3 and 4 actual output falls short of normal production by 100 and 200 units, respectively. Under absorption costing, these output variations lead to fixed overheads being over- absorbed to the extent of £200 and £400 in years 1 and 2 and under-absorbed to the extent of £200 and £400 in years 3 and 4. Corresponding fluctuations occur in the net profit figures.

By contrast, the net profit calculated using marginal costing remains unaffected by fluctuations in production levels and stays constant at £750 throughout the 4-year period.

(c) Summary of impact on profit of marginal and absorption costing

The impact on net profits of these two alternative methods of product costing may be summarized as follows:

(i) Where sales and production levels are constant through time, the net profit is the same under both methods.
(ii) Where production remains constant through time, but sales fluctuate, the resulting fluctuations in net profits will be greater with marginal costing than absorption costing, assuming that prices and costs remain unchanged.
(iii) Where sales are constant but production fluctuates, net profit will remain constant with marginal costing but will fluctuate under absorption costing.
(iv) Where production exceeds sales, net profit is higher under absorption costing than under marginal costing. This is because fixed production overhead costs relating to the unsold output are carried forward in closing stocks to the next period.
(v) Where sales exceed production, net profit is higher under marginal costing than under absorption costing. This is because fixed overhead costs that would otherwise have been included in the valuation of opening stocks have already been charged against the profit of the previous accounting period.

12.4 MARGINAL COSTING AND VARIABLE NON-PRODUCTION EXPENSES

Product costing under both absorption and marginal costing include only factory costs. Non-factory expenses, such as selling and administrative expenses are excluded from the definition of cost of goods sold for profit reporting purposes.

Profit and loss accounts based on marginal costing emphasize the contribution margin. In this respect, they are different from those prepared on the basis of absorption costs. The contribution margin is calculated by deducting both production and non-production variable overhead expenses from sales revenue. Fixed factory overheads and fixed selling and administrative expenses are set-off against the contribution margin in the process of calculating the net profit.

EXAMPLE 12.4:
Ponds Ltd used marginal costing for product costing and financial reporting purposes. There were no opening or closing stocks. The following data relates to the year ended 31 December 19X2:

	£000	£000
Sales revenue		100
Production costs:		
Fixed	15	
Variable	50	65
Selling and administrative expenses:		
Fixed	5	
Variable	10	15

The profit and loss account drawn up on the basis of marginal costing is as follows:

	£000	£000
Sales revenue		100
Variable costs of good solds		50
Manufacturing contribution		50
Selling and administrative expenses		10
Contribution margin		40
Fixed costs:		
Production costs	15	
Selling and administrative expenses	5	20
Net profit for the year		20

12.5 ADVANTAGES AND DISADVANTAGES OF MARGINAL COSTING

There is considerable controversy over the use of marginal costing. Its advantages and disadvantages are as follows:

12.5.1 ADVANTAGES OF MARGINAL COSTING

(a) It provides management with information that is appropriate and relevant to decision making.
(b) It eliminates the confusion and misunderstanding that may occur by the presence of over- or under-absorbed overhead costs in the profit and loss account.
(c) Profit varies in accordance with sales, and is not distorted by changes in stock levels.
(d) Profit–volume analysis using profit graphs and break-even analysis is facilitated.
(e) The profit performance of different product lines can be more easily evaluated. The need to use allocation bases for both allocating and apportioning overhead costs to product lines under absorption costing can in itself lead to distortions. Moreover, absorption costing obscures the impact on profit of changes in stock levels.
(f) More efficient pricing decisions can be made, since their impact on the contribution margin can be measured.
(g) Marginal costing is particularly helpful when making decisions in the face of limiting factors, where there is a need to know the contribution margin per key factor. This is important for budgeting and production planning.
(h) Marginal costing can be adapted to all costing systems.

12.5.2 Disadvantages of marginal costing

(a) It does not conform to the matching principle which constitutes a basic financial accounting principle. It cannot be used for external reporting purposes. SSAP 2 Disclosure of Accounting Policies requires that 'revenues and costs are matched with one another so far as their relationship can be established or justifiably assumed'. In this regard, SSAP 9 Stocks and Work-in-Progress restated the traditional accounting view with regard to stock valuations, namely that the aim should be to match revenues and costs 'in the year in which revenue arises rather than the year in which cost is incurred', cost being defined as including 'all related overheads, even though some of these may accrue on a time basis'.
(b) As was noted in Chapter 11, difficulty may be experienced in trying to segregate the fixed and variable elements of overhead costs for the purpose of marginal costing.
(c) The misuse of marginal costing approaches to pricing decisions may result in setting selling prices that do not allow the full recovery of overhead costs.

Questions

1. Explain the nature of marginal costing.
2. What cost classification is used for marginal costing? How does it compare with the classification used for absorption costing?
3. Why is marginal costing claimed to be more 'relevant' for product costing purposes?
4. Explain the significance of marginal costing for profit planning.
5. Compare and contrast marginal and absorption costing under the following conditions:

   (a) when production and sales are running at the same levels;
   (b) when opening stocks and closing stocks are the same.

6. Explain the impact of marginal costing on net profit results when sales exceed production during the year.
7. Would the net profit for the year be greater under absorption costing than under marginal costing if:

   (a) overhead costs were under-absorbed?
   (b) production was greater than sales?
   (c) stock levels were lower at the end of the year than at the beginning?

8. Explain how non-production overheads are accounted for under marginal costing.
9. List five advantages associated with marginal costing.
10. Would you agree that product cost information based on marginal cost leads to better pricing decisions?
11. What is the standard accounting external reporting practice with respect to marginal costing?

Problems

1. (a) A company manufactures and sells two products, A and B. The following information is available.

		A	*B*
Sales price (each)		£15	£20
Labour (unit)		£2 (1 hour)	£4 (2 hours)
Variable production overheads		£3	£6
Material		£4	£5
Production quantities:	November	700	800
	December	350	500
Quantities sold:	November	600	700
	December	400	400
Fixed overheads:	November	£4600	
	December	£2700	

Required:
Prepare statements for November and December showing profit and closing stock valuations using the following methods:
(i) marginal costing; (7 marks)
(ii) absorption costing. (7 marks)

(b) Discuss absorption costing as a method of costing factory output.

(8 marks)
(Total 22 marks)

(*Association of Accounting Technicians*)

2. (a) XY Ltd is operating at a normal level of activity of 80 per cent which represents an output of 5600 units. The statement shown below gives basic details of cost and sales at three operating levels of activity. In view of the depressed market in which the company may have to operate in the near future, the production director believes that it may be necessary to operate at 60 per cent level of activity.

As cost accountant of XY Ltd, you are required to prepare a forecast statement to show the marginal costs and contribution at the proposed level of activity of 60 per cent.

	Level of activity		
	70%	*80%*	*90%*
	£	£	£
Direct materials	73 500	84 000	94 500
Direct wages	44 100	50 400	56 700
Overhead	45 400	49 600	53 800
Sales	196 000	224 000	252 000

(b) Explain the meaning of contribution and discuss its relevance in a marginal costing system.

(20 marks)

(*Chartered Institute of Management Accountants*)

3. Rumbles Ltd manufactures a single product, with a variable manufacturing cost of £12 per unit and a selling price of £20 per unit. Fixed production overheads are £90 000 per period. The company operates a full absorption costing system and the fixed overheads are absorbed into the cost of production, on the basis of a normal activity of 15 000 units per period, at a rate of £6 per unit. Any under- or over-absorbed overheads are written off to the profit and loss account at the end of each period. It may be assumed that no other expenses are incurred.

Summarized below are the company's manufacturing and trading results showing quantities only, for periods 2 and 3.

	Period 2	*Period 3*
Opening stock	5 000 units	11 000 units
Production	17 000 units	13 000 units
	22 000 units	24 000 units
Less closing stock	11 000 units	6 000 units
Sales	11 000 units	18 000 units

The managing director of Rumbles Ltd, who has recently returned from a course on marginal costing, has calculated that as sales have increased by 7000 units in period 3, the company's profits should increase by £56 000. However, the results produced by the accountants show that profits in period 2 were £34 000 and in period 3 were £24 000. The managing director is somewhat surprised!

Required:

(a) Produce columnar revenue accounts, for both periods, showing how the profits of £24 000 and £34 000 were obtained. (5 marks)

(b) Carefully explain, with supporting calculations:

  (i) the reasons for the reduction in reported profits between the two periods; (5 marks)

  (ii) how the managing director has calculated that profits should increase by £56 000 in period 3; (2 marks)

  (iii) why profits have not increased by £56 000 in period 3. (5 marks)

(Total 17 marks)

(*Chartered Association of Certified Accountants*)

4. (a) Comment briefly on the two most important features which you consider distinguish marginal costing from absorption costing.

(b) For decision-making purposes, a company uses the following figures relating to product B for a 1-year period.

Activity	*50%*	*100%*
Sales and production (000)	200	400
	£000	£000
Sales	1000	2000
Production costs:		
Variable	400	800
Fixed	200	200
Selling, distribution and administration expenses:		
Variable	200	400
Fixed	300	300

The normal level of activity for the current year is 400 000 units. The fixed costs are incurred evenly throughout the year and actual fixed costs are the same as budgeted.

There were no stocks of product B at the start of the quarter in which 110 000 units were produced and 80 000 units were sold.

From each of the questions (i)–(iv) below, you are required to select the appropriate answer. You must support each answer with an explanatory calculation.

(i) The amount of fixed production costs absorbed by product B in the first quarter, using absorption costing is:

	£
1	80 000
2	40 000
3	110 000
4	55 000
5	None of these

(ii) The over- or under-absorption of fixed production costs in the first quarter is:

	£
1	(5 000)
2	5 000
3	10 000
4	15 000
5	None of these

(iii) The net profit (or loss) for the first quarter using absorption costing, is:

	£
1	(115 000)
2	50 000
3	(175 000)
4	125 000
5	None of these

(iv) The net profit (or loss) for the first quarter, using marginal costing, is:

	£
1	35 000
2	(340 000)
3	65 000
4	(115 000)
5	None of these

(20 marks)

(*Chartered Institute of Management Accountants*)

5. At a recent conference on 'cost control in a period of reduction in demand', your managing director was impressed by the remarks of one of the speakers who advocated a marginal costing system of management reporting.

The managing director has now asked you to compare the present absorption costing system with an alternative marginal costing system.

Required:

(a) Tabulate the merits of:
  (i) a marginal costing system; and
  (ii) an absorption costing system.

(b) Prepare for presentation to your board of directors two statements showing the budgeted results for the year in:
  (i) an absorption costing form;
  (ii) a marginal costing form;

  paying particular attention to the layout of your presentation, which should be based on the data shown below.

(c) Present ratios with each statement which will show the relative profitability of each product and comment briefly on these ratios.

The company produces two products; the standard cost data for one of each are as follows:

Product	*A*	*B*
Direct materials:		
Units required	20	5
Price per unit	£0.50	£1.00
Direct labour:		
Hours allowed	5	10
Rate per hour	£2.00	£1.50

Budgeted data for the year are as follows:

Direct labour hours	55 000
Production overhead	£220 000

Product	*A*	*B*
Sales (£000)	375	300
Profit as a percentage of selling price	20%	10%

Overhead absorption:

production overhead is absorbed by a direct labour hour rate;
administration overhead is absorbed on a basis of 20 per cent of production cost;
selling and distribution overhead is absorbed on a basis of 30 per cent of production cost.

For the purpose of this presentation it has been decided that in order to facilitate the preparation of the marginal cost statement, it can be assumed that, using the overhead absorption cost per unit as a base, 20 per cent of the production overhead can be regarded as variable, and 33⅓ per cent of the selling and distribution overhead can be regarded as variable.

(30 marks)

(*Chartered Institute of Management Accountants*)

13 Short-run Tactical Decisions

This chapter deals with the following topics:

- **13.1 The nature of short-run tactical decisions.**
- **13.2 Cost analysis for short-run tactical decisions.**
- **13.3 Contribution margin analysis.**
- **13.4 Opportunity costs.**
- **13.5 The drop or keep decision.**
- **13.6 The sell or process further decision.**
- **13.7 The make or buy decision.**
- **13.8 The operate or lease decision.**
- **13.9 Contribution margin analysis applied to limiting factors.**
- **13.10 Linear programming and short-run tactical decisions.**

13.1 THE NATURE OF SHORT-RUN TACTICAL DECISIONS

Short-run decisions for which cost information is required fall into two categories:

(a) Those that relate to short-run output planning, involving determining the required output level for the budget period. Such decisions are recurrent and remain valid only for the duration of the budget period.

(b) Those that relate to 'one-off' situations, which are non-recurrent. They are sometimes referred to as *special decisions* or as *tactical decisions*. They reflect a response to a particular event. The nature of that response is said to be 'tactical', since it is an adjustment by the firm to a new situation.

It was noted in Chapter 11 that short-run output planning decisions relied on cost–volume–profit (c–v–p) analysis indicating the impact on profits of changes in activity levels. Consequently, with a given cost structure, the firm is assumed to seek profit improvement through the expansion of the volume of activity.

Short-run tactical decisions apply to a broad range of issues, as follows:

(a) the acceptance of a special order;
(b) dropping an existing product line, or adopting a new product line;
(c) closing a branch, distribution network or factory, ceasing to trade in a particular market, or vice versa, opening a new branch, distribution network or factory, entering a new market, and similar decisions that affect methods of operating;
(d) making or buying a part, component or product;
(e) operating or leasing assets;
(f) selling a product or processing further with a view to improving its selling price or changing its market.

Short-run tactical decisions do not have as their objective purpose the intention to influence the short-run output level. With one exception, namely the acceptance of a special order, the short-run tactical decisions listed above do not have immediate implications for current output levels.

Indeed, the character of these decisions is much more significant to the operations of the firm in the longer term, for they involve particularly changes in methods of operation or the management of assets. In this respect, they have important implications for long-run output levels and long-run profits.

Finally, unlike short-run output decisions, short-run tactical decisions do not have an impact limited to one accounting period, and they are not easily reversed in the following accounting period.

13.2 COST ANALYSIS FOR SHORT-RUN TACTICAL DECISIONS

It was noted in Chapter 2 that different types of decisions require different cost information. Pricing decisions require information about product costs. Such information is obtained by a cost analysis that focuses on direct and indirect costs. This is because profit per unit is seen as the difference between the sale price per unit and the product cost per unit. Short-run output planning decisions require knowledge of cost behaviour over the planned level of activity, for such decisions relate aggregate profit to the level of activity.

In a sense, therefore, product pricing and short-run output planning decisions require relevant cost information. In cost accounting, however, the term *relevant costs* as defined in Chapter 2 have a special meaning. Relevant costs are costs required for the purpose of making decisions involving *choice*, where the choice is the preference of one clearly stated alternative against other less desirable alternatives. In this analysis, relevant costs are costs that will enable the preferred alternative to be identified.

Relevant costs may be distinguished from product costs and activity level costs as follows:

(a) relevant costs are future costs;
(b) relevant costs are differential costs.

13.2.1 Relevant costs as future costs

Relevant costs are costs that have not yet been incurred, since they will come into existence when a decision will have been made regarding the preferred alternative. In this sense, they may be contrasted with product costs and activity level costs which are assumed to be actual costs. It may be argued that this difference is purely semantic when decisions of whatever nature imply future events and future costs.

A more cogent reason why relevant costs are categorized as future costs is to make it plain that past costs or sunk costs are not relevant costs, and therefore not included in relevant costs. By contrast, product costing as we discussed in Parts I and II brings all expenditure incurred in the normal course of business in bringing the product to its present location into the definition of 'cost'.

The significance of the exclusion of past or sunk costs from relevant costs is seen in the following example:

EXAMPLE 13.1:
High Tech Development Ltd has invested £50 000 in developing a new process. A revised forecast of future investment expenditure required to complete the development work indicates that the initial forecast of £200 000 was an underestimate. According to the new forecast, a further £300 000 is required.

The short-run tactical decision that has to be made is a choice between two alternatives, as follows:

(a) Alternative A: Complete the development work and expend £300 000.
(b) Alternative B: Abandon the project and do not expend £300 000.

It should be noted particularly that the prior expenditure of £50 000 is an irrelevant factor in the decision whether or not to spend a further £300 000. Relevant cost information focuses narrowly on the *costs that will be affected by the decision.* In this sense, the decision cannot affect the costs of £50 000 already sunk in the project.

Note well the different reasoning that would come into play upon a decision to sell the process after completion. The decision then becomes a product sale. The intention is to make a profit through sale. For this purpose, the product costs (that is, the costs of developing the process to completion) would be established as the full costs incurred, namely £350 000.

13.2.2 Relevant costs as differential costs

Relevant costs are costs that are *both* future costs *and* differential costs. The added requirement that relevant costs should be differential costs is a strict condition that adds a further dimension to the nature of relevant costs. Differential costs are those that differ depending on the alternative selected. It is especially important to note that not all future costs are necessarily relevant costs. Example 13.2 illustrates this point.

EXAMPLE 13.2:

Alpha Ltd is a precision engineering company that is about to tool up in order to manufacture a new instrument, which will require a special machine. Two rival companies produce the machines that perform the same functions. The following data is available.

	Rival Model A	*Rival Model B*
	£	£
Cost of acquisition	200 000	250 000
Installation costs	5 000	5 000
Annual operating costs for standard output of 25 000 units	20 000	15 000
Expected residual value at end of estimated useful life of 5 years	10 000	10 000

The relevant costs for the purpose of choosing one of these two alternative machines are the future costs that will be differential costs. All the costs detailed above are future costs, since they will be incurred as the result of a decision yet to be made. Those future costs that remain the same irrespective of which alternative is chosen are irrelevant costs. They are the installation costs of £10 000. Likewise, the end of life residual value may be ignored since both machines have the same estimated residual value. Accordingly, the relevant costs are:

	Rival Model A	*Rival Model B*
	£	£
Cost of acquisition	200 000	250 000
Annual operating costs for standard output of 25 000 units over 5 years	100 000	75 000
Total differential costs	300 000	325 000

Note that differential costs are costs that change under different alternatives. This does not mean that variable costs are always differential costs nor that fixed costs are never differential costs. As Example 13.2 shows, differential costs may consist both of fixed asset costs and annual operating costs, the latter comprising both fixed, variable and semi-variable costs.

13.3 CONTRIBUTION MARGIN ANALYSIS

Short-run tactical decisions are not made solely by reference to relevant costs, but rather by comparing the contribution to profits that will result from preferring one alternative to all other alternatives. Therefore, determining the relevant cost is only one aspect of the decision problem.

The contribution margin plays an important role in short-run tactical decisions that relate to making the best use of resources. The following decisions rely on contribution margin analysis:

(a) the special order;
(b) closing or keeping a branch, product line, market or process;
(c) making or buying a part or component;
(d) operating or leasing an asset;
(e) selling or processing further.

In the context of short-run tactical decisions, the contribution margin is defined as *the excess of the revenue associated with a decision alternative over its relevant costs that is available as a contribution towards the firm's fixed costs and profit.*

The contribution margin is a better guide than accounting profit in certain circumstances, as explained in Example 13.3.

EXAMPLE 13.3:
Gadget and Sons Ltd manufactures a device selling for £10 per unit. The device is marketed under the brand name Ploof. Fixed costs

are £2 500 000 per annum. The variable costs relating to Ploof amount to £5 per unit. Current production of Ploof is running at 1 000 000 per annum, representing 50 per cent of productive capacity. A West German company is interested in buying 100 000 units, but is not willing to pay more than £6 per unit. Mr Gadget Snr has always been willing to negotiate a price with a prospective client, but has never agreed to sell below full-product cost. As part of the price negotiation, full-product costs per unit have been recalculated to take account of the size of the potential order, as follows:

	£
Variable costs per unit	5
Allocated fixed costs per unit	
£2 500 000/1 100 000 units	2.27
Full-product cost per unit	7.27
	7.27

This analysis of relevant costs has led Mr Gadget Snr to the firm conclusion that his bottom line in the negotiations is a selling price of £7.27, at which he is just covering costs. His only reason for accepting the deal on this basis is to introduce Ploof in the West German market. The client refuses to raise his bid price beyond £6. Negotiations are deadlocked.

An alternative analysis suggested by the West German client during the negotiations as evidence of the adequacy of his bid price on a special order of that magnitude is as follows:

	£
Sales revenue generated by the order	
£6 × 100 000	600 000
Less: Relevant costs	
£5 × 100 000	500 000
Contribution margin	100 000

According to the West German client, Gadget and Sons Ltd stand to lose £100 000 in profit by turning down his bid price. In his view, fixed costs should not be taken into account in determining product costs in this case since they are not relevant costs. All this is new to Mr Gadget Snr who suspects that he is being fooled.

It is clear from the above example that there is justice in both points of view. Mr Gadget Snr is right on insisting that his regular market price should cover full-product costs, but a special order requires a different approach based on relevant costs and the contribution margin analysis. Given that fixed costs are not affected by the decision to accept or reject the special order, they are irrelevant costs. Consequently, relevant costs are reduced to £5 per unit, and the rejection of the special order will result in a lost contribution of £100 000.

13.4 OPPORTUNITY COSTS

It has been assumed so far that costs are incurred expenses. Accordingly, product costs are costs that are identified as incurred in manufacturing a product; activity level costs are costs incurred at different levels of activity. Relevant costs in relation to a decision such as the acceptance of a special order have also been assumed to refer to expenses expected to be incurred. Irrelevant costs have been disregarded on the basis that they would have been incurred irrespective of the decision.

The accounting process restricts the accumulation of costs to product costs. Activity level costs and relevant costs result from alternative cost classifications that are required for decision making. Such costs are not recorded as such in the cost accounts. An opportunity cost is a concept that is alien to accounting. It is used in economic analysis for the purpose of assessing the relative advantage gained as a result of choosing one alternative against another. It is defined as *the value of the next best opportunity lost as the result of preferring the chosen alternative to the rejected alternative.* Since accounting is able to deal only with money values, an opportunity cost may be redefined as *the net cash inflows or cash savings lost as the result of preferring the chosen alternative to the rejected alternative.*

EXAMPLE 13.4:

Realty Investment Corporation plc has £5 million available for investment. The board of directors is considering two alternative investment projects. The annual rate of return forecasted for project A is 10 per cent per annum, that for project B is 8 per cent. In every other respect, both projects are comparable.

The relevant cost of choosing project A lies in the opportunity cost resulting from not having the cash inflows from project B. The justification for preferring project A to project B may be seen only in terms of the comparative advantage associated with project A, as follows:

	£
Estimated annual return from project A	500 000
Less: Relevant costs	
Opportunity cost of losing the annual return from project B	450 000
Advantage resulting from choosing project A	50 000

By their nature, opportunity costs arise only at the moment when a choice is being made, and their usefulness lasts only as long as a decision has not been reached. Relevant costs must include opportunity costs whenever the objective of making a short-run tactical decision is to place the firm in a better position as the result of choosing one alternative rather than another. The inclusion of opportunity costs in relevant costs is illustrated in the four following decisions, namely:

(a) drop or keep;
(b) sell or process further;
(c) make or buy;
(d) operate or lease.

13.5 THE DROP OR KEEP DECISION

The drop or keep decision is an entire category of decisions that includes such decisions as dropping a product line, closing a department, branch, factory, or process, withdrawing from a market or activity. The analysis used in the drop or keep decision is equally valid in the reverse sense, that is, to adopt a new product, to open a new department, factory or process, to enter a new market or undertake a new activity.

EXAMPLE 13.5:
Eatup Restaurants Ltd operates three restaurants in Southwold, a county town in Eastern England. The profit and loss account for the year ended 31 December 19X5 shows the following analysis of results:

Restaurant	*A*	*B*	*C*	*Total*
	£	£	£	£
Gross receipts	200 000	100 000	150 000	450 000
Variable costs	100 000	70 000	80 000	250 000
Fixed costs	60 000	40 000	50 000	150 000
Net profit/loss	40 000	(10 000)	20 000	50 000

Restaurant B has made a similar loss for the last two years. By closing it down, the board of directors believes that not only would it increase the company's total profit by £10 000, but also make an additional saving since fixed costs amounting to £10 000 are direct fixed costs to restaurant B and would be eliminated. The remaining £30 000 represented allocated fixed costs that would have to be apportioned to restaurants A and B.

The analysis of the consequence on the company's profit of the decision to close or to keep the restaurant B is as follows:

	Close B	*Keep B*
Gross receipts	350 000	450 000
Variable costs	180 000	250 000
Contribution margin	170 000	200 000
Fixed costs	140 000	150 000
Net profit	30 000	50 000

From this analysis, it is seen that the consequence of closing B is not an increase of £10 000 in total profits as a result of eliminating an accounting loss, but a reduction of £20 000 in profits resulting from the loss of the contribution generated by B, as follows:

Restaurant B	£
Gross receipts	100 000
Variable costs	70 000
Contribution margin	30 000
Relevant fixed costs	10 000
Net contribution	20 000

The decision to keep or to close restaurant B may now be examined as follows:

	£
Total profits if B is kept open	50 000
Opportunity cost of closing B (net contribution lost)	20 000
Total profits if B is closed	30 000

Hence, the best alternative between keeping or closing B is to keep B open. The net advantage of keeping B open is £20 000. The opportunity cost of closing B would be the loss of the net contribution £20 000 generated by B.

13.6 THE SELL OR PROCESS FURTHER DECISION

Like the drop or keep decision, the sell or process further decision is also an entire category of managerial decisions. These decisions have one common characteristic, namely, doing something additional with a view to adding value. The most obvious example is a decision to process a semi-finished product further rather than selling it in its present condition. The justification for processing further must be a net advantage over the decision to sell now. Other common examples of the sell or process further decision lie in the marketing of products, such as in improving the presentation of a product by improved packaging, boxing soap in sets of three bars, etc., and selling a product in a differentiated market at a higher price. The sell or process further decision is another example of choice involving two mutually exclusive alternatives. The decision to sell now is an alternative that precludes the possibility of further processing. Likewise, the decision to process further precludes the possibility of selling now. Given the exclusive nature of these alternatives, the preferred alternative is the one that yields the highest return. The costs relevant to the decision of choosing the preferred alternative are the opportunity costs of losing the returns associated with the rejected alternative.

EXAMPLE 13.6:

A company sells, for £10 per unit, a semi-finished product costing £4 to make. The product could be sold as a finished product for £22 in a different market by further processing costing £5. The analysis of the choice decision is as follows:

	Sell	*Process further*
	£	£
Revenue/unit specific to each decision	10	12
Costs specific to each decision	4	5
Differential profit per unit	6	7

The nature of the decision to be made is a choice now between two mutually exclusive alternatives. Once the decision has been made, one of the alternatives will no longer be available. The problem, therefore, is one of identifying the alternative that yields the highest differential profit. The relative advantage of the choice will take account of the opportunity of losing the other alternative, as follows:

	£
Return per unit of process further decision	7
Opportunity cost of losing the return per unit associated with the sell decision	6
Comparative advantage of choosing the process further decision	1

13.7 THE MAKE OR BUY DECISION

Industrial specialization has favoured the growth of satellite subcontracting companies making parts and components for incorporation in other intermediate products or as subunits installed in major products sold on the market. Nonetheless, whether to make a part or component, or to buy it from another company is a question that frequently arises throughout industry at all types of manufacturing concerns. Policy considerations may induce a company to prefer to make rather than buy: cost considerations may compel subcontracting the making of a part. The inclusion of opportunity costs in relevant costs for decision making assists in the selection of the best alternative.

EXAMPLE 13.7:
Aerojet plc specializes in making components for the aircraft industry. Casings Ltd has made an offer to supply casings for Aerojet plc at a price of £275 per unit. At present, Aerojet plc is making these units at a cost of £380 each, as follows:

	£
Unit variable costs	180
Direct fixed costs	90
Allocation fixed costs	110
Product cost per unit	380

Assume that the productive capacity released as a result of ceasing to make the casings will remain idle. Assume also that the monthly production of casings affected by the decision to buy totals 500. The relative advantage of buying rather than making can be stated as follows:

	£
Variable costs	90 000
Direct fixed costs	45 000
Relevant costs	135 000
Cost of buying	137 500
Advantage of making	2 500

Assume now that the productive capacity released as a result of selecting the buy decision will not remain idle, but can be employed to extend the production of components yielding an additional monthly profit of £10 000. The relevant costs associated with the make decision have to be revised to include the opportunity cost of losing the monthly profits of £10 000 that would otherwise have been realized by making additional components.

	£
Cost of making	
Variable costs	90 000
Direct fixed costs	45 000
Relevant manufacturing costs	135 000
Opportunity costs	10 000
	145 000
Cost of buying	137 500
Advantage of buying	7 500

As may be seen, the introduction of the opportunity cost of not buying has reversed the previous conclusion that favoured the selection of the buy decision.

13.8 THE OPERATE OR LEASE DECISION

The operate or lease decision is also frequently encountered in business, not only with regard to the use of fixed assets such as buildings, but also intangible assets such as patents, licences, copyrights and trademarks. The operate or lease decision is a choice between using such assets in productive operations or ceding their use to others in return for a periodic payment in the form of rent or royalty. British companies commonly find it more profitable to allow a foreign company to exploit a British invention under a licensing agreement rather than setting up foreign distribution or manufacturing operations.

The operate or lease decision is another classic example of the use of opportunity costs as relevant costs for decision making.

EXAMPLE 13.8:
Finkst Ltd is a small private company formed by two brothers for the purpose of exploiting a new invention. The patent right is the principal asset of the company. After 3 years of successful operations, Finkst Ltd is currently making profits of £100 000 per annum. Further successful growth is being hampered by lack of finance and of an appropriate distribution network. Grabit plc, a large multinational corporation is willing to negotiate a licensing agreement with Finkst Ltd, under which the worldwide exclusive use of the patent would be granted to Grabit plc in return for a yearly royalty amounting to £200 000. The choice between the alternative of operating or leasing may be expressed as follows:

	£
Royalty income under lease	200 000
Opportunity cost being profits from operating	100 000
Net advantage of leasing	100 000

An alternative method of comparing the two alternatives is to determine their present value, and select the alternative that has the highest present value. For such a calculation, it would be necessary to know the cost of capital.

13.9 CONTRIBUTION MARGIN ANALYSIS APPLIED TO LIMITING FACTORS

The foregoing examples illustrate the various ways in which the contribution margin and the opportunity cost concepts are useful for a wide variety of short-run tactical decisions. The contribution margin analysis has further applications, notably in the area of short-term decisions made in the face of limiting factors. One such example is the problem of optimizing profitability in the face of limiting factors.

It was assumed in Chapter 11, that given a particular cost structure, short-run profits were entirely dependent upon the volume of activity. Further constraints may exist that restrict short-run profit, such as limited factors of production or limited demand for particular products. In these situations, the naive conclusions of c–v–p analysis will not help the firm to make choice decisions as to how to use limited resources or how to plan the output of particular products in such a way as to optimize overall profits.

Contribution margin analysis allows such choices to be made, as shown in Examples 13.9 and 13.10.

13.9.1 Profit optimization with limited resources

Limited resources that may restrict the level of activity arise in different ways, for example, shortage of labour, material, equipment or factory space. Faced with such shortages, the firm will seek to optimize profits in the manner in which existing resources are allocated between products. In effect, the firm will optimize profits by allocating the limited resources in such a way as to obtain *the highest contribution margin per unit of the limited resources.*

EXAMPLE 13.9:

Threeproducts Ltd manufactures three different products that are made using the same machine. The contribution margin per unit of the products is as follows:

	£
Product A	9
Product B	7
Product C	5

In the light of this information. Threeproducts Ltd should concentrate machine use on the production of only product A, since that product yields the highest contribution margin.

If the number of machine hours available is limited, the firm should concentrate on producing only that product which optimizes profits in the face of this limiting factor. Assume that the machine hours required to produce one unit of each of the products is as follows:

	Machine hours required
Product A	3
Product B	2
Product C	1

On this basis, the contribution margin per unit of the limited factor is as follows:

		£
Product A	(£9 ÷ 3 hours)	3.00
Product B	(£7 ÷ 2 hours)	3.50
Product C	(£5 ÷ 1 hour)	5.00

Evidently, the firm should now reverse the earlier decision, and produce only product C.

13.9.2 Profit optimization in the face of limited demand

Profit optimization in the face of limited demand can be seen as another level of complexity in running a manufacturing company, as shown in Example 13.10.

EXAMPLE 13.10:
Suppose that machine hours capacity is limited to 450 hours per week. On this assumption, Threeproducts Ltd will concentrate producing only product C from which the highest contribution margin per unit is obtained.

However, the market demand for each of the products is limited as follows:

	Market demand in units
Product A	100
Product B	100
Product C	100

If Threeproducts Ltd were to attempt to satisfy this market demand, it would require 600 machine hours, as follows:

Product	*Maximum demand in units*	*Machine hours equivalent*
A	100	300
B	100	200
C	100	100
		600

The product mix that would, at once, optimize on the limited availability of machine hours and the limited market demand for the product is as follows:

Product	*Output units*	*Machine hours*	*Contribution per machine hour*	*Total contribution*
			£	£
A	100	100	5.00	500
B	100	200	3.50	700
C	50	150	3.00	450
		450		1650

This allocation of machine hours to products having restricted market demand levels pushes product C at the highest level of priority, followed by product B and last by product A.

13.10 LINEAR PROGRAMMING AND SHORT-RUN TACTICAL DECISIONS

Linear programming is a mathematical technique that is applicable to business decisions having profit maximization or cost minimization objectives in the face of constraints or limiting factors.

One typical example of the application of linear programming to short-run tactical decisions is the case of the manufacturing firm seeking to optimize profits within the constraints of limited plant capacity. As explained in Chapter 11, the short-term production capacity level and the cost structure is assumed not to be susceptible to change.

EXAMPLE 13.11

Anchor Steel plc manufactures two products in respect of which the following data is given:

Product	*A*	*B*
Selling price per unit	£30	£20
Variable costs per unit	£15	£10
Contribution margin per unit	£15	£10

Machining hours required per unit

Milling	5 hours	1.5 hours
Grinding	2 hours	2 hours

Total machine capacity is as follows:

Milling (3 machines at 200 hours per month) 600 hours
Grinding (2 machines at 200 hours per month) 400 hours

The linear programming problem may be stated as:

(a) maximizing profits;
(b) recognizing the production constraint.

These two aspects of the problem may be stated algebraically, as follows:

(a) The objective is to maximize the contribution to fixed overheads and profit. This objective is called the objective function, and may be expressed thus:

$$\text{Maximize } C = 15A + 10B$$

where C is the total contribution with A and B being the total number of units of the two products which must be manufactured to maximize the total contribution. This equation is subject to the limits that:

$$A \geqslant 0$$
$$B \geqslant 0$$

for it is not possible to produce negative quantities of either A or B.

(b) The constraints on production arising from the machine capacity limits of the milling department (600 hours) and of the grinding department (400 hours) may also be expressed in algebraic terms as follows:

$$5A + 1\tfrac{1}{2}B \leqslant 600$$
$$2A + 2B \leqslant 400$$

The first inequality states that the total number of hours used on milling must be equal to or less than 600 hours; the second inequality states that the total hours used on grinding machines must be equal to or less than 400 hours.

The problem may now be summarized in the form:

$$\text{Maximize } C = 15A + 10B$$

subject to the constraints:

$$\begin{aligned} 5A + 1\tfrac{1}{2}B &\leqslant 600 \\ 2A + 2B &\leqslant 400 \\ A &\geqslant 0 \\ B &\geqslant 0 \end{aligned}$$

It is possible to solve the problem by means of a graph (Exhibit 13.1) showing the manufacturing possibilities for the two departments, viz.:

Milling department	
Product A	$600 \div 5 = 120$ units
or Product B	$600 \div 1\tfrac{1}{2} = 400$ units
Grinding department	
Product A	$400 \div 2 = 200$ units
or Product B	$400 \div 2 = 200$ units

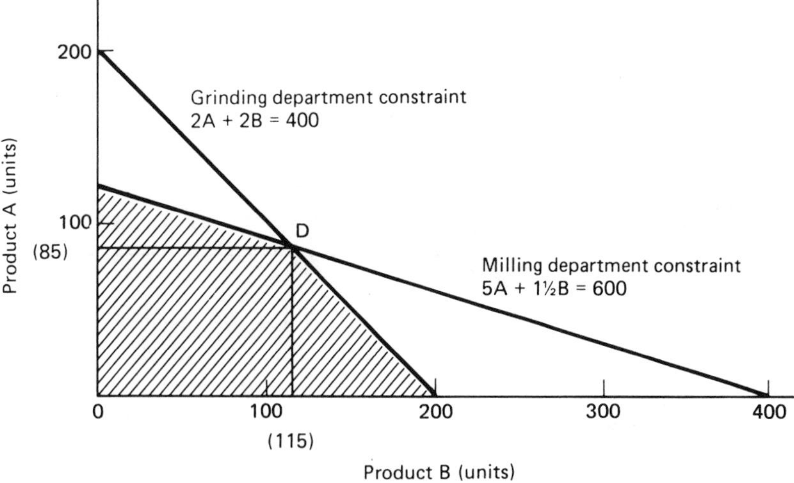

Exhibit 13.1

Hence, the optimal combination of products A and B is 85 units and 115 units, respectively, in terms of the limited machine capacity which will be utilized as follows:

	Milling department	*Grinding department*
	(hours)	(hours)
Product A: 85 units	425 (85 × 5)	170 (85 × 2)
Product B: 115 units	172.5 (115 × $1\frac{1}{2}$)	230 (115 × 2)
Total hours used	597.5	400
Total hours available	600	400

The optimal combination will produce a total contribution to overheads and profits of £2425 as follows:

Product A:	85 units at £15 =	1275
Product B:	115 units at £10 =	1150
		£2425

We may verify that this combination of products is the optimal one in terms of profits and available machine capacity, as follows:

(a) Altering the product combination from 85 units of A and 115 units of B to 84 units of A and 116 units of B, which would affect machine use as follows:

	Milling department	Grinding department
	(hours)	(hours)
Product A: 84 units	420 (84 × 5)	168 (84 × 2)
Product B: 116 units	174 (116 × $1\frac{1}{2}$)	232 (116 × 2)
Total hours used	594	400
Total hours available	600	400

Hence, this combination is as efficient in the utilization of the grinding department but less efficient in the utilization of the milling machines. It is less profitable also yielding a contribution of only £2420 as against £2425 as follows:

Product A:	84 units at £15 =	1260
Product B:	116 units at £10 =	1160
		£2420

(b) Altering the product combination from 85 units of A and 115 units of B to 86 units of A and 113 units of B, which would affect machine use as under:

	Milling department	Grinding department
	(hours)	(hours)
Product A: 86 units	430 (86 × 5)	172 (86 × 2)
Product B: 113 units	$169\frac{1}{2}$ (113 × $1\frac{1}{2}$)	226 (113 × 2)
Total hours used	$599\frac{1}{2}$	398
Total hours available	600	400

The shaded region of Exhibit 13.1 contains all the combinations of products A and B which are feasible solutions to the problem, hence its name – the feasibility region. The optimal solution, that is, the product combination of A and B which is the best of all the feasible solutions lies at the intersection of the lines at point D, and may be read off as 85 units of A and 115 of B. It will be observed that the optimal solution lies on a tangent which is the furthest away from the point of origin. The graphical method of solving the problem is susceptible to error unless carefully plotted, and a more reliable answer may be obtained by solving the problem mathematically.

The optimal combination of products A and B may be found by solving the simultaneous equation given above, that is,

$$(1)\ 5A + 1\tfrac{1}{2}B = 600$$
$$(2)\ 2A + 2B = 400$$

The solution is obtained by multiplying (1) by 4 and (2) by 3 to give us the value of A, as follows:

$$\begin{aligned} 20A + 6B &= 2400 \\ -6A + 6B &= 1200 \\ \hline 14A &= 1200 \\ A &= 85\tfrac{5}{7}\text{ths} \end{aligned}$$

Since we are concerned only with completed units of A, the optimal production of product A is 85 units. The optimal number of units of B may be calculated by inserting the known value of A into the equation, as follows:

$$\begin{aligned} 6 \times 85 + 6B &= 1200 \\ \text{i.e. } 510 + 6B &= 1200 \\ 6B &= 1200 - 510 \\ B &= 115. \end{aligned}$$

Hence, whereas this combination is more efficient in the use of the milling machines than the optimal combination, it is less efficient in the use of the grinding machinery. Moreover, to keep within the capacity limits of the milling department we have had to forgo the production of two units of product B to expand the manufacture of product A by one unit. The consequential contribution to profits is also only £2420 as against the optimal contribution £2425, which may be calculated as follows:

Product A:	86 units at £15 =	1290
Product B:	113 units at £10 =	1130
		£2420

It is noteworthy, also, that the linear programming approach to the best product combination mix gives a solution which is more profitable than the one which relates the contribution margin to the machine capacity limits, which we discussed on page 274, and which suggested that only product B should be made so that 200 units of B would be manufactured to yield a contribution of £2000.

We have so far only discussed simple cases involving at the maximum only two resource constraints. In real life, a firm may be faced with more than two constraints, but mathematical techniques exist for coping with larger numbers of limits. The simplex method, for example, which is based on matrix algebra may be employed in such cases and it is ideally suited for solutions using a computer.

Questions

1. What are short-run tactical decisions?
2. Give examples of short-run tactical decisions.
3. Do short-run tactical decisions have limited short-run effects?
4. State the nature of relevant costs.
5. Distinguish the following categories of costs:

   (a) product costs;
   (b) activity level costs;
   (c) relevant costs.

6. What do you understand by the term 'differential costs'?
7. Define the contribution margin.
8. What is an 'opportunity cost'?
9. List four short-run tactical decisions in which opportunity costs are used.
10. Explain how the contribution margin may be useful to short-run output planning decisions.
11. What is linear programming? Give an example of the application of linear programming.

Problems

1. Mr Belle has recently developed a new improved video cassette and shown below is a summary of a report by a firm of management consultants on the sales potential and production costs of the new cassette.

   Sales Potential

   The sales volume is difficult to predict and will vary with the price, but it is reasonable to assume that at a selling price of £10 per cassette, sales would be between 7500 and 10 000 units per month. Alternatively, if the selling price was reduced to £9.00 per cassette, sales would be between 12 000 and 18 000 units per month.

   Production Costs

   If production is maintained at or below 10 000 units per month, then variable manufacturing costs would be approximately £8.25 per cassette and fixed costs £12 125 per month. However, if production is planned to exceed 10 000 units per month, then variable costs would be reduced to £7.75 per cassette, but the fixed costs would increase to £16 125 per month.

   Mr Belle has been charged £2000 for the report by the management consultants and, in addition, he has incurred £3000 development costs on the new cassette.

If Mr Belle decides to produce and sell the new cassette it will be necessary for him to use factory premises which he owns, but are leased to a colleague for a rental of £400 per month. Also he will resign from his current post in an electronics firm where he is earning a salary of £1000 per month.

Required:

(a) Identify in the question an example of
 (i) an opportunity cost;
 (ii) a sunk cost. (3 marks)

(b) Making whatever calculations you consider appropriate, analyse the report from the consultants and advise Mr Belle of the potential profitability of the alternatives shown in the report.
 Any assumptions considered necessary or matters which may require further investigation or comment should be clearly stated. (19 marks)
 (Total 22 marks)

(*Chartered Association of Certified Accountants*)

2. From one basic raw material a company produces two different grades of a product known as 'crude' and 'refined'. The company's direct labour wage rate is £3 per hour and it absorbs overhead into the cost of its two grades of product by means of variable and fixed overhead rates per 100 kg produced. The budgeted costs and selling prices for each grade are as follows:

	Crude 100 kg	Refined 100 kg
	£	£
Direct material	20.0	20.0
Direct wages	18.0	30.0
Variable production overhead	3.6	7.5
Fixed production overhead	24.0	40.0
	65.6	97.5
Selling prices	80.0	105.0

For the year ending 30 June 19X5, the company's effective annual production capacity is 120 000 labour hours and its estimated fixed production overhead costs total £480 000. Its sales policy is to sell 75 per cent of its capacity in the more profitable grade and 25 per cent in the less profitable grade.

Required:

(a) State on which grade of product the company should concentrate to obtain the highest profit – show your calculation.

(b) Present a statement for management which shows the expected sales, variable costs (by element of cost) and contribution for each grade of product together with the overall net profit which can be expected for the year ending 30 June 19X5, if the company's present sales policy is followed. Budgeted fixed selling and administration costs are £90 000.

(c) Comment on the principle you have followed to determine the highest profit in your answer to (a) above. Could this same principle be used in a retailing organization and if so, how? (20 marks)

(*Chartered Institute of Management Accountants*)

3. (a) Explain the purpose of a 'make' versus 'buy' exercise and detail how this purpose may be achieved.

(10 marks)

(b) A company manufactures and sells three components, but has requested its purchasing manager to investigate the prices of an overseas producer. The following costs and prices are made available:

Component	*X*	*Y*	*Z*
Production (units)	20 000	40 000	80 000
Direct material cost, per unit	£0.80	£1.00	£0.40
Direct labour cost, per unit	1.60	1.80	0.80
Direct expense cost, per unit	0.40	0.60	0.20
Fixed cost per unit	0.80	1.00	0.40
Selling price each	4.00	5.00	2.00
Imported price	2.75	4.20	2.00

Required:

(i) Your recommendation to management as to whether any component should be purchased on the basis of cost only.

(4 marks)

(ii) The profit figure the company will make by producing all the components itself.

(2 marks)

(iii) State if your recommendation in (i) above is likely to affect the profit and by how much.

(2 marks)

(iv) Assuming management proposes to go ahead and import some of the components, what matters would you bring to their attention.

(4 marks)

(c) One of the component European agents has placed orders which were not previously anticipated, for 4000 of component Y and 8000 of component Z. If these are produced the purchasing manager will be able to negotiate a 10 per cent reduction on all material costs providing these and the original quantities of X, Y and Z are manufactured. Overtime will have to be worked on the export order involving a 25 per cent premium.
Evaluate the new situation. (6 marks)

(Total 28 marks)

(*Association of Accounting Technicians*)

4. Machine Repairs Ltd, which is currently working at about two-thirds of full capacity, has been invited to quote for reconditioning a planing machine, and the estimator has submitted the following figures:

Direct materials:	
80 kg of 'A' at £0.75 per kg	
4 pieces of 'B' at £5.00 each	
2 pieces of 'C' at £2.50 each	
2 litres of paint at £2.00 per litre	
Direct labour:	
Machine shop:	20 hours at £3.25
Fitting shop:	10 hours at £3.00
Paint shop:	2 hours at £3.00

Variable and fixed overheads are absorbed on the basis of direct labour hours, separate rates being used for each department. Twenty-five per cent is normally added to total cost for profit.

The following data are taken from the annual budget:

Department	*Direct labour hours*	*Variable overhead*	*Fixed overhead*
		£	£
Machine shop	40 000	16 000	80 000
Fitting shop	20 000	4 000	34 000
Paint shop	10 000	—	15 000

Required:

(a) Prepare the cost estimate and show the price that would be quoted for reconditioning the planing machine.

(15 marks)

(b) If the customer rejects the quotation and offers £250 for the work, state whether you consider that such an offer should be accepted or declined, giving the reasons for your decision.

(5 marks)

(Total 20 marks)

(*London Chamber of Commerce and Industry*)

5. (a) The current average weekly trading results of the Swish Restaurant in Sumtown are shown below:

	£	£
Turnover		2800
Operating costs:		
Materials	1540	
Power	280	
Staff	340	
Building occupancy costs	460	
		2620
Profit		£180

The average selling price of each meal is £4; materials and power may be regarded as a variable cost varying with the number of meals provided. Staff costs are semi-variable with a fixed cost element of £200 per week; the building occupancy costs are all fixed.

Required:

Calculate the number of meals required to be sold in order to earn a profit of £300 per week.

(3 marks)

(b) The owners of the restaurant are considering expanding their business and using under-utilized space by diversifying into:

either (1) Take-away foods.

or (2) High-quality meals.

The estimated sales and costs of each proposal are shown below:

	Take-away foods	*High-quality meals*
Sales volume, per week	720 meals	200 meals
	£	£
Average selling price, per meal	1.60	6.00
Variable costs, per meal	0.85	4.66
Incremental fixed costs, per week	610.00	282.00

The sales estimate for both of the above proposals is rather uncertain and it is recognized that actual sales volume could be up to 20 per cent either higher or lower than that estimated.

If either of the above proposals were implemented it has been estimated that the existing restaurant's operations would be affected as follows:

(i) As a result of bulk purchasing, material costs incurred would be reduced by 10p per meal. This saving would apply to all meals produced in the existing restaurant.

(ii) Because more people would be aware of the existence of the restaurant it is estimated that turnover would increase. If the 'take-away food' section were opened then for every ten take-away meals sold the existing restaurant's sales would increase by one meal, alternatively if the 'high-quality meals' section were opened then for every five such meals sold the existing restaurant's sales would increase by one meal.

A specific effect of implementing the 'take-away food' proposal would be a change in the terms of employment of the staff in the existing restaurant, the result of which would be that the staff wage of £340 per week would have to be regarded as a fixed cost.

Required:
Calculate, for each of the proposed methods of diversification:

(i) the additional profit which would be earned by the owners of the restaurant if the estimated sales were achieved; (8 marks)

(ii) the sales of volume at which the owners of the restaurant would earn no additional profit from the proposed diversification. (5 marks)

(c) Carefully consider the conclusions which may be drawn from your calculations in (b) above.

(6 marks)
(Total 22 marks)

(*Chartered Association of Certified Accountants*)

6. (a) Next year's forecasted trading results for Caribee Ltd, a small company manufacturing three different types of product, are shown below.

Product	*A*	*B*	*C*	*Total*
Selling price, per unit	£10	£12	£8	
	£000	£000	£000	£000
Sales	100	96	32	228
Variable cost of sales:				
Prime cost	40	38	13	91
Variable overhead	20	18	11	49
Share of general fixed overhead	30	27	10	67
Profit/(loss)	10	13	(2)	21

Required:

(i) Explain how the company's forecasted profits would be affected if product C were discontinued. It should be assumed that sales of the remaining products would not be affected, any other assumptions made should be included with your explanation.

(4 marks)

(ii) Additional advertising for product B would cost £8000 next year, this amount is not included in the forecasts shown above. Calculate the minimum extra sales, in units, of product B required to cover this additional cost.

(4 marks)

(iii) Calculate the increase in sales volume of product A necessary to compensate for a 10 per cent reduction in the selling price of the product. Carefully explain why the increase in volume is proportionately greater than the reduction in selling price. (5 marks)

(b) The production director of Caribee Ltd has just been informed that next year's supplies of a material used in the manufacture of each of the three products will be restricted to 92 000 kg, no substitute material is available and the estimated consumption of this restricted material, per product, is:

Product A	8 kg per unit
Product B	4 kg per unit
Product C	1 kg per unit

The sales director estimates that the maximum demand for each product is that which is shown in the original forecast in (a) above; he also decides that advertising or adjustments to selling price are not possible.

Assume that stocks of materials, work-in-progress or finished goods cannot be carried.

Required:
Calculate the optimum quantities of products A, B and C which should be manufactured next year in order to maximize company profits.

(9 marks)
(Total 22 marks)

(*Chartered Association of Certified Accountants*)

7. Clamart Company Ltd operates a car valet scheme. They accept bookings from clients who wish to have their cars thoroughly cleaned and offer two services, the 'normal' and the 'super'. The processes involved are split into two operations: first, external cleaning and second, internal cleaning. Because of the type of polishing and buffing machinery used, the operations are separate, and resources cannot be switched from one process to the other. The number of hours available in the interior cleaning section is 360 in any week and a normal service takes 4 hours in this section whilst a super service takes 5 hours. The number of hours available in the exterior cleaning section in any week amounts to 540. In this department a normal service takes 10 hours while a super service takes 6 hours.

After allowing for the variable cost element in each service, the contribution amounts to £2.00 for a normal service and £3.00 for a super service. Before accepting bookings, Clamart Company Ltd wishes to know how many of each type of service it should accept as there are known to be many potential clients waiting to use both of the services.

Required:
(a) Set out a linear programme which clearly indicates the company's objectives and constraints.

(b) Graph the data set out in the above problem.
(c) Suggest a use of resources compatible with the company's objectives, based on:
   (i) graphical methods;
   (ii) algebraic methods.

14 Budgetary planning and control

This chapter deals with the following topics:

14.1 The nature of budgetary planning.
14.2 The nature of budgeted expenses.
14.3 The budget process.
14.4 The nature of budgetary control.
14.5 Essentials of a budgetary control system.
14.6 The budget committee and budgetary control.
14.7 Constraints in setting budgets.
14.8 Master, functional and departmental budgets.
14.9 The importance of the sales forecast.
14.10 Preparing the master budget.
14.11 Evaluating budget proposals.
14.12 The revision of budgets.

14.1 THE NATURE OF BUDGETARY PLANNING

As explained in Part III, cost accounting has a major concern with product costing and with establishing cost accounting systems for accumulating product costs for management purposes, such as pricing products and costing contracts. Additionally, cost accounting data is used for a variety of other management decisions. As was noted in Chapter 12, the relationship of cost, volume and profit plays a vital role in understanding the nature of short-term profitability. These notions lie at the heart of budgetary planning.

Budgetary planning involves determining the desired volume of activity for the firm in the period immediately following the end of the current accounting period. It finds its expression in the 'annual operating plan' or 'budget'. A budget is defined as:

> 'a plan quantified in monetary terms, prepared and approved prior to a defined period of time, usually showing planned income to be generated and/or expenditure to be incurred during that period and the capital to be employed to attain a given objective.' (*Chartered Institute of Management Accountants' Terminology*)

A basic assumption of the budget is that the firm's productive capacity cannot be increased beyond the limits imposed by existing capital assets.

Budgetary planning should be distinguished from long-term planning, where the firm is able to consider changing the productive capacity by adding to existing plant through the process known as 'capital budgeting'. Budgetary planning integrates product cost information and product cost behaviour for the following purposes:

(a) determining the total level of expenditure at the desired activity level;
(b) expressing the desired output in terms of forecasted revenue;
(c) estimating the net operating profit on the basis of budgeted assumptions relating to expenditure and revenues.

The essence of budgetary planning lies in the setting of targets that the firm seeks to achieve in these three areas.

14.2 THE NATURE OF BUDGETED EXPENSES

The budget process begins with an attempt to forecast the level of activity or output that the firm should undertake. This is followed by an analysis of the expenditure implied by the desired output level. Accordingly, the cost elements that enter into the calculation of budgeted expenses are those that relate to product costing. Indeed, it would be impossible to prepare a budget without forecasts of product costs that would be incurred during the budget period.

Budgeted expenses and product costs differ in one important respect. Product costs are required to be expressed at the *unit level* for such management decisions as pricing. Budgeted expenses are required to be stated *at the cost centre level* for the purposes of enabling management to provide cost centre managers with an 'expense' or 'spending' allowance. Each cost centre has a budget: the firm's budget is the aggregate of the budget of its various cost centres. *At the firm level*, budgeted expenses are equal to forecasted product costs at the unit level multiplied by the budgeted output.

It will be recalled that product costs are determined by reference to the direct/indirect cost classification. The accumulation of product cost data is based on cost centres. Service cost centre costs have to be apportioned to production cost centres. Production cost centre costs are either direct or indirect to different products manufactured in production cost centres. Indirect production cost centre costs have to be apportioned to products and accumulated with direct costs in each production cost centre. It is seen, therefore, that the process of obtaining product cost information requires *breaking down* cost centre costs into product costs. By contrast, the process of determining budgeted expenses requires *building up* from product costs into cost centre costs by forecasting the direct and indirect costs that would be incurred at cost centre level at the budgeted volume of activity.

14.3 THE BUDGET PROCESS

The budget process is a cycle of management planning activity that is structured through a budget committee responsible for preparing budget estimates. It begins its work well in advance of the budget period, which is generally a period of 12 months that coincides with the firm's accounting year.

The budget cycle describes the manner in which agreement on budget proposals is obtained. The initial budget target may be proposed by the board of directors and passed through the lower managerial echelons before returning up for comment and decision. This type of budget cycle is described as 'top down'. 'Bottom up' means that the initial budget target is proposed by the lower echelons and moves up for discussion and final approval by the board of directors.

The term 'fixed budgeting' means that the firm's output level is fixed in terms of the expenses expected to be incurred by the budgeted output level. The budgeted volume is determined by taking into consideration all relevant factors, such as the level of market demand, the firm's productive capacity during the budget period and its profit expectations.

The budgeted expenses are estimates of cost centre costs expected to be incurred during the budget period. Estimates prepared by cost centre managers in response to requests formulated by the budget committee usually are closely examined by that committee to prevent cost centre managers from overstating their budget requirement and, as a result, obtaining a budget allowance greater than is needed for the budgeted level of output or activity. The manner is which cost centre budgets are prepared is critically important for achieving efficient cost performance. There are two ways in which such budgets can be prepared:

(a) By relying on past cost experience and projecting this experience forward into the budget by adjusting for price level increases. This approach assumes that cost centres are already operating at efficient levels of resource use.
(b) Exposing cost centre budgets to the requirement that budgeted expenses should represent an efficient level of resource use. This approach assumes that cost and expense standards have been set and that these standards reflect an acceptable level of efficiency in the use of resources.

14.4 THE NATURE OF BUDGETARY CONTROL

Budgetary planning assumes that there will be an effective system of budgetary control. Budgetary control may be given an extended meaning that refers not only to the manner in which the budget plan is prepared, but also the procedures that ensure that planned targets are attained. The Chartered Institute of Management Accountants (CIMA Terminology) defines budgetary control as:

> 'The establishment of budgets relating the responsibilities of executives to the requirements of a policy, and the continuous comparison of actual with budgeted results, either to secure by individual action the objectives of that policy, or to provide a basis for its revision.'

The term 'budgetary planning and control' is often used to describe the entirety of budget planning and control procedures that are concerned with the following interdependent functions:

(a) planning;
(b) co-ordination;
(c) communication;
(d) motivation;
(e) control.

14.5 ESSENTIALS OF A BUDGETARY CONTROL SYSTEM

The essential requirements for an effective budgetary control system needed to support the functions stated above are:

(a) Clearly defined organizational objectives.
(b) An organizational structure that clearly defines areas of authority and responsibility. Such a structure allows managers at all levels to be given specific responsibilities for particular functions or operations, but also for their related costs.
(c) Efficient accounting records and procedures. This implies a costing system that records, analyses and classifies actual costs by particular cost centres, thereby allowing actual cost performance to be compared with budgeted expenses by means of timely reports.
(d) Top management commitment to ensuring that the budgetary control procedures function effectively.
(e) Participation by cost centre managers in the budget process, thereby securing their commitment to attaining budget targets they have agreed.
(f) Flexibility in the manner in which budget targets are modified adjusted as circumstances change during the evolution of the budget period.

14.6 THE BUDGET COMMITTEE AND BUDGETARY CONTROL

Generally, the budget committee is appointed to steer the budget preparation to a final budget recommendation, which is presented to the board of directors for approval. It is composed of managers representing major functions in the firm. Its exact status and authority is defined by the board of directors, but generally, it will be a standing committee charged with an on-going responsibility for budget preparation and for overseeing its evolution. Its principal functions are:

(a) establishing budget procedures and timetables;
(b) requesting, obtaining and scrutinizing budget estimates supplied by managers responsible for spending departments;
(c) suggesting revisions of budget estimates;
(d) preparing the final budget proposals for approval by the board of directors;
(e) exercising overall budgetary control by comparing budgeted targets with periodic reports of actual performance;
(f) recommending corrective action to deal with variances between budgeted and actual performance.

Day-to-day responsibility for budget administration lies with the *budget officer*, whose duties are as follows:

(a) acting as secretary to the budget committee;
(b) co-ordinating all budget activities;
(c) issuing budget instructions in accordance with the budget programme;
(d) providing the forms and schedules in which budget details are to be accumulated;
(e) establishing timetables for submission of budget estimates;
(f) assisting departmental managers in preparing budget estimates for their department;
(g) assembling and publishing the master budget and its supporting schedules;
(h) comparing actual performance with budgeted targets;
(i) evaluating, interpreting and reporting to the budget committee;
(j) regularly reviewing the budget manual (see below) and making such modifications as are necessary to improve budgetary control procedures.

14.6.1 The budget manual

It is common practice for the budget officer to prepare a budget manual as a reference guide for all staff connected with the budgetary control system. The budget manual includes:

(a) a description of the budgetary control system and its objectives;
(b) the procedures to be followed in determining budgets;
(c) the organizational structure defining the responsibilities of specific personnel for aspects of budgetary control procedures;
(d) bases and methods for calculating budgets estimates, as well as supporting accounting policies;
(e) reports required for each reporting period.

14.6.2 Budget centres

Budgetary control requires that budget centres be established. These are similar to cost centres, save that they must relate to areas of authority and individual responsibility. For example, a cost centre under the management of a foreman would be a budget centre, as would be likewise an office in the charge of an office manager. Therefore, a budget centre is a segment of an organization for which a separate budget can be prepared.

14.6.3 The budget period

The budget period should be short enough to permit reasonably accurate predictions to be made. Yet, it should also be long enough to allow time for implementation. For practical purposes, the budget period should coincide with the firm's fiscal year to allow actual results obtained from accounting records to be compared to budget estimates.

Usually, the operating budget is prepared for a full year. Supporting schedules are broken into monthly or quarterly periods. Capital expenditure budgets or project budgets are usually developed for the longer periods of time over which long-lived assets or large projects last.

14.7 CONSTRAINTS IN SETTING BUDGETS

Two important constraints have to be considered when setting budgets, as follows:

(a) limiting factors;
(b) human relations.

14.7.1 Limiting factors

Restrictions on the ability of the firm to develop profit maximizing budgets are known as 'limiting factors'. Such limiting factors may be in the form of market, production constraints or other obstacles that prevent the firm from attaining its maximum profit potential. The failure to recognize limiting factors when setting budgets will negate completely the main objective of budgetary planning, which is to provide the firm with a realistic and attainable annual operating plan.

EXAMPLE 14.1:
X plc has established a sales organization capable of selling 10 000 units of product A at a price that would yield a high profit margin. Existing use of plant capacity limits output of product A to 7000 units. The budget committee is faced with dealing with this limiting factor when setting budget targets for the marketing department and the factory, as follows:

(a) limit the sales budget to 7000 units of product A; or
(b) expand factory production of product A by altering the existing use of plant capacity.

A limiting factor of such over-riding importance that it affects the entire budget planning process is known as the *principal budget factor* or *key factor*. It must be taken into account at the beginning of the budgeting cycle.

Examples of limiting factors and means of dealing with them are as given in Exhibit 14.1.

Exhibit 14.1 Limiting factors and their elimination

Limiting factor	*Means of elimination*
Demand for product	Extra advertising, new products or new markets
Supply of skilled labour	Higher pay rates or increased mechanization
Supply of materials	New sources of supplies, or alternative materials
Plant capacity	Expand capacity or subcontract

14.7.2 Human relations in budgeting

Budgets are intended to co-ordinate and motivate managerial effort throughout the firm towards attaining budgeted targets. Budgetary control procedures are also used to evaluate managerial performance. Hence, effective budgetary planning and control requires the active co-operation of staff and their commitment to budget objectives. Mistrust will lead to dysfunctional behaviour in the form of budget biasing resulting from the exaggeration of spending estimates and distorted performance reports. The reasons for such mistrust are related generally to the management style found in different firms. The reduction of areas of conflict between the objectives of the firm expressed in the budget and a manager's own personal objectives will depend on the extent to which the firm allows participation in fixing budget targets.

14.8 MASTER, FUNCTIONAL AND DEPARTMENTAL BUDGETS

The master budget for the firm as a whole takes the form of:

(a) a projected profit and loss account for the budget period;
(b) a projected balance sheet at the end of the budget period;
(c) in most cases, a projected funds statement for the budget period.

Functional budgets for the different functions, such as sales, production, material purchases, etc., are segments of the master budget. They aggregate budget estimates developed for the various departments that have been defined as budget centres. The number and size

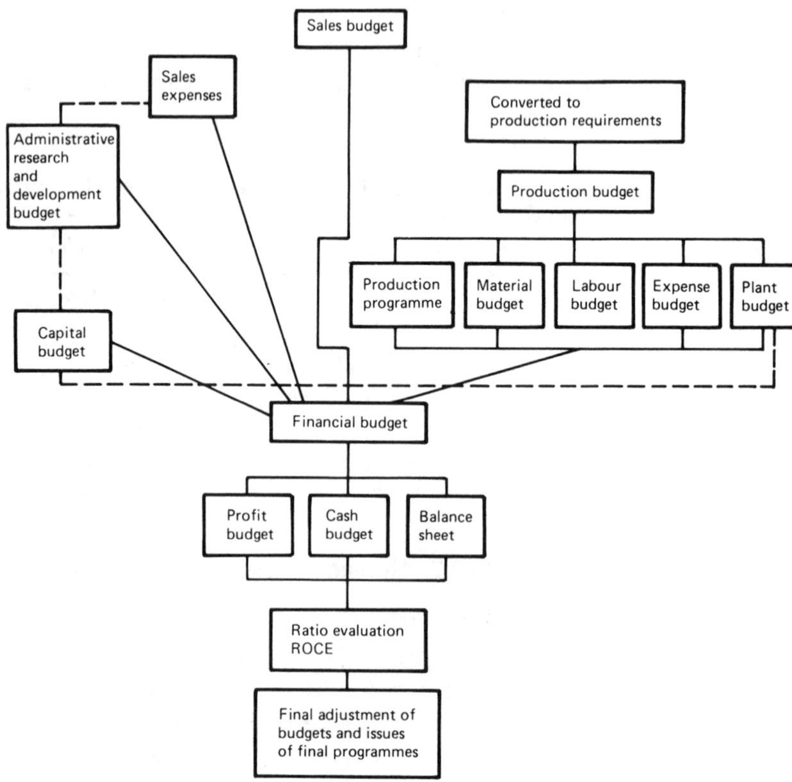

Exhibit 14.2 Interrelationship of master and functional budget.

of budget centres will depend on the nature of the firm's business. Exhibit 14.2 illustrates the interrelationship of master and functional budgets.

Exhibit 14.2 shows the flow of information relevant to budget planning. The process begins with the sales budget, which is based on the sales forecast. Thereafter, the sales expenses budget and the production budget can be prepared. On the production side, five functional budgets are dependent on fixing the production budget. Capital budgets that are concerned with increasing productive capacity over longer time periods are brought in as separate considerations that affect the financial budget. Exhibit 14.2 also shows how the financial budget leads into an overall evaluation of budgeted profitability expressed as a return on capital employed.

14.9 THE IMPORTANCE OF THE SALES FORECAST

Knowledge of the likely level of demand for the firm's products and services is critically important for budgetary planning and control. Indeed, the entire financial viability of the firm is at stake. If market demand is overstated, the firm may have committed itself to producing surpluses that cannot be sold and will face consequent financial losses. If market demand is underestimated, the firm may not be able to supply all its clients, and in addition to losing the opportunity to make profits, it may lose part of its market to competitors.

Difficulties in forecasting accurately the level of demand for the budget period lie in the nature of factors that are mostly outside the firm's control. These include market trends, the economic climate and the intentions of competitors.

The sales forecast is the initial stage in preparing the sales budget. It requires, among other things, a knowledge of market demand for the firm's goods and services at different prices. In view of business risks attached to incorrect sales forecasting, particular efforts have been made in recent years to develop improved forecasting techniques. Commonly known methods of sales forecasting include:

(a) *The sales force composite method*, in which individual salesmen participate in developing estimates of market demand for their own estimates of what clients will require in the budget period.
(b) *Analysis of market and industry factors*, in which factors outside the knowledge of salesmen are taken into account for modifying salesmen's estimates. These factors include forecasts of gross national product, personal incomes, employment and price levels.

(c) *Statistical analyses of market trends.* Four basic factors affect sales forecasts: growth trends, business cycle fluctuations, seasonal fluctuations and irregular variations in demand. Time series analyses are useful for examining the impact of these factors on sales, and for testing the quality of the sales forecast.
(d) *Computer-based sales forecasting analyses,* using various mathematical techniques for arriving at sales projections for the budget period.

14.10 PREPARING THE MASTER BUDGET

From the perspective of budgeting, the firm is assumed to be 'sales-led'. The forecasted level of market demand for the firm's goods and services in turn determine the firm's own output target and its resource needs. For the purpose of the annual operating budget or plan, it is assumed that productive capacity is relatively fixed.

The budgeting process for the forthcoming period begins during the current period. The experience of actual performance against budget for the current period will influence the budget preparation to the extent to which cost and other figures will have to be adjusted. Moreover, price level changes will also have to be anticipated. For these reasons, the preparation of budgets will encounter quite sophisticated forecasting problems.

The budgeting cycle can best be understood through a simplified illustration in which budget components are bought together in constructing the master budget.

EXAMPLE 14.2:
Bostow Industries Ltd is a privately controlled engineering company manufacturing two products known as Rextran and Straco. The company has a budget organization consisting of five budget centres. The factory is organized into three budget centres, as follows:

(a) two budget centres that are also production cost centres: the machining department and the finishing department;
(b) one budget centre for overhead costs.

The two non-factory budget centres are:

(a) administrative expenses;
(b) selling expenses.

The budget period coincides with the accounting year that ends 31 December 19X4. The budget cycle begins on 1 September 19X4 prior to the end of the current budget period, and the master budget is agreed at the monthly meeting of the board of directors that takes place on 1 December 19X4. Thereafter, the budget officer issues formal budget instructions to managers responsible for budget centres.

The budget forecasts for the current budget period ending 31 December 19X4, adjusted for changes in forecast results as at 1 September 19X4 are as follows:

Exhibit 14.3 Budget forecast 19X4

Bostow Industries Ltd
Forecast results for the year ending 31 December 19X4

Profit and loss account

	£	£	£
Sales		135 000	
Cost of goods sold		80 000	
Gross margin		55 000	
Selling and administrative expenses		25 000	
Income before tax		30 000	
Tax at 40%		12 000	
Profit after tax		18 000	

Balance sheet

Fixed assets			
Plant and machinery		250 000	
Less: Accumulated depreciation		30 000	220 000
Current assets			
Stocks			
Finished goods		6 025	
Raw materials		1 650	
		7 675	
Debtors		20 000	
Cash		5 325	
		33 000	
Less: Current liabilities			
Sundry creditors	5 000		
Tax	12 000	17 000	
Net current assets			16 000
			236 000
Capital and reserves			
Ordinary share capital		210 000	
Retained profit		26 000	
			236 000

From these forecasts, the budgeted profitability of the company for the year 19X4 may be calculated as follows:

$$\text{return on shareholders' equity: } \frac{\pounds 18\ 000}{\pounds 236\ 000} = 7.6\%$$

$$\text{return on capital employed: } \frac{\pounds 18\ 000}{\pounds 253\ 000} = 7.1\%$$

The budget committee holds its regular meeting on the first Monday of each month. Timetabling requires the sales forecast to be agreed at the October meeting of the budget committee. The following sales forecast has been confirmed at the October 19X4 meeting as the basis for preparing the budget period ending 31 December 19X5:

Exhibit 14.4 Sales forecast 19X5

	Rextran	*Straco*
Expected selling price per unit	£11	£14
Sales volume forecast:		
1st quarter	1500 units	2000 units
2nd quarter	1000 "	2000 "
3rd quarter	1000 "	2000 "
4th quarter	1500 "	2000 "
Total for the year	5000 "	8000 "

The company's budget manual contains specific instructions relating to the preparation of functional budgets and budgeted financial results. The relevant chapters in the budget manual are as follows:

Exhibit 14.5 Budget manual

Chapter 1. The sales budget.
Chapter 2. The production budget.
Chapter 3. The direct materials usage budget.
Chapter 4. The materials purchases budget.
Chapter 5. The budgeted direct labour costs.
Chapter 6. The overhead costs budget.
Chapter 7. The closing stocks budget.
Chapter 8. The selling and administrative costs budget.
Chapter 9. The capital expenditure budget.
Chapter 10. The cost of goods sold budget.
Chapter 11. The cash budget.
Chapter 12. The budgeted profit and loss account.
Chapter 13. The budgeted balance sheet.

14.10.1 Preparing the sales budget

The sales budget was prepared from the sales forecast for 19X5 as follows:

Exhibit 14.6 Sales budget

		1st quarter	*2nd quarter*	*3rd quarter*	*4th quarter*	*Total*
Units						
Rextran		1 500	1 000	1 000	1 500	5 000
Straco		2 000	2 000	2 000	2 000	8 000
Value						
Rextran	(£11)	£16 500	£11 000	£11 000	£16 500	£55 000
Straco	(£14)	28 000	28 000	28 000	28 000	112 000
		£44 500	£39 000	£39 000	£44 500	£167 000

14.10.2 Preparing the production budget

The budgeted output volume comprises the units required by the sales forecast and the units required by the stock forecast. The opening stock is estimated as follows:

Rextran: 750 units
Straco: 1000 units.

Exhibit 14.7 Production budget

	1st quarter	*2nd quarter*	*3rd quarter*	*4th quarter*	*Year*
Rextran			(Units)		
Desired closing stocks (units)	500	500	750	750	750
Add: Sales	1500	1000	1000	1500	5000
Total required	2000	1500	1750	2250	5750
Less: Opening stocks	750	500	500	750	750
Production required	1250	1000	1250	1500	5000
Straco					
Desired closing stocks (units)	1000	1000	1000	1000	1000
Add: Sales	2000	2000	2000	2000	8000
Total required	3000	3000	3000	3000	9000
Less: Opening stocks	1000	1000	1000	1000	1000
Production required	2000	2000	2000	2000	8000

The closing stock stock level for both products at the end of each quarter is to be maintained at a level equal to half the expected sales for the next quarter. The production requirement is given in Exhibit 14.7.

14.10.3 Budgeted factory costs

Estimates required for the preparation of the budgeted factory costs have to be made available for approval at the November meeting of the budget committee. These estimates are as follows:

(a) Materials purchase budget
The purpose of this budget is to determine the quantities and value of raw material purchases required to meet the production budget. The following information is available:

Standard quantities:
Raw material X: Two units for each unit of Rextran.
Raw material Y: Three units for each unit of Straco.
Estimated costs:
Raw material X: £0.50 per unit.
Raw material Y: £0.30 per unit.
Opening raw material stocks:
Raw material X: Estimated at 1500 units.
Raw material Y: Estimated at 3000 units.
Closing raw material stocks:
Raw material X: Estimated at 1500 units.
Raw material Y: Estimated at 3000 units.

The usage rate of raw materials is obtained from the production budget and is stated in the direct materials usage budget in Exhibit 14.8.

Exhibit 14.8 Direct material usage budget

	1st quarter	*2nd quarter*	*3rd quarter*	*4th quarter*	*Year*
Material X					
(2 units for Rextran)	2 500	2 000	2 500	3 000	10 000
Material Y					
(3 units for Straco)	6 000	6 000	6 000	6 000	24 000

The materials purchases budget is prepared as shown in Exhibit 14.9.

Exhibit 14.9 Material purchases budget

	1st quarter	*2nd quarter*	*3rd quarter*	*4th quarter*	*Year*
Raw Material X					
Desired closing stocks	1 000	1 000	1 500	1 500	1 500
Add: Material usage (Chap 3)	2 500	2 000	2 500	3 000	10 000
Total required	3 500	3 000	4 000	4 500	11 500
Less: Opening stocks	1 500	1 000	1 000	1 500	1 500
Purchases required (units)	2 000	2 000	3 000	3 000	10 000
Price per unit	£0.50	£0.50	£0.50	£0.50	£0.50
Total purchases (value)	£1 000	£1 000	£1 500	£1 500	£5 000
Raw Material Y					
Desired closing stocks	3 000	3 000	3 000	3 000	3 000
Add: Material usage (Chap 3)	6 000	6 000	6 000	6 000	24 000
Total required	9 000	9 000	9 000	9 000	27 000
Less: Opening stocks	3 000	3 000	3 000	3 000	3 000
Purchase required (units)	6 000	6 000	6 000	6 000	24 000
Price per unit	£0.30	£0.30	£0.30	£0.30	£0.30
Total purchases (value)	£1 800	£1 800	£1 800	£1 800	£7 200
Total purchases (value)	£2 800	£2 800	£3 300	£3 300	£12 200

(b) Budgeted direct labour costs

This budget is based on a calculation of the direct labour requirement per product unit, forecast of labour rates during the budget period and the production requirement indicated by the production budget. The direct labour requirement and the direct labour budget are shown in Exhibits 14.10 and 14.11.

Exhibit 14.10 Direct labour requirement per unit

	Direct labour required per unit of product		*Departmental wage rate*	*Direct labour cost per unit of output*	
	in labour hours		£	£	
	Rextran	Straco		Rextran	Straco
Preparation department	1/5	1/2	£2 per hour	£0.40	£1.00
Machining department	1/2	1/2	£2 per hour	£1.00	£1.00
				£1.40	£2.00

Exhibit 14.11 Budgeted direct labour costs

	1st quarter	*2nd quarter*	*3rd quarter*	*4th quarter*	*Year*
Production (Chap 2)					
Rextran	1 250	1 000	1 250	1 500	5 000
Straco	2 000	2 000	2 000	2 000	8 000
Labour hours					
Preparation department					
Rextran (1/5)	250	200	250	300	1 000
Straco (1/2)	1 000	1 000	1 000	1 000	4 000
Total	1 250	1 200	1 250	1 300	5 000
Machining department					
Rextran (1/2)	625	500	625	750	2 500
Straco (1/2)	1 000	1 000	1 000	1 000	4 000
Total	1 625	1 500	1 625	1 750	6 500
Direct labour costs					
Preparation department					
Labour hours	1 250	1 200	1 250	1 300	5 000
Wage rate/hour	£2	£2	£2	£2	£2
Direct labour cost	£2 500	£ 2400	£2 500	£2 600	£10 000
Machining department					
Labour hours	1 625	1 500	1 625	1 750	6 500
Wage rate/hour	£2	£2	£2	£2	£2
Direct labour cost	£3 250	£3 000	£3 250	£3 500	£13 000
Total direct labour cost	£5 750	£5 400	£5 750	£6 100	£23 000

(c) Overhead costs budget

This budget relies on forecasts of variable and fixed overhead costs. They are given in Exhibit 14.12.

Exhibit 14.12 Overhead cost forecast

Fixed overheads		
Depreciation	£10 000	per annum
Rates and insurances	4 000	
Supervisory salaries	6 000	
	£20 000	

Variable overheads

	Cost per unit of output Rextran	Straco
	£	£
Indirect labour Indirect material Repairs and maintenance Power	£0.50	£1.00

Budgeted variable costs are calculated from the estimated variable costs per unit multiplied by the planned quarterly output. Fixed overhead costs are incurred in equal quarterly amounts. Exhibit 14.13 shows the overhead cost budget.

Exhibit 14.13 Overhead costs budget

	1st quarter	*2nd quarter*	*3rd quarter*	*4th quarter*	*Year*
Production (Chap 2)					
Rextran (units)	1 250	1 000	1 250	1 500	5 000
Straco (units)	2 000	2 000	2 000	2 000	8 000
Variable costs					
Rextran					
(£0.50 per unit)	£625	£500	£625	£750	£2 500
Straco					
(£1.00 per unit)	2 000	2 000	2 000	2 000	8 000
Total	2 625	2 500	2 625	2 750	10 500

	1st quarter	*2nd quarter*	*3rd quarter*	*4th quarter*	*Year*
Fixed costs					
Depreciation	2 500	2 500	2 500	2 500	10 000
Rates and insurance	1 000	1 000	1 000	1 000	4 000
Supervisory salaries	1 500	1 500	1 500	1 500	6 000
Total	5 000	5 000	5 000	5 000	20 000
Total overhead costs	£7 625	£7 500	£7 625	£7 750	£30 500

14.10.4 Preparing the closing stock budget

The closing stock budget is composed of:

(a) raw material stock;
(b) finished goods stock.

(a) Closing raw material stock

Exhibit 14.14 Budgeted closing raw material stock

Raw material	*X*	*Y*	
Closing stocks (units)	1500	3000	
Cost per unit	£0.50	£0.30	
Value of closing stocks	£750	£900	
Total			£1650

(b) Closing stock of finished goods

Closing stocks of finished goods are to be valued on a variable costing basis as follows:

	Rextran	*Straco*
	£	£
Raw materials	1.00	0.90
Direct labour	1.40	2.00
Variable overheads	0.50	1.00
	2.90	3.90

The value of the closing stock of finished goods is shown in Exhibit 14.15.

Exhibit 14.15 Budgeted finished goods stock

Product	*A*	*B*	
Closing stocks (units)	750	1000	
Cost per unit	£2.90	£3.90	
Value of closing stocks	£2175	£3900	
Total			£6075

14.10.5 Preparing the budgeted profit and loss account

The budgeted profit and loss account is prepared from the following component budgets:

(a) the sales budget;
(b) the cost of goods sold budget;
(c) the selling and administrative expenses budget.

The sales budget has already been prepared.

(a) The cost of goods sold budget
This budget is prepared as shown in Exhibit 14.16.

Exhibit 14.16 Cost of goods sold budget

	£
Opening raw materials stocks (balance sheet 31/12/19X0)	1 650
Add: Materials purchases	12 200
Raw materials available for production	13 850
Less: Planned closing stocks of raw materials	1 650
Cost of raw materials to be used in production	12 200
Cost of direct labour	23 000
Factory overhead costs	30 500
Cost of goods to be manufactured	65 700
Add: Opening stocks of finished goods (balance sheet 31/12/19X0)	6 025
	71 725
Less: Planned closing stocks of finished goods	6 075
Budgeted cost of goods sold	£65 650

(b) The selling and administrative expenses budget
This budget is prepared from data given in Exhibit 14.17.

Exhibit 14.7 Administrative and selling costs budget

	£	£
(a) *Administrative costs*		
Office salaries	18 000	
Stationery	1 000	
Other	1 000	20 000
(b) *Selling costs*		
Salaries	15 000	
Advertising	5 000	20 000
		40 000

These three budgets are combined to produce the budgeted profit and loss account budget of Exhibit 14.18.

Exhibit 14.18 Budgeted profit and loss account

Sales	£167 000
Cost of goods sold	65 650
Gross margin	101 350
Selling and administrative expenses	40 000
Net income before tax	61 350
Tax (40%)	24 540
Net profit after tax	£36 810

14.10.6 The cash budget

The importance of the cash budget is that it integrates the financial implications of the totality of the firm's activities during the budget period. It defines and describes key expenditure accounts by nature and indicates the financing requirement across the budget period. Hence, its significance is as a basic tool for financial management analysis across the budget period. It shows the time profile of cash receipts and cash payments. Forecast cash balances at the end of each month or quarter are incorporated with the cash receipts and cash payments to indicate the net borrowing requirement that has to be financed or the net cash surplus for which suitable short-term investments will have to be found.

Three major sector activities are brought together in the cash budget:

(a) The financial implications of the operations budget or plan that stem from the budgeted output volume.
(b) The financial implications of the 'capacity growth plan' or capital expenditure budget, agreed by the board of directors.
(c) The tax implications that define the firm's overall tax liability and take into account both (a) and (b) above. Regulations relating to actual tax payments will determine when payments actually fall due.

(i) Cash implications of budgeted operations

These are derived from the cash receipts and cash payments related to operations and include cash receipts from debtors and cash payments to creditors as follows:

(*a*) *Sales receipts*
50% of sales received in cash during month of sale.
50% of sales received in cash in the following month.

(*b*) *Cash expenditure*
Production costs
Direct labour, direct materials and variable overheads paid in the month in which incurred. Fixed overheads paid in equal amounts quarterly.
Administrative and selling costs
Paid in equal amounts quarterly.
Other costs
Tax outstanding amounting to £12 000 will be paid off in equal quarterly instalments over the year.

(*c*) *Sundry creditors*
The balance outstanding to sundry creditors will remain at a constant amount of £5000 throughout the year.

(ii) Capital expenditure budget

The capital expenditure budget prepared from information given is as shown in Exhibit 14.19.

Exhibit 14.19 Capital expenditure budget

Capital expenditure	
1st quarter	£10 000
2nd quarter	15 000
3rd quarter	8 000
4th quarter	20 000
Total for the year	£53 000

The cash budget is as shown in Exhibit 14.20.

Exhibit 14.20 Cash budget

	1st quarter	*2nd quarter*	*3rd quarter*	*4th quarter*	*Total*
	£	£	£	£	£
Opening cash balance	5 325	10 900	11 450	15 275	5 325
Receipts:					
Debtors (balance sheet)	20 000	—	—	—	20 000
50% of current sales	22 250	19 500	19 500	22 250	83 500
50% of previous quarter	—	22 250	19 500	19 500	61 250
Total receipts	42 250	41 750	39 000	41 750	164 750
Total cash available	47 575	52 650	50 450	57 025	170 075
Payments:					
Purchases	2 800	2 800	3 300	3 300	12 200
Direct labour	5 750	5 400	5 750	6 100	23 000
Factory overheads (excluding depreciation)	5 125	5 000	5 125	5 250	20 500
Selling and administrative expenses	10 000	10 000	10 000	10 000	40 000
Capital expenditure	10 000	15 000	8 000	20 000	53 000
Tax (balance sheet)	3 000	3 000	3 000	3 000	12 000
Total payments	36 675	41 200	35 175	47 650	160 700
Closing cash balances	10 900	11 450	15 275	9 375	9 375

14.10.7 Budgeted balance sheet

The budget planning process ends with a forecast of the financial status of the firm at the close of the budget period (Exhibit 14.21).

Exhibit 14.21 Budgeted balance sheet

Fixed assets	*Cost*	*Provision for depreciation*		
	£	£	£	£
Plant and machinery	303 000	40 000	263 000	
Current assets				
Stocks		£		
Raw materials		1 650		
Finished goods		6 075		
Debtors		22 250		
Cash		9 375		
		39 350		

Fixed assets	*Cost*	*Provision for depreciation*		
Total b/d	£	£	£	£
		39 350	263 000	
Less: Current liabilities				
Sundry creditors	5 000			
Tax outstanding	24 540			
		29 540		
Net current assets			9 810	
				272 810
Capital and reserves				
Ordinary share capital			210 000	
Retained profit			62 810	
				272 810

14.11 EVALUATING BUDGET PROPOSALS

The budget may be evaluated as a financial plan interpreted in terms of profitability. This may be seen from the viewpoint of shareholders, as a planned return on shareholders' equity, and also as a planned return on capital employed, as follows:

$$\text{return on shareholders equity: } \frac{£36\ 810}{£272\ 810} = 13.5\% \text{ (previous 7.6\%)}$$

$$\text{return on capital employed: } \frac{£36\ 810}{£302\ 350} = 12.2\% \text{ (previous 7.1\%)}$$

Evaluated in these terms, it is evident that the budget proposals reflect the firm's intentions to improve profitability considerably in the year 19X5.

14.12 THE REVISION OF BUDGETS

To be an effective means of control, budgets should reflect closely the underlying conditions that influence the activities and costs. If these conditions change during the budget period, and as a result, actual activities and actual costs differ from budget, the budget's usefulness as an instrument of control is undermined. For example, changes in sales or production volume or in production costs may completely invalidate budgeted profitability. Hence, budget revisions are required when conditions on which the budget is based change.

Questions

1. Explain the nature of budgetary planning.
2. What is an annual operating plan?
3. What is the essence of budgetary planning?
4. What cost elements enter into the budgetary planning process?
5. Explain the nature and purpose of budgeted expenses.
6. Define the budget process.
7. Distinguish product costs and cost centre costs in the context of budgetary planning.
8. What is the role of the budget committee?
9. Define budgetary control.
10. Explain the term 'budgetary planning and control'.
11. What are the essentials of a budgetary control system?
12. List the duties of the budget officer.
13. Explain the purposes of the following:

    (a) the budget manual;
    (b) budget centres;
    (c) budget period.

14. Name two important constraints in setting budgets.
15. What is meant by the term 'principal budget factor'?
16. What is the role of the following budgets:

    (a) the master budget;
    (b) functional budgets;
    (c) departmental budgets.

17. Explain the importance of the sales forecast.
18. List three commonly known methods of sales forecasting.
19. Describe briefly the contents of the following budgets:

    (a) the sales budget;
    (b) the production budget;
    (c) the material usage budget.

20. What difficulties could be found in determining the overhead cost budget?
21. What is the purpose of the cash budget?
22. What methods exist for evaluating budgets?

Problems

1. Discuss the advantages you would expect to result from the introduction of a system of budgetary control into a small factory producing a variety of products. Detail the difficulties you are likely to encounter in setting up and operating such a system.
2. The managing director of a small manufacturing company has

recognized the benefits to the company, of introducing a formal and comprehensive system of budgeting and he has asked for your advice on how to implement the system.

Required:
To assist the managing director:
(a) Discuss the role of the budget committee, and explain the duties of an accountant responsible for administering the company's budgeting system. (9 marks)
(b) As an indication of the data and sequencing requirements of the budgeting process describe the information required to construct the materials purchase budget. (8 marks)
(Total 17 marks)

(Chartered Association of Certified Accountants)

3. A company manufactures three products X, Y and Z. The budgets are currently being prepared for 19X7 and estimates have been submitted for sales, costs and output.

From the data provided below you are required to prepare two statements to show:
(i) the expected profit if the original budget is pursued;
(ii) the expected profit at maximum sales demand.

The standard cost per unit is as follows:

Product	*X*	*Y*	*Z*
Direct materials: Aye	8	6	6
Bee	2	4	2
Cee	6	2	4
Direct wages	8	10	12
Variable overhead	6	8	8
Fixed overhead	12	15	18

Fixed overhead is absorbed as a percentage of direct wages and is based on the original budget.

	Units	*Units*	*Units*
Budgeted output for 19X7	8 000	6 000	10 000
Maximum sales demand (estimated)	10 000	7 500	12 500
	£	£	£
Sales price	40	50	60

(15 marks)

(Chartered Institute of Management Accountants)

4. R Ltd manufactures three products, A, B and C.

Required:

(a) Using the information given below, prepare budgets for the month of January for:

(i) sales in quantity and value, including total value;
(ii) production quantities;
(iii) material usage in quantities;
(iv) material purchases in quantity and value, including total value;

(N.B. Particular attention should be paid to your layout of the budgets.)

(b) Explain the term principal budget factor and state what it was assumed to be in (a) of this question.

Data for preparation of January budgets

Sales	*Product*	*Quantity*	*Price each (£)*
	A	1000	100
	B	2000	120
	C	1500	140

Materials used in the company's products are:

Material		M1	M2	M3
Unit cost		£4	£6	£9
Quantities used in:		units	units	units
Product: A		4	2	—
B		3	3	2
C		2	1	1
Finished stocks:	*Product*	*A*	*B*	*C*
Quantities:				
1 January		1 000	1 500	500
31 January		1 000	1 650	550
Material stocks:		M1	M2	M3
		units	units	units
1 January		26 000	20 000	12 000
31 January		31 200	24 000	14 400

(20 marks)

(*Chartered Institute of Management Accountants*)

5. Shown below are extracts from next year's budget for a company manufacturing two products using only one grade of direct labour.

	1st quarter	*2nd quarter*	*3rd quarter*	*4th quarter*
	Units	Units	Units	Units
Sales: Product M	9 000	20 000	14 000	8 000
Product N	10 000	16 500	11 000	7 000
Finished goods stocks have been provisionally budgeted for each quarter end as follows:				
Product M	5 000	5 000	4 000	4 000
Product N	4 000	4 000	2 000	2 000

The stock of finished goods at the beginning of the first quarter is expected to be 3000 units of product M and 1000 units of product N. Stocks of work-in-progress are not carried.

Inspection is the final operation for product M and it is budgeted that 20 per cent of production will be scrapped. Product N is not inspected and no rejects occur.

The company employs 210 direct operatives working a basic 40-hour week for 12 weeks in each quarter and the maximum overtime permitted is 12 hours per week for each operative. The company has an agreement with the union that operatives will not be made redundant, temporarily paid off, or any more recruited for the next 2 years.

The standard direct labour hour content of product M is 5 hours per unit and for product N, 3 hours per unit. The budgeted productivity (or efficiency) ratio for the direct operatives is 90 per cent.

It should be assumed that both products are profitable.

Required:

(a) Calculate the budgeted direct labour hours required in each quarter of next year and show the extent to which the direct labour hours available can meet these budgeted requirements. (8 marks)

(b) (i) Examine alternative courses of action which may minimize the shortfall or surplus of labour hours available and which also allows the company to achieve each quarter's sales budget whenever possible. Where appropriate, calculations should be shown to support your analysis. Use only the information available in the question.

(10 marks)

(ii) Assuming that the budgeted sales cannot be achieved in every quarter explain how you could minimize the effect of the labour shortfall on the company's profits. Briefly comment upon any reservations you may have concerning your recommendations.

(4 marks)

(Total 22 marks)

(Chartered Association of Certified Accountants)

6. (a) (i) Explain the purpose of a cash budget;

(3 marks)

(ii) From what principal source is the cash budget prepared?

(3 marks)

(b) On 31 December 19X4, the summary balance sheet of Kingsley & Dickens Ltd. booksellers, was as follows:

	£		£
Capital	10 000	Shop equipment	3 750
Creditors	5 000	Stock of books	6 000
Proposed dividends	750	Debtors	3 750
		Cash in bank	2 250
	15 750		15 750

The following transactions are anticipated for the next three months:

	Credit sales	*Cash sales*	*Credit purchases*	*Cash purchases*
Jan.	£3750	£3500	£6000	£500
Feb.	4500	1250	5750	250
March	5000	3000	6750	250

Additionally, you are informed:

Wages paid will be £250 per month.

Postage and packing is to be 20 per cent of credit sales, and paid in the month of sale.

Debtors normally pay 1 month after books are sold to them.
Creditors are paid 1 month after receipt of books.
Shop equipment will be replaced on 1 January. The new equipment will cost £6000 and payment will be made in equal instalments in February, March and April. The old equipment will realize £2000 in February.
Depreciation of the new equipment will be 10 per cent per annum and charged to accounts monthly.
Half the dividends proposed will be paid in March, half in July next. The company expects a gross profit of 33⅓ per cent on selling price.

Required:

(i) A cash budget for 3 months ending 31 March 19X5; (6 marks)

(ii) a forecast trading and profit and loss account; (6 marks)

(iii) a forecast balance sheet at 31 March 19X5. (6 marks)

(c) Miss Kingsley cannot understand why the cash balance does not equate with the profit and loss account surplus. How would you respond? (4 marks)

(Total 28 marks)

(*Association of Accounting Technicians*)

7. James Johnson, a skilled engineer with many years experience of his trade, has recently been made redundant, but proposes to start his own small business commencing on 1 July 19X2. He is aware that money will be a problem and asks you to help him produce a cash forecast in the form of a budget over the next 6 months.

He provides you with the following actions he proposes to take:

(i) The business will commence with £75 000 in the bank made up of his personal savings, redundancy pay and a loan of £10 000 obtained to aid small businesses. This is the maximum obtainable and cannot be increased in the 6 month period. He will immediately pay a deposit of £30 000 on a building for conversion into a workshop and commencing 15 July, a £250 per month mortgage repayment. He will also purchase plant, valued at £18 000 and a motor van for £8000. Other immediate payments to cover lubricating oil, stationery, a typewriter, etc. will be £2000 and he expects to pay £150 per month on such items from August onwards.

(ii) Four staff will be employed, each paid £500 per month paid on the last day of the month. Staff costs will be 10 per cent of salaries and this is due the month after payment of salaries.

(iii) Purchases of raw materials on credit and paid 1 month after receipt will be:

July	*Aug.*	*Sept.*	*Oct.*	*Nov.*	*Dec.*
£18 000	£13 000	£16 000	£16 000	£16 000	£18 000

(iv) Another machine costing £14 000 will be paid for in October.

(v) Sales (in units)

July	*Aug.*	*Sept.*	*Oct.*	*Nov.*	*Dec.*
2000	2500	2500	2000	3000	3000

Fifty per cent of units will be sold for £10 each and cash received in the month following sale, 50 per cent will sell at £12 each, receivable 2 months after sale.

(vi) Johnson will draw £600 per month and there will be an additional £70 per month payable 1 month in arrears.

(vii) Advertising will be £2000 per month for the first 3 months and £100 per month thereafter, paid for in the month incurred.

(viii) Interest on the loan is 1½ per cent per month, payable on the 15th of each month commencing July, but half the loan capital will be repaid on 31 October and the balance on 31 December.

Required:

(a) Construct a cash budget showing clearly the cash at bank position at the end of each month. (16 marks)

(b) Advise Johnson as to the results in the form of a brief report. (6 marks)

(Total 22 marks)

(*Association of Accounting Technicians*)

8. Mr Flower is a baker specializing in the production of his famous individual meat pies which he sells to shops throughout the area. Shown below is a summary of the previous year's budgeted and actual trading results, which Mr Flower has just received from his accountant.

	Budget		*Actual*	
	£	£	£	£
Sales		50 000		54 000
Operating costs:				
Materials	20 000		26 000	
Power	5 000		5 500	
Fixed overheads	15 000	40 000	17 000	48 500
Profit		£10 000		£5 500

Mr Flower is extremely worried by the above results, as at the beginning of the year, after the budget specified above had been prepaed he had decided to make several changes which he had anticipated would have increased the profitability of this business. The changes which he had made were:

(i) In order to increase the number of pies sold he reduced the selling price per pie from the budgeted 25p each to 22½p each.

(ii) In order to reduce operating costs he changed his supplier of materials and obtained a 20 per cent price reduction compared with that budgeted. Mr Flower was aware that the materials from the new supplier were of a lower quality and there would be a little more waste.

(iii) In an attempt to reduce power costs, which he regards as variable, he changed his method of working from that implied in the budget.

Required:

(a) Analyse the effect of the above changes on the year's profit, and produce a statement reconciling budgeted and actual profit in a manner which you consider would be most helpful to Mr Flower.

It should be assumed that the original budget shown above was an accurate estimate of the likely results based on the original assumptions.

(16 marks)

(b) Briefly comment on your analysis in (a) above.

(3 marks)

(c) Explain how you would measure the profitability of Mr Flower's business and identify any additional information which would be required in order to make the appropriate calculations.

(3 marks)
(Total 22 marks)

(Chartered Association of Certified Accountants)

9. Next year's preliminary budget workings for Scrunchie, a breakfast cereal, the only product manufactured by H.F. Ltd, are shown below.

H.F. Ltd.
Budgeted revenue account for the year ended 30 September 19X0

		£
Sales (20 000 boxes, containing standard packets)		600 000
	£	
Direct materials	240 000	
Direct labour	102 000	
Variable overhead	70 000	
Fixed overhead	122 200	534 200
Profit		£65 800

H.F. Ltd
Budgeted net assets as at 30 September 19X0

		£
Fixed Assets (net of depreciation)		310 000
Working capital:	£	
Debtors	50 000	
Stocks	65 000	
Creditors	(25 000)	90 000
Net assets employed		£400 000

The existing plant and equipment is considerably underutilized and a proposal being considered is to extend sales to supermarkets, where the product would be sold under a different brand name.

Estimated effects of this proposal are:

(i) additional annual sales, to supermarkets, 8000 boxes at £25 per box;

(ii) cost of direct materials will be reduced as a result of a 5 per cent quantity discount on all purchases;
(iii) extra supervisory and clerical staff will be required at a cost of £16 000 per annum;
(iv) market research has indicated that sales to existing outlets will fall by approximately 10 per cent, there will be no change in selling price to these customers;
(v) stocks and creditors will increase by £25 000 and £15 000, respectively, and the credit period extended to supermarkets will be double that given to existing customers.

Required:
Present data to assist in the evaluation of the proposal. Specifically you should:

(a) Prepare a revised budgeted revenue account and statement of net assets employed incorporating the results of the proposal.

(8 marks)

(b) Calculate the effect on profit of each of the changes resulting from the proposal and reconcile the total of these with the difference in budgeted profits.

(5 marks)

(c) Advise management on the suitability of the proposal making any further calculations you consider necessary and adding any other comments or reservations you think relevant.

(9 marks)
(Total 22 marks)

(*Chartered Association of Certified Accountants*)

15 Standard Costing and Variance Analysis

15.1 THE NATURE OF STANDARD COSTS

So far, it has been assumed that product costs are based on actual production costs, defined as costs actually incurred by the firm. Costs accounting records of actual production costs are in the form of invoices for goods and services used in the manufacturing process and in payroll records in respect of labour costs. Direct actual costs in the form of direct materials and direct labour costs are immediately identified with particular products: indirect actual costs are estimated on the basis of the expected volume of activity and allocated to products on an appropriate basis.

The problem of product costing on the basis of actual costs is that such costs may reflect inefficiencies in the use of resources. In effect, two types of inefficiencies may be hidden in actual costs. First, there may be purchasing inefficiencies whenever the 'best deal' is not obtained. This will arise whenever purchasing departments are not functioning effectively. Second, there may be inefficiencies in the use of resources in the production process. This will occur if the usage of raw materials, supplies and services is not exposed to some control, or if the factory workforce is not properly supervised.

Competition in the market place forces firms to be cost-conscious. Where prices are market-determined, firms compete on costs. To the extent that costs can be controlled at the firm level, management will seek production efficiency and profits through cost economies.

Standard costing is product costing that is based on the notion of 'efficient costs'. The notion of cost efficiency is introduced in standard product costs in two ways. First, spending on production resources is exposed to predetermined standards of efficiency. Second, the usage of production resources is required to be efficient in quantity terms.

EXAMPLE 15.1:
Axon Ltd manufactures a product for which actual costs are £20 per unit. Actual direct material costs are £7.50 per unit. The ruling market price is £21. Several firms are producing the same product, and appear to have more satisfactory profit levels than Axon. The product uses only one raw material. Data recorded in the costing system based on invoices received are analysed and show that actual purchase price is £1.50 per kg and that on average 5 kg are used in each unit of the product. On close investigation, it is found that the raw material could be purchased at £1.25 per kg. Consulting engineers report that there is excessive usage of 10 per cent, due to inexperienced operatives and faulty machine settings. Following these studies, corrective measures are taken to reduce direct material costs from £7.50 to £5.625 per unit. Proper training is given to operative and machine settings are adjusted and regularly checked.

A standard cost has two important characteristics. First, it represents an 'efficient cost' as explained in Example 15.1 Second, it is used to maintain an on-going control over production costs to prevent inefficiencies occurring. The control feature of standard costs is imported directly into the costing system itself, which consequently becomes a 'standard costing system'. *A standard cost is a predetermined production cost that is set before production actually occurs.*

EXAMPLE 15.2:
Spedwich Ltd is a small privately owned engineering company that manufactures garden tools. Heretofore, it has used a costing system based on actual costs. As a result of obtaining new sources of capital, is about to launch into an expansion programme. Management consultants have advised on the replacement of the actual costing system by a standard costing system. Cost and engineering studies

result in standard costs being calculated for each product line. The standard cost of the Spedwich garden spade has been calculated as follows:

	£	£
Standard direct costs:		
Raw materials	1.00	
Labour	0.50	
		1.50
Standard overhead costs:		
Variable costs	0.20	
Fixed	0.25	
		0.45
Standard product cost per unit		1.95

It is particularly important to note that in a standard costing system actual costs are *replaced* by standard costs. This means that the standard costing system only records standard costs. In effect, standard costs are accumulated in the standard costing system by a triggering process that is activated as units of the product enter the manufacturing process.

EXAMPLE 15.3:
Betral plc is a manufacturing company making a variety of standardized products. It operates a standard costing system. The standard costs established for the 19X5 budget year in respect of the Zeon product line are as follows:

	£	£
Standard direct costs per unit		
Raw materials	2.50	
Labour	1.50	
		4.00
Standard overhead cost per unit		
Variable overheads	2.00	
Fixed overheads	1.00	
		3.00
		7.00

There were no opening stocks of Zeons at 1 January 19X5. During the budget year ended 31 December 19X5, 60 000 Zeon units were produced, and there remained 5000 units in stock at the year-end. The costing and financial accounting records will be based on the standard costs that were established prior to the beginning of the budget period, and will provide the following information:

(a) *Cost of sales*:
55 000 units at standard unit cost of £7.00 = *£385 000*
(b) *Closing stock*:
5000 units at standard unit cost of £7.00 = *£35 000*

The actual costs involved in producing 60 000 Zeon units will not be recorded as product cost.

15.2 STANDARD COSTS AND BUDGETED EXPENDITURE

Standard costs impose predetermined standards of cost efficiency at the product level. As was noted in Chapter 14, budgeted expenditure aims to control spending at the cost centre level. Therefore, the relationship between standard costs and budgeted expenditure in manufacturing businesses that have standard costing systems is as follows:

(a) Production cost centres will have budget allowances fixed in terms of budget output expressed in units terms.

EXAMPLE 15.4:

Betral plc has two production cost centres engaged in manufacturing Zeons – a machining and a finishing cost centre. The budgeted output for budget year 19X5 was fixed at 60 000 units. Standard production costs per unit established for the machining department are as follows:

	£	£
Standard direct costs per unit		
Raw materials	2.50	
Labour	0.75	
		3.25
Standard overhead cost per unit		
Variable overheads	1.00	
Fixed overheads	0.50	
		1.50
		4.75

Accordingly, the budget allowance for the year 19X5 for the machining department will be fixed at £4.75 × 60 000 units = *£285 000*. This sum will allow the machining department to spend only £285 000 for a required output of 60 000 Zeon units.

(b) Non-production cost centres will have budget allowances that will have been determined as efficient spending levels for the activity levels that such cost centres are expected to support during the budget period.

EXAMPLE 15.5:
Betral plc has three non-production cost centres – factory maintenance cost centre, factory administration and the cafeteria. The budget allowance for the cafeteria has been determined on the basis of one meal a day for 250 factory employees at a cost of £1.25 per standardized meal. Holidays, public holiday and weekends mean that, on average, employees work a 240-day year. Accordingly, the budget allowance for the cafeteria is established at £75 000 (£1.25 × 250 × 240).

15.3 STANDARD COSTS, BUDGETED EXPENDITURE AND ACTUAL COSTS

A budgetary planning and control system will set up budget allowances for all cost centres. As explained above, product costs will be standardized at the cost until level. In the case of production cost centres, product costs per unit will be determined and the budget allowance will be a multiple of the standard costs and the budgeted output in units. Both the standard costs and budgeted expenditure will have been determined *before* the beginning of the budget period and will become operative as from the first day of that period.

Actual costs will be incurred as financial expenses in the form of invoices and payroll payment. These actual costs will reflect the level of spending incurred in respect of the actual output that is being generated by production cost centres, and the actual activity level of non-production cost centres. In the exceptional case that budet forecasts are completely realized, actual cost centre spending will be equal to the budgeted spending allowance. In that unique case, production costs debited in the costing profit and loss account will have their corresponding credits in various creditor accounts, such as creditors for raw material supplies, payroll, etc.

EXAMPLE 15.6:
Terta Ltd has a standard costing system. The budgeted total expenditure for the 19X6 year was fixed at £850 000, based on the following budgeted output and standard cost per unit:

(a) Budgeted output: 100 000 units.
(b) Standard unit costs:

	£
Direct materials	2.00
Direct labour	2.50
Variable overheads	2.00
Fixed overheads	2.00
	8.50

Actual output was 100 000 units and was entirely sold.
Actual costs incurred amounted to £850 000, as follows:

	£
Direct materials	200 000
Direct labour	250 000
Variable overheads	200 000
Fixed overheads	200 000
	850 000

The entries in the financial accounts were as follows:

	£	£
Cost of sales at standard cost	850 000	
Sundry creditors		850 000

There were no outstanding sundry creditors at the year-end. Therefore, the following transactions will have occurred during the year:

	£	£
Sundry creditors	850 000	
Cash		850 000

For a variety of reasons, total actual production costs will generally differ, if only by relatively small margins, from budgeted total costs. Actual output will have been recorded at standard cost, and the difference between budgeted costs and actual costs will appear as a budget variance.

EXAMPLE 15.7:
During the year 19X7, Tetra Ltd expected to maintain output at

100 000 units. Inflation in the economy was expected to average 10 per cent across the board, and standard costs were adjusted upwards by 10 per cent as follows:

	£
Direct materials	220 000
Direct labour	275 000
Variable overheads	220 000
Fixed overheads	220 000
	935 000

Actual output, which was entirely sold, was valued at standard cost and recorded as amounting to £1 000 000, an excess of £65 000 over-budget. The budget itself proved to be an underestimate of actual expenditure, which was recorded in the financial accounts as amounting to £1 200 000. The overall difference (variance) between budget and actual was £265 000 (£1 200 000 – £935 000). It is described as an *unfavourable budget variance*, since it represents excessive actual expenditure over budget. There were no sundry creditors outstanding at the year-end. The accounting entries would be:

	£	£
Cost of sales at standard cost	1 000 000	
Unfavourable budget variance	265 000	
Sundry creditors		1 265 000
Sundry creditors	1 265 000	
Cash		1 265 000

As Example 15.7 illustrates, variances between actual expenditure and the standard cost of actual output are revealed whenever creditor's accounts show actual costs *in total* running at a different level than actual output recorded only at standard cost. It follows that the usefulness of actual cost information in the context of cost control is to provide *feedback* information to allow variances to be identified and investigated.

15.4 SETTING STANDARD COSTS

To be effective for the purpose of cost control, standard costs should reflect attainable standard of cost performance. This means that the process of setting standard costs is of critical importance if a standard costing system is to be effective as a means of cost control.

Setting standard costs implies:

(a) Establishing procedures for setting standards with respect to the price at which resources are acquired and their usage. This suggests the employment of specialist engineers and consultants to determine relative levels of cost efficiency that should be within the firm's reach.
(b) Establishing procedures for allowing participation by cost centre managers in setting attainable standards. This suggests that there may be resistance to cost standards that are too harshly set, in the form of negative reactions by personnel.

Cost standards are set for all categories of costs. Setting cost standards for direct costs, such as direct material and direct labour costs, focuses upon price and usage as the two key cost components. Setting cost standards for indirect costs is relatively more difficult since there is no direct output against which standard costs can be set. This problem is resolved by a surrogate measure of output in respect to which overhead costs can be related. As will be seen later in this chapter, the *standard hour* is used in this context. Overhead costs are considered to vary with activity levels expressed in standard hours. Further problems associated with standard overhead costs are as follows:

(a) An appropriate overhead rate must be selected for allocating standard variable and standard fixed costs per unit.
(b) In the case of fixed overhead costs, the overhead rate selected must be calculated by reference to a standard activity level for the budget period.

15.5 STANDARD DIRECT MATERIAL AND DIRECT LABOUR COSTS

Setting standard costs for direct material and direct labour involves two aspects:

(a) quantifying an efficient input of resources;
(b) acquiring that input at the best price.

15.5.1 Standard direct material costs

The quantity of raw material required for a standard unit is determined by engineers. The standard quantity should include an appropriate allowance for normal wastage in production.

Responsibility for purchasing rests with the purchasing department. The standard price should reflect the best price that the purchasing department can obtain, and be the price expected to be paid during the budget period.

15.5.2 Standard direct labour costs

Before standard labour costs can be set, operatives have to be graded according to standardized categories of skills. Labour time standards are set by time and motion study engineers. The standard wage rates are those that are expected to be paid during the budget period.

15.6 VARIANCE ANALYSIS FOR DIRECT COSTS

The control of direct costs through variance analysis is based on two principles:

(a) *Management by exception.* Actual expenditure is assumed to be in line with standard costs, unless this is contradicted by information showing that variances are occurring between the budget allowance, based on standard costs, and actual expenditure being recorded in the financial accounts through the process of recording invoices.
(b) *Accounting responsibility.* Responsibility for the control of costs is located with the manager having the responsibility for cost centre costs.

The first sign that standard costs are not being respected is the appearance of a *budget variance* on direct material or direct labour. A budget variance is *defined as a difference between the budget allowance for the output achieved and actual spending on the output achieved.* It requires further analysis, before its causal factors may be identified, investigated and, if possible, corrected. The analysis of the budget variance necessitates splitting up the budget variance into the two components of standard costs, namely the quantity standard and the price standard. As a result, it is possible to attribute the problem to the occurrence of excessive usage or excessive price, or both.

Variances fall into two categories:

(a) *Unfavourable variances* that arise when the standard allowance is exceeded by actual expenditure.
(b) *Favourable variances* that are due to actual expenditure being less than the standard allowance.

Clearly, management will be more immediately concerned with possible inefficiencies arising as a result of *unfavourable* variances. *Favourable variances* may arise out of fortuitous events occurring in the firm's favour, for example, a fall in market prices for raw materials. However, favourable variances may also indicate that standards should be adjusted upwards to reflect actual performance more accurately. The truth remains that, under ideal conditions, favourable or unfavourable variances should not occur if standards have been correctly set.

15.6.1 Direct material variances

The analysis of the direct material variance begins by identifying the direct material budget variance. The material budget variance is *the difference between the actual expenditure and budgeted expenditure.* It provides a measure of the overall difference that has to be investigated. It is composed of two elements:

(a) *Price variance* explains the proportion of the budget variance that is caused by paying more or less than the standard price for actual purchase.
(b) *Usage variance* explains the proportion of the budget variance that is due to using more or less material in production than the standard quantity.

The principle of accounting responsibility means that responsibility for the price variances is laid on the purchasing department, whereas responsibility for the usage variance lies with the manager of the appropriate production cost centre.

EXAMPLE 15.8:

Peam Ltd is a small manufacturing company making a product known as Platron. It has a standard costing system, and standard direct material costs per unit of Platron have been set for the budget year 19X6 as follows:

Standard material quantity per unit	3 kg
Standard price per kg	£0.50

During the month of January 19X6, 4000 units of Platron were produced. The following information was obtained by the costing department:

Quantity used during January	11 000 kg
Quantity purchased during January	15 000 kg
Purchase price per kg	£0.55

The following points are immediately brought to our attention:

(a) *Price*. The purchase price turned out to be 5p per kg higher than estimated.
(b) *Quantity*. An output of 4000 Platrons should have required a consumption of 12 000 kg of material according to the standard usage on which the standard cost of £1.50 per Platron was estimated. As only 11 000 kg were actually used, a saving in material usage of 1000 kg was realized.

The accounting analyses of these differences are made in terms of a material price variance and a material usage variance, as shown in Exhibit 15.1.

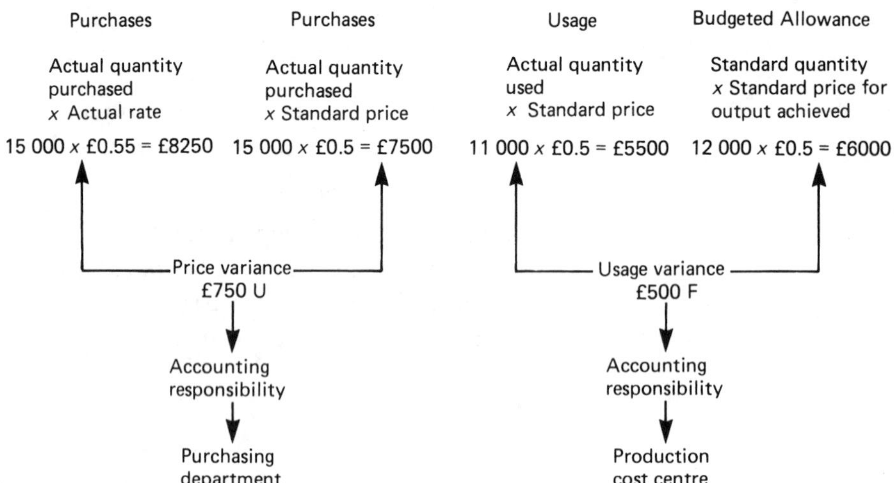

Exhibit 15.1 Analysis of direct material variances.

The material price variance is best calculated when raw materials are purchased and before they are committed to production. In this way, the variance is highlighted at the earliest possible stage so that action may be taken immediately to deal with future purchases should it turn out to be necessary. For example, the buyer may have purchased at a high price, while alternative sources may be available at the old price. A further advantage of this method is that it enables stocks to be valued in the accounts at standard cost, thereby reducing the clerical effort which is necessary if stocks are valued at actual cost. The material price variance results, therefore, from a comparison of the price of raw materials purchased with an estimate of what these purchases should have cost.

15.6.2 Direct labour variance

The analysis of the direct labour variance begins by determining the *direct labour budget variance* defined as *the differences between the actual payroll and the budgeted payroll.* The major difference between the analysis of direct material and direct labour variances is in the stocking of direct materials in excess of usage. The terminology is slightly different, though the same meaning is retained. The notion of price is expressed in the labour wage rate; and the notion of usage is stated in labour efficiency. Accordingly, once the direct labour budget variance has been calculated, it is split into *the direct labour wage rate variance* and *the direct labour efficiency variance.*

EXAMPLE 15.9:
Standard costs established by Peam Ltd for the 19X6 budget year were as follows:

Standard direct labour hour per unit	0.25 hour
Standard direct labour rate per unit	£4.00 per hour

The actual output for the month of January 19X6 was 4000 Platrons. The following additional information is given:

Actual hours	900 hours
Actual expenditure	£3690

The direct labour budget variance is analyzed into its two components, as shown in Exhibit 15.2.

15.7 STANDARD OVERHEAD COSTS

Setting standard overhead costs poses more difficult and complex problems than the setting of standard direct costs in the following respects:

(a) setting cost standards;
(b) selecting an overhead rate for both standard fixed and variable overhead cost allocation;
(c) determining the standard volume for the purpose of recovering standard fixed overhead costs.

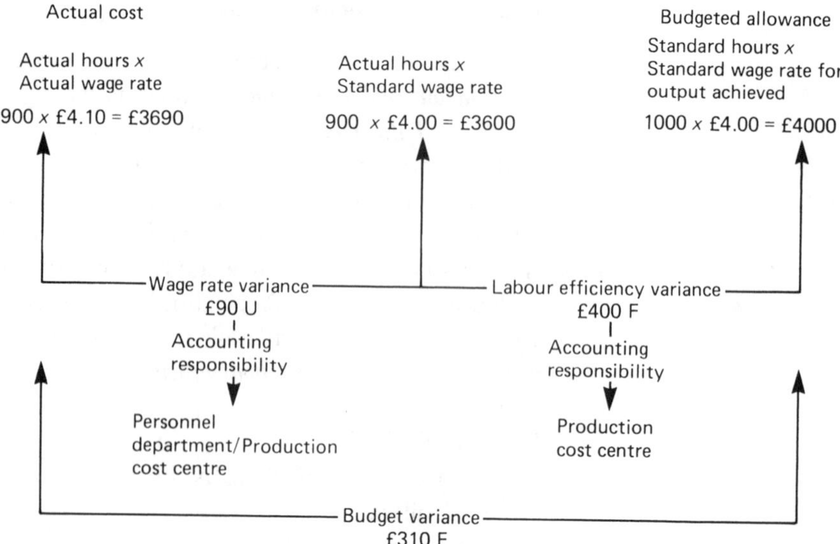

Exhibit 15.2 Analysis of direct labour variances.

15.7.1 Setting cost standards

The setting of efficient cost standards for overheads requires ensuring that the acquisition of resources classified as fixed and variable overheads has been subjected to efficient purchasing, and that the usage of these resources corresponds to an efficient utilization. Efficient purchasing implies that the responsible departments will have secured resources at the best price, and that the budget allowance is a spending level that reflects such purchasing. In this respect, the budget allowance for fixed and variable overheads has a component element that is similar to the standard price and standard wage rate used for setting standard direct material and direct labour costs.

The budget allowance also has another component that assumes that there will be an efficient usage made of variable and fixed costs. This implies that such costs will support a standard level of activity. Therefore, setting efficient usage levels for variable overheads consists in finding what type of activity provokes variations in variable overheads, and then attempting to impose expenditure limits on variable overheads with respect to activity. For example, if the simplifying assumption is made that machine repair and maintenance costs vary with machine hours, the problem is not simply to ensure that repair charges are the best obtainable, but that in relation to machine hours, repairs themselves are not excessive but reflect good machine usage.

15.7.2 Selecting a standard overhead rate

The difficulty in establishing an appropriate level of activity in relation to variable and fixed costs lies in that overhead costs are not directly related to output expressed as units of product. As discussed earlier in Chapter 5, an overhead rate has to be selected for the purposes of allocating standard variable and fixed overheads to products.

The most convenient overhead rate is the *standard hour* defined as *a unit of measurement representing the quantity of any product or service which can be produced or performed in 1 hour by any process, machine or operative.*

15.7.3 The standard hour and cost control

The standard hour is not a measure of time but a measure of performance in a period of 1 hour.

EXAMPLE 15.10:
If the estimated time required to write 200 letters is 20 hours, a standard hour represents ten letters. Similarly, if 48 units of product A can be produced in 12 hours, a standard hour of that product represents four units.

The standard hour constitutes not only a convenient base for establishing standard overhead rates, but can also be applied to all types of cost centres where it is useful to have a common measure through which the output of diverse products can be expressed. The standard hour may also be used to develop overhead rates both for variable and fixed overheads.

Three production control ratios are derived from the standard hour:

(a) *The efficiency ratio* measures the efficiency of direct labour and is expressed as follows:

$$\text{efficiency ratio} = \frac{\text{standard hours of production achieved}}{\text{actual direct working hours}} \times 100$$

(b) *The production volume ratio* compares actual output with budget and is expressed as follows:

$$\text{production volume ratio} = \frac{\text{standard hours of production achieved}}{\text{budgeted standard hours}} \times 100$$

(c) *The capacity ratio* compares actual hours with budgeted hours and is expressed as follows:

$$\text{capacity ratio} = \frac{\text{actual hours worked}}{\text{budgeted hours}}$$

EXAMPLE 15.11:

Extrust Ltd manufactures tables and chairs. It is estimated that 2 hours are required for one table and 1 hour for one chair. In March, 19X2, actual production was 50 tables and 150 chairs. Budgeted production for the period was 40 tables and 160 chairs. Actual hours worked were 230 and actual output in terms of standard hours was:

Tables:	50 units × 2 hours per unit	=	100 hours
Chairs:	150 units × 1 hour per unit	=	150 hours
			250 standard hours

Budgeted production in terms of standard hours:

Tables:	40 units × 2 hours per unit	=	80 hours
Chairs:	160 units × 1 hour per unit	=	160 hours
			240 standard hours

$$\text{efficiency ratio} = \frac{250}{230} \times 100 = 108.7\%$$

$$\text{production volume ratio} = \frac{250}{240} \times 100 = 104.2\%$$

$$\text{capacity ratio} = \frac{230}{240} \times 100 = 95.8\%$$

These results may be checked as follows:

$$\text{production volume ratio} = \text{capacity ratio} \times \text{efficiency ratio}$$

$$104.2\% = \frac{230}{240} \times \frac{250}{230}$$

15.7.4 Determining the standard output

Variable overhead costs vary directly with output. Hence, if the output is expressed in standard hours, variable overheads will be applied to actual output in accordance with the predetermined rate.

Fixed costs, however, do not vary with output. Hence, a normal or standard output must be budgeted to enable a fixed overhead rate to be calculated. The standard fixed overhead rate will be applied to the number of standard hours fixed in the budget.

The term *fixed budgeting* refers to budgets prepared on the basis of a standard output for the purposes of establishing budget allowances throughout the firm. Under fixed budgeting, standard fixed overheads will be over- or under-applied whenever actual output is greater or less than the standard output, giving rise to favourable or unfavourable volume variances.

Firms will always need to plan their financing requirements on the assumption that they will attain the budgeted output level. In this sense, the financial budget will always be a *fixed budget*. The disadvantages of using the fixed budget for control purposes lies in the inability to control costs under fluctuating output conditions.

15.8 FLEXIBLE BUDGETING

Flexible budgeting is intended to overcome the difficulties posed by fixed budgeting for controlling overhead costs. Flexible budgeting does not replace fixed budgeting for planning the financing requirement purposes. It only replaces fixed budgeting for control. The particular difficulties that make fixed budgeting redundant for control are:

(a) Overhead allowances are budgeted in respect of only one output volume, namely, the standard output.
(b) Fixed overheads will generally be under- or over-applied, but responsibility for volume variances cannot be attributed to cost centre managers, since they are not responsible for output variations.

15.8.1 Flexible budget allowances

Flexible budgeting allows fluctuations in output levels to be taken into account for cost control purposes by means of flexible budget allowances.

EXAMPLE 15.12:

Jobin Ltd is a small manufacturing company that has a budgetary planning and control system based on the fixed budgeting principle. The fixed budget overhead allowance for assembly cost centre A is £20 000 for a period during which the standard output was represented by 5000 standard hours. The budgeted allowance was calculated as follows:

Indirect material	£5 000
Indirect labour	2 500
Repairs and maintenance	5 000
Insurance	1 500
Rates	3 000
Depreciation	3 000
	£20 000

The overhead costs per unit are:

£20 000 ÷ 5 000 = £4

The firm has experienced severe fluctuations in demand for its products over several months. As a result, actual costs have diverged significantly from budget allowances. It has now been decided to introduce flexible budgeting making it possible to match any given actual output with a corresponding budget allowance. During the month of June, actual activity level of cost centre A was 4000 standard hours, for which the following flexible budget allowance was calculated:

	Total variable costs	*Fixed costs*	*Total budget allowance*
	£	£	£
Indirect materials	4 000		4 000
Indirect labour	2 000		2 000
Repairs and maintenance	2 400	2 000	4 400
Insurance	800	500	1 300
Rates		3 000	3 000
Depreciation		3 000	3 000
	9 200	8 500	17 700

Flexible budgeting improves the control of overhead costs by establishing a flexible budget allowance for each output level, once that output is known. In effect, cost centres are allowed to incur overhead costs at a predetermined standard rate. Control is applied routinely for each management reporting period, usually monthly, when the flexible overhead allowance for the actual output achieved is calculated.

EXAMPLE 15.13:

Jobin Ltd has a fixed financial budget providing for a monthly output of 5000 units. On this basis, each cost centre has been given a monthly budget allowance corresponding to predetermined standard costs per unit. Jobin Ltd uses flexible budgeting for cost control. During the month of June, actual output was 4500 units. Actual overhead costs incurred amounted to £19 150. The following overhead cost control report was prepared.

	(1) Actual cost of production	(2) Total budget allowance	(3) Original budget	(4) Variation from original budget	(5) Variation from budget allowance
Units produced	4 500	4 500	5 000	(1)–(3)	(1)–(2)
Indirect materials	£4 700	£4 500	£5 000	£300F	£200U
Indirect labour	£2 400	2 250	2 500	100F	150U
Repairs and maintenance	4 600	4 700	5 000	400F	100 F
Insurance	1 450	1 400	1 500	50F	50U
Rates	3 000	3 000	3 000	—	—
Depreciation	3 000	3 000	3 000	—	—
	£19 150	£18 850	£20 000	£850F	£300U

15.9 VARIANCE ANALYSIS FOR OVERHEAD COSTS

The analysis of overhead cost variances fall into two parts:

(a) the analysis of variable overhead costs;
(b) the analysis of fixed overhead costs.

15.9.1 Variable overhead cost variance

The analysis of the variable overhead cost variance begins by identifying the variable overhead budget variance, which is *the difference between the actual expenditure and budgeted expenditure.* It provides a measure of the overall difference that has to be investigated. It is composed of two elements:

(a) *Expenditure variance* explains the proportion of the budget variance that is caused by differences in the price paid to services charged as overhead costs. It is calculated as follows:

expenditure variance = actual overheads − (actual hours × standard variable overhead rate)

(b) *Efficiency variance* explains the proportion of the budget variance that is due to differences in the usage of service charged as overhead costs. It is calculated as follows:

efficiency variance = (actual hours − standard hours) × standard variable overhead rate.

EXAMPLE 15.14:
Setract Ltd has an assembly cost centre that is budgeted for an output of 5000 standard hours. The following information is given with respect to October 19X3:

(a) actual hours worked: 4800
(b) variable costs incurred: £11 600
(c) standard variable overhead rate per standard hour: £2.3

The expenditure and efficiency variances are calculated as is shown in Exhibit 15.3.

15.9.2 Fixed overhead cost variances

Fixed overhead cost variances fall into two types:

(a) *Expenditure variance* is calculated as follows:

fixed overhead cost expenditure variance = actual fixed overheads − budgeted fixed overhead costs,

(b) *Volume variance* is calculated as follows:

fixed overhead cost volume variance = budgeted fixed overheads − (standard fixed overhead rate × standard hours in the output achieved)

EXAMPLE 15.15:
Refer to Example 15.13, where the assembly department is budgeted for an output of 5000 standard hours and actual hours worked were 4800. The following fixed overhead cost information is given with respect to October 19X3:

	£
(a) actual fixed overhead costs	8 900
(b) budgeted fixed overhead costs	6 000
(c) standard fixed overhead rate per standard hour	1.7

The analysis of the fixed overhead cost variance is given in Exhibit 15.4.

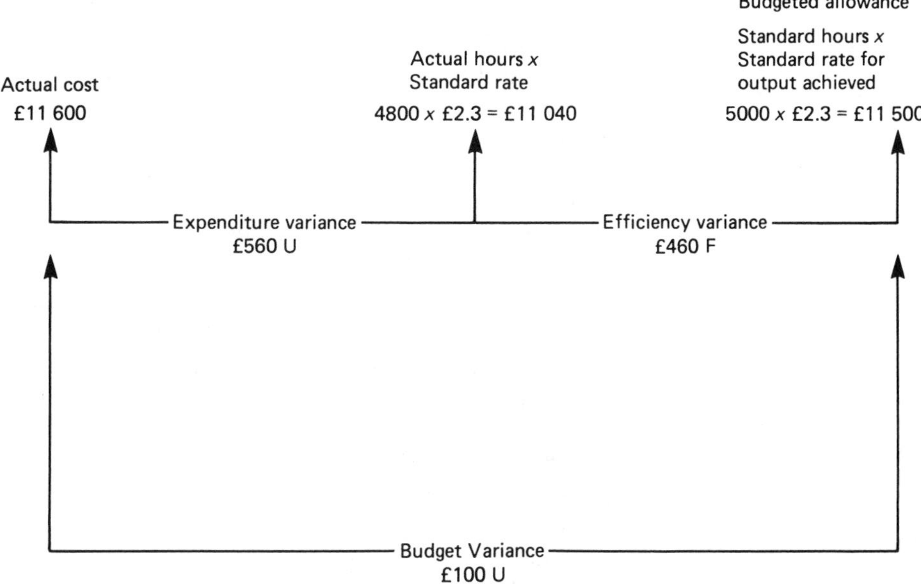

Exhibit 15.3 Analysis of variable overhead variances.

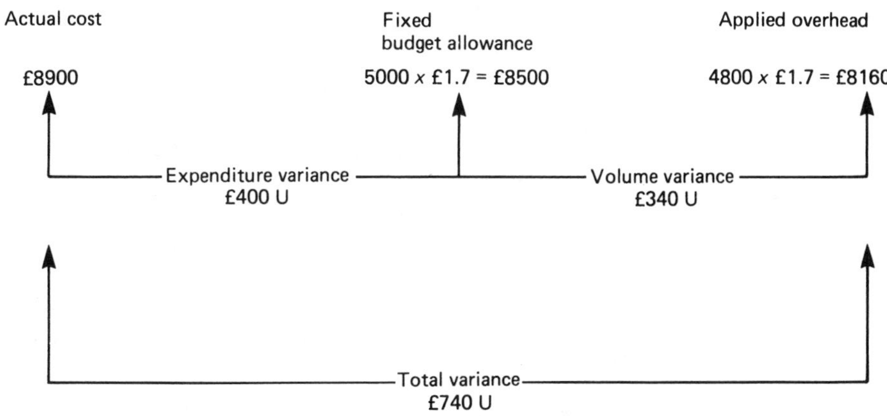

Exhibit 15.4 Analysis of fixed overhead variances under fixed budgeting.

15.10 VARIANCE ANALYSIS AND THE CONTROL OF REVENUE

A business has less control over its revenues than it has over its costs. This is because the market will dictate how much the firm can sell at given prices. By contrast, a firm can seek to establish standards of cost efficiency in relation to usage, even though prices at which resources are acquired are dictated by market prices. Nevertheless, the following budgetary planning and control procedures are routinely applied to sales revenues:

(a) developing an annual sales forecast and corresponding sales budget;
(b) monthly management report of variances between budgeted and actual sales;
(c) analysis of sales variances;
(d) implementation of corrective measures.

The real concern of management regarding sales variances is the impact on profits, rather than the impact on sales revenues. For this reason, the analysis of sales variances is directed at investigating *the difference between budgeted (standard) contribution margin and the actual contribution margin derived from sales.* This analysis is broken into the following three components:

(a) *Sales price variance* indicates the extent to which the contribution margin has been affected by price adjustments.
(b) *Sales volume variance* reveals the extent to which the contribution margin has been affected by changes in quantities sold on the market.
(c) *Sales mix variance* shows how changes in market demand for different products sold by the firm has affected the total contribution margin.

15.10.1 Sales price variance

This variance expresses the difference between the budgeted contribution margin and the actual contribution margin that results from selling the actual quantity sold at the actual price rather than the standard price. It is calculated as follows:

sales price variance = units sold × (actual unit contribution margin less the standard contribution margin per unit)

15.10.2 Sales volume variance

This variance expresses the difference between the budgeted contribution margin and the actual contribution margin that results from volume rather than price changes. It is calculated as follows:

sales volume variance = standard contribution margin per unit × (actual number of units sold less the budgeted number of units)

15.10.3 Sales mix variance

As was noted in Chapter 11, improvements in the contribution margin are possible simply by altering the sales mix away from products with relatively low unit contribution margins towards those with relatively higher unit contribution margins. The sales mix variance measures the impact on the total contribution margin that results from such changes. It is calculated as follows:

sales mix variance = standard contribution per unit of each product × (actual units of each product sold less actual sales in budgeted mix proportions)

EXAMPLE 15.16:

Twintrick Ltd sells two products X and Y. The following data relates to the quarter ended 31 March 19X4:

Budgeted sales:	Product X	5000 units at £10 unit standard contribution margin £4
	Product Y	5000 units at £5 unit standard contribution margin £2
Actual sales:	Product X	4000 units for £44 000
	Product Y	8000 units for £32 000

These data may be tabulated as follows:

	(a) *Actual contribution*	(b) *Actual quantity*	(c) *Standard contribution margin*	(d) *(b) × (c) Value*	(e) *Actual quantity in standard proportions*	(f) *Standard contribution margin*	(g) *(e) × (f) Value*	(h) *Budgeted margin*
	£	Units	£	£	Units	£	£	£
X	20 000	4 000	4	16 000	6 000	4	24 000	20 000
Y	8 000	8 000	2	16 000	6 000	2	12 000	10 000
	28 000	12 000		32 000	12 000		36 000	30 000

Notes:

1. Column (a) is derived from the following formula:

actual contribution = actual sales less (actual units × standard cost)
= £44 000 − (4000 × £6)
= £20 000

2. Column (e) is derived by taking total actual sales of 12 000 units and applying the budgeted mix proportions. According to the

budget, 50 per cent of X and 50 per cent of Y should be sold. Total sales were 12 000 units, which expressed in budgeted mix proportions amount to 6000 units of X and 6000 units of Y.

The variances which may be extracted from these data are as follows:

(a) *Sales price variance*

x = units sold × (actual contribution per unit less standard contribution)
= column (a) − column (d)
= £28 000 − £32 000
= £4000 U

The sales price variance is unfavourable to the extent of £4000 because 3000 units of Y were sold at a price which was £1 lower than the standard, whilst only 1000 units of X were sold at a price which was £1 higher than the standard price.

(b) *Sales volume variance*

x = standard contribution per unit × (actual number of units sold less budgeted units of sales)
= column (g) − column (h)
= £36 000 − £30 000
= £6000 F

This variance reflects the fact that 12 000 units were actually sold as against a budgeted volume of only 10 000 units. Its value is the contribution which the extra 2000 units would have brought if they were at standard price and mix.

(c) *Sales mix variance*

= (standard contribution per unit of each product × the actual quantities of units sold) − (standard contribution per unit of each product × actual total sales in budgeted mix proportions)
= column (d) − column (g)
= £32 000 − £36 000
= £4000 U

This variance discloses the reduction in budgeted profits caused by selling a greater proportion of units having a lower contribution margin than the standard.

15.11 ACCOUNTING DISPOSITION OF VARIANCES

Once variances have been investigated and corrective measures taken, they have to be disposed of in the financial accounts. The rule is that during the year cost of sales and stock values should be retained at standard cost, even though there may have been substantial variances. The significance of this rule is that it highlights the extent to which variances were significant events during the year. Moreover, it reinforces the essential purpose of standard costing, namely, that the firm should seek to be cost competitive in the market. Consequently, standard costs should be retained for pricing purposes, and variances should be treated as period costs and not reflected in product costs.

Accordingly, variances are accounted for in separate variance accounts:

Materials price variance
Materials usage variance
Labour wage rate variance
Labour efficiency variance
Variable overhead expenditure variance
Variable overhead efficiency variance
Fixed overhead expenditure variance
Fixed overhead volume variance

Unfavourable variances are debited and favourable variances are credited to the variance accounts. Sales variances do not appear in the books; sales are recorded in the sales account at actual invoiced value.

There are two methods for treating year-end balances on the variance accounts:

(a) Apportioning the variances between the three cost elements with which such variances are associated, namely:

   (i) work-in-progress closing stock;
   (ii) finished goods closing stock;
   (iii) cost of sales.

   Apportionment is based on the proportionate value of each element of stock to total stock. This conforms with the matching principle, and involves carrying forward variances that have been apportioned to work-in-progress and finished goods stocks.

(b) Writing-off the variance account to cost of sales. This conforms with the prudence principle, which would treat unfavourable variances as incurred in the year in which they occur.

15.12 RESPONSIBILITY FOR VARIANCES

In variance analysis it is necessary that the precise cause of a variance be determined and that the cause be traced to the individual responsible. It is the function of the individual in charge of each responsibility centre to act promptly upon reports of variances which are within this control. Therefore, variances are not ends in themselves. Rather, they raise the questions why did the variance occur? What must be done to eliminate them? Obviously the importance of these questions depends on the significance of the deviations.

The material usage and labour efficiency variances respectively reveal that the quantities of material and labour used in production are either more or less than planned, depending on whether the variances are unfavourable or favourable. If more material is being used than planned, the cause may lie elsewhere than in the production department, for example in the purchase of inferior materials by the purchasing department. The fault, however, may lie in the production department and may be found to be attributable to careless supervision, or the use of untrained staff, or faulty machines. An unfavourable labour efficiency variance may be due to poor control by the foreman, bad labour relations, health factors, production delays, inferior tools and badly trained staff. Again the responsibility for the variance should be located. For example, if due to badly trained staff this may be caused by inefficiency on the part of the personnel department; but if, on the other hand the variance is caused by the economic conditions prevailing at the time which had produced a shortage of specialized labour, the variance is considered to be uncontrollable.

Price and wage rate variances may not be controllable by the firm, and this is particularly true of raw material prices and wages agreed nationally with trade unions. On the other hand, variances may occur in the negotiation of contracts for materials which are the responsibility of the purchasing department. Purchasing department controls prices by getting several quotations, taking advantage of economic lots and securing cash discounts. Inefficiency in these areas will reveal unfavourable variances for which that department should be held responsible.

With regard to overhead variances, spending variances are usually the responsibility of the departmental head, because they are usually controllable by him. The volume variance is not normally controllable by the departmental manager; it is usually the responsibility of the sales department or production control.

Questions

1. Why are actual costs not useful for control?
2. What are standard costs? Explain how the notion of 'cost efficiency' is introduced in standard costs.
3. State the uses made of standard costs.
4. What is a standard costing system?
5. Explain the relationship between budgeted costs and standard costs.
6. Define a budget allowance.
7. Explain the term 'unfavourable budget variance'.
8. Describe the role of actual cost information in a standard costing system.
9. Describe briefly how cost standards are set.
10. What do you understand by the standard hour?
11. Discuss the principles involved in the control of direct costs when using standard costing.
12. How do the following variances arise:

    (a) direct material variance;
    (b) direct labour variance?

13. What problems are involved in setting standard overhead costs?
14. Explain the relevance of the standard hour in setting overhead cost standards.
15. Compare and contrast fixed budgeting and flexible budgeting in the context of overhead cost control.
16. Describe briefly how a flexible budget allowance is calculated.
17. Define the following:

    (a) variable overhead cost variance;
    (b) fixed overhead cost variance.

18. How are the following variances calculated:

    (a) variable overhead expenditure variance;
    (b) variable overhead efficiency variance;
    (c) variable overhead budget variance;
    (d) fixed overhead budget variance;
    (e) fixed overhead expenditure variance;
    (f) fixed overhead volume variance?

19. Describe how variance analysis is applied to control revenue.
20. How are the following variances calculated:

    (a) sales price variance;
    (b) sales volume variance;
    (c) sales mix variance?

21. Describe the accounting treatment that may be applied to the disposition of cost and revenue variances.

Problems

1. (a) Briefly explain the term 'standard cost'. (2 marks)
   (b) Outline the benefits which a company may obtain from a standard costing system. (9 marks)
   (c) Discuss the problems which may arise in the development and operation of a standard costing system. (6 marks)
   (Total 17 marks)

   (*Chartered Association of Certified Accountants*)

2. (a) Explain, briefly, what is meant by each of the following terms:
      (i) standard hour;
      (ii) productivity (or efficiency) ratio;
      (iii) production volume ratio.
   (b) Using the information given below, you are required to calculate the productivity ratio and the production volume ratio for each of the two production departments X and Y.

	Product D	*Product* G
Department X		
Budgeted production, in units	18 000	4 000
Standard minutes required to produce one unit:	20	30
Actual units produced	15 000	10 000
Total actual hours worked on both products: 11 111		
Department Y		
Budgeted standard hours	10 000	
Actual hours worked	9 000	
Standard hours produced	9 450	

   (15 marks)

   (*Chartered Institute of Management Accountants*)

3. (a) Calculate the material and labour variances from the following data:

Standard cost of component XY	
Material cost	£0.60 per kg
Material weight to produce one component	1½ kg
Wages rate, per hour	£3.80
Time required to manufacture one component	36 min
Standard selling price, per component	£3.50

The following was recorded in the month of May 19X3:

Components manufactured and sold		3 510
Sales income		£12 285
Materials purchased and issued:	(i)	2 740 kg at £0.58
	(ii)	2 315 kg at £0.62
Wages paid for the production:	(i)	880 hours at £3.90 hour
	(ii)	1 300 hours at £3.65 hour

(12 marks)

(b) Present the answers to the above information in a statement to management disclosing the reasons for the differences between standard and actual gross profit.

(8 marks)

(c) A consultant recently stated that: 'past performance is the best guide to ascertaining standard costs'. Analyse this statement in detail and indicate whether or not you agree with it.

(8 marks)
(Total 28 marks)

(*Association of Accounting Technicians*)

4. Shown below is the standard prime cost of a tube of industrial adhesive, which is the only product manufactured in one department of Gum plc.

Industrial adhesive

	£ per tube	£ per tube
Materials: Powder	1.50	
Chemicals	0.60	
Tube	0.30	2.40
Labour: mixing and pouring		1.80
Total standard prime cost		£4.20

The standard material allowance for each tube of adhesive is 2 lbs of powder, ¼ litre of chemical and one tube. The standard wage rate for mixing and pouring is £4.50 per hour.

During the previous month 4500 tubes of adhesive were produced, there were no work-in-progress stocks at the beginning or end of the month, and the receipts and issues of materials during the month are shown below:

	Powder	*Chemicals*	*Tubes*
Opening stock	1 500 lb	200 litres	100 tubes
Purchases	10 000 lb at 70p per lb	600 litres at £2.30 per litre	200 tubes at 40p each
		600 litres at £2.50 per litre	5000 tubes at 30p each
Issues	9800 lb	1050 litres	4520 tubes

The above materials are used exclusively in the production of the adhesive and it is the policy of the company to calculate any price variance when the materials are purchased.

The direct employees operating the mixing and pouring plant worked a total of 2050 hours during the previous month and earned gross wages of £8910.

Required:

(a) Calculate for the previous month the following variances from standard cost:

materials price variance, analysed as you consider appropriate;
materials usage variance, analysed as you consider appropriate;
direct labour efficiency variance;
direct wages rate variance. (12 marks)

(b) Discuss the possible causes of the material variances and the direct labour efficiency variance.

(10 marks)
(Total 22 marks)

(*Chartered Association of Certified Accountants*)

5. For a product the following data are given:

Standards per unit of product		
Direct material	4 kg at £0.75 per kg	
Direct labour	2 hours at £1.60 per hour	
Actual details for given financial period		
Output produced in units		38 000
Direct materials:		£
Purchased	180 000 kg for	126 000
Issued to production	154 000 kg	
Direct labour	78 000 hours worked for	136 500

There was no work-in-progress at the beginning or end of the period.

Required:

(a) Calculate the following variances:
  - (i) direct materials cost;
  - (ii) direct materials price, based on issues to production;
  - (iii) direct materials usage;
  - (iv) direct wages cost;
  - (v) direct wages rate;
  - (vi) direct labour efficiency.

(b) State whether in each of the following cases, the comment given and suggested as the possible reason for the variance, is *consistent* or *inconsistent* with the variance you have calculated in your answer to (a) above, supporting each of your conclusions with a brief explanatory comment.

Item in

(a)
  - (ii) direct materials price variance: the procurement manager has ignored the economic order quantity, and, by obtaining bulk quantities, has purchased material at less than the standard price;
  - (iii) direct materials usage variance: material losses in production were less than had been allowed for in the standard;
  - (v) direct wages rate variance: the union negotiated wage increase was £0.15 per hour lower than expected;
  - (vi) direct labour efficiency variance: the efficiency of labour was commendable.

(25 marks)

(*Chartered Institute of Management Accountants*)

6. A company manufactures two products called 'Kob' and 'Kleg'. Each uses two kinds of materials, 'alloy' and 'composite', and two grades of labour, grade I and grade II.

At the beginning of a 4-week period the following stocks were recorded:

Kob	*Kleg*	*Alloy*	*Composite*
16 units	9 units	187 kg, value £935	60 kg, value £480

Planned specifications for each product are:

	Kob	*Kleg*
Alloy (£5 kg)	3 kg	1 kg
Composite (£8 kg)	1 kg	4 kg
Grade I labour (£4 hour)	30 min	15 min
Grade II labour (£5 hour)	24 min	48 min

Overheads are recovered at 100 per cent of labour cost.

Actual transactions for the 4-week period were:

Material purchases	Alloy	900 kg costing £5400
	Composite	870 kg costing £6003
Materials issued to production:	Alloy	890 kg
	Composite	810 kg
Grade I labour	142 hours costing £568	
Grade II labour	200 hours costing £960	
Overheads total	£1596	

	Kob	*Kleg*
Transfer to finished stock	208 units	152 units
Sales	210 units	135 units

There was no work-in-progress at the beginning or end of the period and no losses in production.

Required:

(a) Calculate the standard cost of one unit of each product. (5 marks)

(b) (i) Calculate material usage variances for each material;

(ii) Calculate material price variances for each material;

(iii) Calculate labour efficiency variance for each grade of labour;

(iv) Calculate wages rate variance for each grade of labour;

(v) Calculate overhead variance in total.

(10 marks)

Note: Assume materials are issued on the FIFO basis.

(c) Calculate the finished goods stock valuation at standard cost at the end of the period. (6 marks)

(d) Calculate the material stock valuation at standard cost at the end of the period.

(7 marks)

(Total 28 marks)

(Association of Accounting Technicians)

7. The information shown below is an extract from the previous period's budget and standard cost data for the machining department in a company manufacturing two products and which operates a full absorption standard costing system.

	Product X	*Product Y*
Budgeted production	6500 units	4200 units
Standard machine hours allowed to process each product in the machining department	4 hours	7 hours

The department's overhead is applied to production by means of a standard machine hour absorption rate and this is calculated at the beginning of each period. The variable element of the previous period's absorption rate was £1.50 per standard machine hour and the department's total overheads for that period were budgeted to be £207 750. The budget assumes that one standard machine hour should be produced in one actual hour of machining time.

The actual results in the machining department for the previous period were:

Actual machining time	54 000 hours
Production: Product X	7 200 units
Product Y	4 000 units
Actual overheads incurred: Fixed £120 550	
Variable £87 600	

Required:

(a) Calculate the following variances from standard/budgeted cost which occurred in the machining department during the previous period:

fixed overhead volume variance;

fixed overhead expenditure variance;
variable overhead expenditure variance. (10 marks)

(b) Discuss in detail the possible reasons for the fixed overhead volume variance.

(7 marks)

(c) Calculate the machining department's total flexed overhead budget for the actual level of production in the previous period and explain the difference between this total budgeted amount and the total production overhead absorbed by the department in the period.

(5 marks)
(Total 22 marks)

(Chartered Association of Certified Accountants)

8. *Required*:
   (a) Comment on the statement that 'for the most managerial purposes the sales margin variances (operating profit variances) are more informative than sales variances'.
   (b) Using the data given in the table below, calculate for each product and in total, the operating profit variances:
      (i) due to sales;
      (ii) due to selling prices;
      (iii) due to sales volume.

Product	*Per unit*			*Totals*		
	Selling price	*Cost*	*Profit*	*Quantity*	*Profit*	*Sales*
	£	£	£	units	£	£
Budget: A	30	16	14	1 500		
B	10	9	1	3 500		
C	20	18	2	1 000		
Actual: A			15	1 100	16 500	34 100
B			1	5 200	5 200	52 000
C			4	1 100	4 400	24 200
Total					26 100	110 300

(20 marks)

(Chartered Institute of Certified Management Accountants)

9. The following are standard cost data for a company manufacturing a single product:

	Quantity	Price	£
Direct materials	50 kg	£4.20 per kg	210
Direct labour	20 hours	£3.50 per hour	70
Variable production overhead	20 hours	£1.20 per hour	24
Fixed production overhead	20 hours	£4.50 per hour	90
			394
Standard selling price			£600

Budgeted production for the month of April was 260 units and this figure was used in calculating the fixed overhead absorption rate. Overhead is absorbed into production on the basis of units produced but the variable overhead is deemed to vary with hours worked.

An abridged trading and profit statement prepared in the conventional way shows the following:

	£	£
Sales		165 000
Materials used	50 200	
Direct wages	22 400	
Production overhead: Variable	6 600	
Fixed	23 500	
		102 700
Gross profit		62 300
Selling and administration		29 300
Net profit		£33 000

Additional information appropriate to April:
Sales and production: 250 units;
There was no work-in-progress;
Actual hours worked by direct labour: 5600;
Materials used cost £4.00 per kg.

Required:

(a) Calculate the following variances:
 (i) due to selling prices;
 (ii) direct materials price;
 (iii) direct materials usage;
 (iv) direct wages rate;

(v) direct labour efficiency;
(vi) variable production overhead expenditure;
(vii) variable production overhead efficiency;
(viii) fixed production overhead expenditure;
(ix) fixed production overhead volume.

(b) Present a profit statement utilizing standard costs and showing the variances.

(c) (i) Comment on *two* possible reasons for each of the variances you show for (a)(ii) and (a)(v) and state who (job title) is responsible for the variance;
(ii) state what ought to be done by the appropriate executive responsible for the direct labour efficiency variance.

(35 marks)

(*Chartered Institute of Management Accountants*)

16 Presentation of Information to Management

This chapter deals with the following topics:

16.1 The nature of management reports.
16.2 Qualitative criteria for management reports.
16.3 Criteria for an effective reporting system.
16.4 Characteristics of a reporting system.
16.5 Classification of reports.
16.6 The preparation and presentation of reports.

16.1 THE NATURE OF MANAGEMENT REPORTS

It was noted in Chapter 1 that the management process involves two major activities, namely planning and control. Information is a critical input requirement for both activities. Effective planning requires requisite information for establishing targets: effective control requires feedback information that allows management to take action to evaluate performance and to correct variances from plan. In effect, information plays a vital role in business enterprises both as its lifeblood and as its motivating force. It is used to shape decisions and to influence behaviour.

Specifically, budgetary planning and control systems are designed to function by means of relevant cost information. Information contained in management reports is immediately useful for control and for evaluating performance in the form of management reports. Feedback information also has a special significance to the planning process by providing evidence of the firm's experience under given planning assumptions. In effect, management reports make it possible for management to function. This suggests that specific criteria apply to:

(a) the quality of information contained in management reports to ensure that they contain information that is both relevant and useful;
(b) the design of a management reporting system to ensure that different management levels receive information in a suitable form and appropriate to their responsibility level.

16.2 QUALITATIVE CRITERIA FOR MANAGEMENT REPORTS

The purpose of management reports is to communicate information. To be of value to management, reports should be simple, clear, accurate, timely and brief. These qualitative criteria constitute a basic set of rules that apply to all reports, and may be explained as follows:

(a) *Simplicity*. Reports should be simple to enable the recipient to understand immediately the relevance of the information that is being communicated. This criterion is a function of the management level to which reports are addressed. Simplicity does not mean that the facts that are being communicated are of themselves evident, but that the manner in which they are presented is simple and not obtuse, and therefore difficult to understand.

(b) *Clarity*. Reports should be sufficiently clear to ensure that information is not misunderstood. They should be presented in an easily readable form. Except where they are addressed to specialists, technical language should be avoided.

(c) *Accuracy*. The information contained in reports should be accurate and not misleading. The term 'accuracy' may be defined at different levels. At the most basic level, it means the information should not contain errors of data, such as arithmetical errors. At a more sophisticated level, accuracy may mean that the interpretation given to the data being communicated is itself accurate. Generally, the accuracy criterion applies to factual accuracy and not to interpretative accuracy.

(d) *Timeliness*. To be useful for management action, reports should be timely. This means that the information should be communicated with the shortest possible delay to enable management to take the required action before it is too late. Timeliness is a function of the particular context of which information is being provided, and of the level of management involved. Generally, the time period allowed for reports increases with the level of management. Daily and weekly reports are required at lower supervisory levels; whereas senior management reports are usually on a monthly basis.

(e) *Brevity*. Reports should be brief and limited to essential facts. Unnecessary detail should be omitted, and such details as are considered relevant should be provided in supplementary schedules.

16.3 CRITERIA FOR AN EFFECTIVE REPORTING SYSTEM

The problem of designing an effective management reporting system centres on the following two aspects:

(a) ensuring that different management levels receive information appropriate to their responsibility;
(b) defining and standardizing the information to be included in management reports at different levels with respect to both content, timing and frequency.

(a) Reporting to different management levels

The following four broad management categories may be distinguished:

(1) Lower management – comprising foremen and supervisors at the operations level.
(2) Middle management – comprising plant managers responsible for operating units.
(3) Top management – comprising functional managers responsible for mainstream functions, such as production, marketing, sales and personnel.
(4) Board of directors – having overall responsibility for all enterprise activity.

(b) Defining the content, timing and frequency of reports

The nature of the management problem at these different levels defines the information that should be made available as to content, timing and frequency, as follows:

(1) Reports to lower management will contain detailed information regarding operations. Such reports will be restricted in scope and will be prepared promptly after the events reported. They will also be prepared with greater frequency, generally for daily or weekly periods.
(2) Reports to middle management will contain summarized, rather than detailed information. Such reports will be more extensive in scope than reports to lower management and will be in the form of condensed analyses of departments or sections under their control. They will be prepared generally at weekly and monthly intervals.
(3) Reports to top management will contain information covering in review form all the activities of the enterprise, highlighting overall performance and trends in relation to current and future plans and targets. Such reports will emphasize financial aspects, and will be prepared on a monthly and quarterly basis.
(4) Reports to the board of directors will be concerned with overall performance of major functions in the context of broad policy decisions. Meetings are usually on a monthly basis, and reports will be prepared on a monthly, quarterly or semi-annual basis as required for review and control purposes.

Reports to lower, middle and top management should be formalized and standardized. Information becomes less detailed as it moves up the hierarchy. Correspondingly, the need for commentary increases. At the board of directors level, reports will have limited factual content and the emphasis will be on review analysis.

16.4 CHARACTERISTICS OF A REPORTING SYSTEM

The purpose of a reporting system is to permit information to flow as an organic function through the enterprise, giving it cohesiveness and allowing control to be exercised over the totality of its activities. Information is a vital enterprise resource that requires to be as well managed as other more obvious enterprise resource factors. Establishing an effective reporting system is a key success factor for any organization. The reports that convey information upwards through the managerial hierarchy have the primary purpose of providing feedback information on the basis of which performance may be evaluated and control decisions may be taken. At the same time, the reporting system frequently links performance evaluation with the reward system. Consequently, human factors are always present that threaten biasing in several ways, as follows:

(a) Information may be distorted unless the content of reports is strictly specified and reports standardized as to content, form, size and layout.
(b) Routine and repetitive reports should be confined to terms, measurement basis and values that are uniform to ensure community of understanding.
(c) Report analysis may be inaccurate if reports are not addressed to the right person or persons.
(d) Report analysis may suffer from inadequacy if several reports touching upon the same subject-matter are not available at the same time.

For these various reasons, the reporting system should be designed with the following characteristics:

(a) Reports should be properly integrated and co-ordinated within a coherent set of reports.
(b) Reports should be in a standardized form and based on uniform terms.
(c) Reports should be related to appropriate responsibility centres.
(d) Reports should allow proper control to be exercised, and for that purpose the reporting system should be under the supervision of a senior executive, such as the accountant or controller.

16.5 CLASSIFICATION OF REPORTS

Different classifications of reports have been suggested. Some authorities distinguish informational or planning reports from control reports. Others distinguish special or non-repetitive reports from periodic, routine or repetitive reports.

(a) Control and informational reports

It may be argued that, fundamentally, the primary and obvious classification should distinguish *control reports* from *informational reports*. Control reports are related to the control of operations, and are intended to indicate the need for corrective actions. They are highly specific as to content. Informational reports are related to policy making and planning, and are intended to present and interpret facts for management. They may be broad in scope, and less detailed as to factual content.

(b) Routine and special reports

The secondary classification distinguishes both control and informational reports into two further categories – *routine reports* and *special reports*. Routine reports are prepared at regular intervals and in a standardized form. Special reports are initiated either by the financial director/chief accountant or at the request of the board of directors.

By their nature, most control reports will be routine reports and may be submitted to all management levels. For example, analysis of budget performance and variances will be in the form of standardized routine reports, and report on such variances will flow upwards through the management hierarchy, being condensed and summarized as it moves up.

By contrast, most informational reports will be special reports, and usually restricted to higher management levels. For example, the analysis of an investment project will be in the form of a special report that will circulate to a limited number of higher level managers.

16.6 THE PREPARATION AND PRESENTATION OF REPORTS

The considerations that apply generally to the manner in which reports should be prepared and presented to management relate to notions of standardization and uniformity, as follows:

(a) *Title*. Reports should have an appropriate title that is descriptive of overall content and purpose. For example, a report on the analysis of overhead cost analysis should be the title 'Analysis of overhead cost variances'.

(b) *Period covered*. The relevance of a report lies in the period to which it applies.

(c) *Date prepared.* The timeliness of a report is indicated by reference to the date on which it was prepared and presented.

(d) *Management level to which addressed.* The manager(s) responsible for acting on the report is an essential feature of every report. It identifies the chain of command with the reporting system. In addition, reports are frequently also referred to other persons on an informational basis. Such persons should always be identified, usually at the end of the report. This identification defines the extent to which information is required to circulate.

(e) *Originating management level.* The manager responsible for originating the report should be identified both in name and managerial responsibility.

(f) *Terms and measurement units.* Routine control reports should use standardized terms and uniform measurements.

(g) *Format.* Routine reports will be prepared in accordance with a standardized format that aims at ensuring clarity of meaning, adequacy of data and brevity of communication. For this reason, the design of a standardized format is a critically important task. A standardized format allows for the proper organization and reporting of statistical data, as well as the orderly development of reports as far as analysis is concerned. A standardized format will also readily make comparisons possible by requiring prior period figures to be entered alongside current figures.

(h) *Timing and frequency.* The report system will impose time schedules for the preparation and presentation of reports. It is essential to the proper co-ordination of the evaluation and review process that reports should be completed on time and that they reach the responsible manager without delay. Daily reports are usually required to be made available by the next day, weekly reports at the beginning of the following week, monthly reports within 7 days of the end of the month. The reporting frequency is a complex issue that has to be determined by taking into account several factors, as follows:

  (i) the frequency of reporting that is required for adequate control;
  (ii) the extent of information that is needed to be reported;
  (iii) the capacity of the reporting unit to undertake frequent reporting. For example, a small subsidiary company may not have the office staff to undertake the same level of reporting as a major divisional corporation.

Questions

1. Explain the nature of management reports.
2. What qualitative criteria apply to management reports?

3. State two conditions required for an effective reporting system.
4. Review the nature of reports provided to different management levels.
5. What factors may introduce bias in a reporting system?
6. Distinguish routine and informational reports.
7. What are the characteristics of routine reports?
8. State the feature of special reports.
9. List the principles that apply to the preparation of reports.

Problems

1. The four products of PQR Ltd are sold through four customer categories. There is only one price list but concessions are effected by means of special discounts. The following details relate to the sales budget for 19X3:

		Budgeted sales at gross list prices (£000)				
Product	*Factory cost % of gross list price*	*Government departments*	*Super-markets*	*Wholesalers*	*Retail shops*	*Total*
A	55%	160	80	100	20	360
B	65%	—	80	100	20	200
C	60%	40	—	40	40	120
D	75%	—	40	60	20	120
		200	200	300	100	800
Trade discounts		25%	20%	15%	nil	
Selling and distribution expenses expressed at gross list prices		10%	12½%	12%	15%	

Required:
Tabulate figures in an orderly manner so that the manager to whom they are presented would be able to see immediately the budgeted net profit for each customer category and in total.

(London Chamber of Commerce and Industry)

2. At the 30 April 19X2 the accounts of a company showed the following actual figures for the first 4 months of the year:

	£
Turnover	1 200 000
Variable costs	780 000
Fixed costs	240 000
Fixed assets	400 000
Working capital	200 000

The company has financial objectives expressed in working ratios as follows:

Pre-tax profit	15% of turnover value
Pre-tax profit	30% of capital employed
Gross profit margin	35%
Margin of safety	43%

The directors require expansion and in the final 4 months of 19X2 have stated that expansion accompanied by cost reduction and more aggressive selling prices should result in an improved performance. Hence, for this period the following changes are to be made:

Output to be increased by 10 per cent. All output is expected to be sold.
Sales prices reduced by 5 per cent.
Variable cost savings for 4 months; £42 000.
Working capital to be increased by 15 per cent.
Fixed assets, unchanged in value.
Fixed costs increased by £19 000 to cover additional insurance and other charges.

Required:

(a) Tabulate comparative figures for the first 4 months and the third 4 months, with appropriate ratios (to the nearest whole number).

(12 marks)

(b) State your opinion as to the worthwhileness of the directors' proposal.

(6 marks)
(Total 18 marks)

(*Association of Accounting Technicians*)

Index